NORMAL PSYCHOLOGY
OF THE
AGING PROCESS

NORMAL PSYCHOLOGY
OF THE
AGING PROCESS

Revised and Expanded Editi *n*

from the

Boston Society for Gerontologic
Psychiatry, Inc.

Edited by

NORMAN E. ZINBERG, M.D.
and
IRVING KAUFMAN, M.D.

With a Preface by Ralph J. Kahana, M.D.

INTERNATIONAL UNIVERSITIES PRESS, INC.
New York

Copyright © 1978, International Universities Press, Inc.

Library of Congress Cataloging in Publication Data

Main entry under title:

Normal psychology of the aging process.

   Previous ed. published in 1963 under the authorship of the Boston Society for Gerontologic Psychiatry.
   Bibliography: p.
   Includes index.
   1. Aged — Psychology. 2. Aging. I. Zinberg, Norman Earl, 1921-   II. Kaufman, Irving, 1917-   III. Boston Society for Gerontologic Psychiatry. Normal psychology of the aging process.
BF724.8.N67 1978   155.67   77-92178
ISBN 0-8236-3641-0

Manufactured in the United States of America

mms
5-6

"Though he has watched a decent age pass by,

A man will sometimes still desire the world."

— SOPHOCLES, *Oedipus at Colonnus*

Contents

PART ONE
Normal Psychology of the Aging Process

PART TWO
Normal Psychology of the Aging Process Revisited — I

PART THREE
Review of the Literature

Contributors

MARTIN A. BEREZIN, M.D.
   Clinical Professor of Psychiatry, Harvard Medical School
   Training and Supervising Analyst, Boston Psychoanalytic
   Society and Institute

DAVID BLAU, M.D.
   Assistant Clinical Professor of Psychiatry, Harvard Medi-
   cal School
   Faculty, Boston Psychoanalytic Society and Institute

ALVIN I. GOLDFARB, M.D.†
   Consultant on Service for Aged for Department of Mental
   Hygiene, New York State

RALPH J. KAHANA, M.D.
   Assistant Clinical Professor of Psychiatry, Harvard Medi-
   cal School
   Faculty, Boston Psychoanalytic Society and Institute

IRVING KAUFMAN, M.D.
   Faculty, Harvard Medical School and Smith College of
   Social Work

SIDNEY LEVIN, M.D.
   Assistant Clinical Professor of Psychiatry, Harvard Medi-
   cal School
   Training and Supervising Analyst, Boston Psychoanalytic
   Society and Institute

MAURICE E. LINDEN, M.D.
Clinical Professor of Psychiatry, Jefferson Medical College

W. W. MEISSNER, S.J., M.D.
Associate Clinical Professor of Psychiatry, Harvard Medical School
Faculty, Boston Psychoanalytic Society and Institute

JOSEPH J. MICHAELS, M.D.†
Faculty, Harvard Medical School
Training Analyst, Boston Psychoanalytic Society and Institute

ADRIAN VERWOERDT, M.D.
Professor of Psychiatry and Director of Geropsychiatry Training, Duke University Medical Center

NORMAN E. ZINBERG, M.D.
Associate Clinical Professor of Psychiatry, Harvard Medical School
Faculty, Boston Psychoanalytic Society and Institute

Acknowledgments

The task of preparing the first symposium of the Boston Society for Gerontologic Psychiatry was made possible by the zeal and dedication of Dr. Martin Berezin who organized the Society. Merck Sharpe & Dohme generously supplied the funds which financed this symposium. That the presentations are worthy of publication is the result of careful and thoughtful selection of the program by Dr. Stanley Cath, Chairman of the Program Committee. He was aided in the arrangements by Miss Elizabeth Bryant and Miss Agnes Goldberg who worked with conscientious thoroughness and ever-present good humor. Mrs. Penelope Wells arranged for the copies of the manuscripts promptly, efficiently, and above all, patiently. The editorial assistance of Miss Sue Annin was invaluable. The other contributors, Drs. Alvin Goldfarb, Maurice Linden, Sidney Levin, and Joseph Michaels, transformed efficiently their spoken, more informal remarks into well-organized manuscripts. Last, but by no means least, is Dr. Irving Kaufman, the coeditor, without whose continuous cooperation and perseverance this volume would not have been published.

The second symposium, included in Part Two of this expanded volume, was made possible by generous contributions from Cooper Laboratories, Inc., Endo Laboratories, Inc., Sandoz Pharmaceuticals, and Smith Kline & French Laboratories.

NORMAN E. ZINBERG, M.D.

[xi]

Preface

Ralph J. Kahana, m.d.

There is an old notion that personality is established in all its essentials during childhood and that later development merely repeats and reworks these foundations. It follows that the inner life of old people is only a continuation of post-adolescent existence without essential differences in normal personality or psychopathology except those caused by organic brain diseases. This viewpoint, while it attempts to pay attention to the lasting importance of early impressions and to life-long continuities in personality, neglects the unique qualities of older persons and the special experiences and problems of later life. In his Foreword to the first edition of *Normal Psychology of the Aging Process*, Berezin expressed the need for an explicit focus on the psychodynamics of older people. The subsequent experience of the Boston Society for Gerontologic Psychiatry has confirmed the value of such a focus for those who work with older people in health care and other social services.

The Boston Society for Gerontologic Psychiatry has made its contribution by concentrating on the psychoanalytic psychology of aging, previously neglected. Other work in gerontology has been concerned with social factors, such as economic conditions and the attitudes of society; with physiological and medical conditions; and with the care of the five percent of older people in institutions. Twice yearly the Society has sponsored symposia in which one or more papers and formal discussions by leaders in geriatric psychiatry center on a specific topic. Subsequent to the first symposium, which is reprinted in this volume, the proceedings of these meetings have been published in two other books — *Grief, Loss, and Emotional Disorders in the Aging Process* (Berezin and Cath, 1965) and *Psychodynamic Studies on Aging: Creativity, Reminiscing, and Dying* (Levin and Kahana, 1967) — and the *Journal of Geriatric Psychiatry*. The symposia have included many contributions to the understanding of psychodynamic factors in the normal psychology of aging and later life, as well as in psychopathology and therapy. Among those dealing directly with normal psychology are papers on the metapsychology of the aging process, reminiscing, reactions to loss, creativity in later life, aging leaders, ethical and cultural considerations in aging, the older person and the family, the transition from middle to old age, widowhood, longevity, and the dying patient. While these contributions have concentrated on normal psychology, they also contain many observations and constructs concerning psychopathology. One must understand the normal in order to comprehend pathology and, conversely, observations of the pathological, with its exaggeration of behavior, often illuminate normal psychology. Other papers, on psychopathology and its treatment, have dealt with depression, suicide and delinquency in later life, aging and the conflict of generations, psychotherapy and psychoanalysis in older people, transference, extended care of the chronically ill, future directions of nursing homes, group therapy, and the use of psychotropic drugs. The symposia have reflected the prevalence of ideas and concerns among those in the forefront of the field at the given time.

When this volume first appeared, the nature and functions of the ego were at the center of psychodynamic interest. The chapters added to the present edition reflect a more recent preoccupation with object relations and narcissism. In psychiatry and psychoanalysis many "advances" simply look at phenomena in a different or more comprehensive way that is helpful for a special group of problems and increases our therapeutic skill. These newer findings and theoretical constructs do not necessarily supersede earlier viewpoints.

What, then, is characteristic of the psychology of later life? The contributors to the first symposium point to specific adaptive challenges that confront older people, especially personal losses, physical disabilities, and cultural prejudices against old age. Changes in basic motivation and in adaptive and defensive capabilities are an important feature of aging. Regression plays a prominent part in behavior in old age.

Zinberg and Kaufman offer an initial overview organized around six components: psychological responses to the physical phenomena of aging; changes in the theoretical mental structures of id, ego, and superego with aging; vicissitudes of sexuality and aggression; interpersonal relations; social and cultural implications of aging; and psychopathology. They consider older people's selective employment of the defenses of regression, isolation, compartmentalization, and denial. The aging person's enhanced need for narcissistic supplies is emphasized. Their discussion of the social and cultural implications of aging reflects on the worship of youth in American society to the detriment of older citizens, describes some personality types who find it particularly hard to retire from employment, and examines the special relationships of physicians and psychiatrists with their older patients. Difficulties in communicating with the older patient and the necessity of involvement with the patient's family are considered. Psychopathology in the aged includes the full spectrum of conditions seen in earlier adult life and is frequently complicated by dependent regression and by organic brain syndromes. Depression is singled out as the most frequent psychoiogical difficulty encountered. Since this chapter was written, there has been some progress in meeting the need for research on sexual life in the aged, a modest increase in the numbers of geriatric patients referred for psychotherapy, and an expansion of the literature on dying and death.

In Goldfarb's view old age and chronic illness are, in many respects, synonymous. True old age, as contrasted to chronological old age, is seen as a condition in which functional efficiency has been lost. It is irreversible although its progress may be slowed. Long experience as a clinician and as a consultant to health administrators has made Goldfarb wary of euphemisms and subterfuges in conceptualizing the problems of aging. Although his definition includes organic illness, he recognizes the tendencies to overemphasize the physiological nature of certain disorders and to push aside their emotional components, their impact on social functioning, and the social corrective action indicated. This tendency to neglect the psychosocial aspects, and treat psychiatric disorders as if they were strictly medical, results in confused planning and implementation of care. Goldfarb cites some of the reasons why psychotherapists have not viewed older people favorably as candidates for psychotherapy and discusses problems posed by the helplessness of aged patients.

Where Goldfarb see organic illness as essential to aging, Berezin emphasizes *regression* as the *sine qua non*—there is no aging without it. Regression is less likely to have pathological significance in an aged person than in a younger one. It is an expected reaction in the older individual, arising out of the diminishing of genital primacy which leaves no choice except to retreat to previous libidinal positions. Regression develops gradually, accompanied by character changes consistent with various libidinal levels of organization. Both Linden and Zinberg in their chapters continue the discussion of regression and elaborate on its pathological and adaptive aspects.

Berezin goes on to consider, among other "Intrapsychic As-

[xvi]

pects of Aging," the timelessness of the unconscious—that is, the lifelong persistence of repressed wishes and drives as well as various defensive and adaptive mechanisms. Another important intrapsychic phenomenon is the wish to be independent which occurs among aged people with startling regularity, in an intense form and sometimes under the most unrealistic conditions. Various meanings and functions of this striving are classified. Berezin considers the question of whether drives diminish with aging or if there is rather a shifting of interests. Finally, he offers the concept of the *consultative position* as representing the image of integrity in old age and a replacement for the lost genital primacy.

In his chapter on "Psychodynamic Considerations in Normal Aging," Kaufman discusses and offers brief illustrations of the timelessness of the unconscious, regressive phenomena, ego-adaptive processes, and countertransference problems as seen in a highlighted form in the therapy of older persons. Linden in his chapter distinguishes between "Regression and Recession in the Psychoses of the Aging." He discusses the concept of the psychic apparatus and details the clinical sequences of its breakdown under the impact of adaptive stresses facing older people, both in more acute psychotic regression and in more gradual senile recession and disability. He concludes with a discussion of goals and prognosis in therapy.

Zinberg identifies some distinctive qualities of psychotherapy with older persons and associates them with the concept of *adaptive regression*. He emphasizes the possibility of assessing quickly the salient personality conflicts accentuated by regression and making constructive use of the older patient's reliance on his intellect and his remembered experiences. The frequent transparency of anxieties and personality structure in old age enables the skilled geriatrician to make an educated guess about how to approach problems in a tactful way which does not further strain the patient's defenses. The aged patient is often able to take a thoughtful, objective view of himself and others, including acceptance of human frailties and vanities. Whenever possible the therapist should find a past solution to problems the patient has already "learned" and can use.

Levin observes the persistent disturbances of *libido equilibrium* are typically accompanied by depressive reactions. This equilibrium may be upset in later life by reduction of opportunities for activity, discharge of feelings, and satisfaction. Disturbing factors include restriction of activities, physical discomfort, major object losses, decline in sexual and intellectual functioning, general weakening of ego functions which makes mastery of new situations more difficult, and cultural prejudices against older people having sexual gratification, making themselves attractive, living with their children, or seeking psychotherapeutic help.

In discussion of these papers Goldfarb further examines the subject of dependence, and both he and Michaels comment on the nature of regression. Michaels observes that the greater the immaturity of the individual, the more pathological the regression will be. Freud's attempt to understand the psychobiological decline of the organism through his concept of the death instinct led to much controversy, particularly a difference of opinion about whether an instinct of aggressiveness exists. Michaels believes that those who meet the inevitability of their own death with equanimity have resolved their castration anxieties and regard death as a natural psychobiological phenomenon free of symbolic meanings.

Since its original publication, the steady demand for *Normal Psychology of the Aging Process* has indicated a continuing need for the orientation it offers and suggests that its contents have not become dated. This second edition includes new chapters by three original authors. Zinberg's paper on "Social Learning and Self-Image in Aging" is discussed by Meissner.[1] Kaufman's presentation of "Marital Adaptation in

[1] Both papers were originally published in the *Journal of Geriatric Psychiatry*, 9:131-160 (1976).

the Aging" has Blau as discussant.[2] Two papers by Berezin reviewing the literature on "Sex and Old Age" are discussed by Verwoerdt.[3] These chapters take us into further aspects of normal psychology and indicate some of the accumulation of knowledge and changes of emphasis that have taken place in dynamic psychiatry during the past 15 years. They suggest that we have learned more about the responses of older people in therapy and about their sexual experiences. We are more cognizant of the impact of social attitudes on the older person. Clinicians have been studying and treating couples and families. Psychoanalytic theorists have been interested in ego autonomy, the internalization and integration of mental "structures," object relations, the self, and narcissism.

Zinberg supports the hypothesis that an aging person's inhibitions result more from acceptance and internalization of the culture's stereotypes and taboos into his or her *self-image* than from any long-standing, unresolved conflicts. On this basis, for example, many older people unconsciously inhibit their sexual activities. The idea that psychotherapy is most effective with the young is another damaging stereotype. The theoretical constructs necessary to study the impact of *social learning* on the individual's lifelong development exist in the work of Hartmann and Rapaport. Rapaport postulated that ego autonomy is always relative. The drives prevent man from being enslaved by the necessity to respond to environmental stimuli, while environmental stimuli moderate the drives by activating and sustaining primary and secondary ego apparatuses. The aging have often lost "stimulus nutriment" and come to feel that it is wrong to seek pleasure and gratification. As a result, their relative autonomy from both the environ-

---

[2] Both papers were originally published in the *Journal of Geriatric Psychiatry*, 9:161-188 (1976).

[3] Berezin's first review appeared in the *Journal of Geriatric Psychiatry*, 2: 131-149 (1969). His second review and Verwoerdt's "Discussion" were published in the *Journal of Geriatric Psychiatry*, 9:189-219 (1976).

[xix]

ment and the drives can become impaired. In two illustrative cases, Rapaport's formulations are used both to explain how adverse social learning can disturb ego autonomy and to guide therapeutic efforts. Thus in one case psychotherapy and his discussion with his granddaughter and her friends, as well as contact with a sympathetic woman, helped a man to overcome sexual inhibitions. Zinberg concludes that an older person who no longer accepts excessively inhibiting cultural dictates needs a new social group with different social rituals to make his "deviance" acceptable.

Meissner points to deficiencies in our theories and stresses the limitations of the Rapaport model of ego autonomy. A theory of social learning and cultural influences cannot stand on its own. A critical variable linking the level of social learning theory to the organization and integration of autonomy has to do with narcissism and object relations. We need a theory of superego and ego integration relevant to the internalization of social value systems. Rather than thinking of ego autonomy as caught between polarities of instinct and environment, it may be more useful to think of it as an internalized attribute, simultaneously independent of both instincts and environment. Psychoanalytic structural theory is derived from conflict between superego and ego, not their integration. In the Hartmann-Rapaport model autonomy has to do with relative independence of specific ego functions, their conflict-free functioning within an average expectable environment. This is not the same as autonomy that has to do with the cohesiveness, integration, and independence of the self. To emphasize stimulus nutriment and social learning runs the risk of thinking that changing social attitudes to the aged and having them accept such changes will solve their problems. The task for old age is not to settle for external conformity, but to achieve that form of internal autonomous growth which enables older people to sustain the trials of old age.

Kaufman draws on his clinical experience with *marital*

problems in older couples and reviews some sociological studies of marriage in order to gain understanding of the adaptation of people who have remained married for a long time. Everyone needs narcissistic support and closeness in marriage, but men and women differ in the ways these needs are met. Men seek "respect" while women emphasize "communication." In these changing times, with greater emphasis placed on individual satisfaction, the institution of marriage is questioned and more frequently interrupted. Interruption is often traumatic. Kaufman describes a couple in their mid-fifties who had a happy marriage until their last child left home, at which time the wife became depressed. The husband, who had foregone greater achievement in his work out of dependence on his wife, felt resentful that she was no longer fun or support and turned his energies to his business. Therapy had to be directed at underlying personality issues in each partner.

After raising questions about the methodology of the main sociological survey cited by Kaufman, Blau agrees that marriage is a dynamic, not a static process and that there is a need for meshing the patterns of marital partners. Kaufman approaches the marital problem in terms of narcissistic and object supplies and the balance of needs of the two partners. Blau takes another direction, emphasizing a central problem common to both partners — the reaction to loss when the youngest child leaves home. He elaborates this thesis with a clinical illustration from his own practice of a couple in their sixties who were treated in six individual and joint interviews.

In two critical reviews of the literature Berezin explores an important aspect of normal psychology, the *sexual life* of old people. The publications surveyed fall between 1925 and 1975, a period that began with scattered scientific reports and then featured the studies of Kinsey et al., Masters and Johnson, and the Duke University longitudinal studies. Many articles are introduced by defensive apologies as if old age should be sexless. Kinsey's observation that "even in the most advanced ages

[xxi]

there is no sudden elimination of any large group of individuals from the sexually active" is substantiated and elaborated. Fewer studies have been made of sex in aging women than in men. For women, as for men, those who were strongly motivated to sexual experience when younger continued to be so in old age. Marriage was an important variable: single individuals did not have nearly as satisfactory a sex life, particularly in older age. In spite of the residue of defensiveness, the general public is becoming more aware through popular literature and other media of some of the facts about sex in old age. At the end of the half-century reviewed, studies on sex in old age continued to be concerned with the physical aspects and masturbation. Still missing is any sense that an aged person's sexual relations are in the service of a love relationship, an object tie in which tenderness and affection are significant. Other topics of studies reviewed include potency after prostatectomy, contributions of dream and sleep research, sexual delinquency among the aged, the need for physicians to be aware of older patients' sexual problems, sexual patterns of older never-married women, the aged homosexual, and postmenopausal sexual interest and activity.

Verwoerdt comments on instances of increased sexual activity in aging men. These are likely to be due to psychological or social factors, such as lessening of inhibitions, the need to overcompensate, increased self-esteem, or a lessening of the burden of economic or family responsibility. Noting that much research has been statistical and quantitative, he takes up considerations bearing on more subjective and qualitative aspects of sex in old age. Finally, he discusses some psychological problems that arise in response to sexual involution and describes the occurrence in later years of sexual symptoms that express nonsexual psychopathology. His comments, like those of the other discussants, suggest that the readers of this book will also be stimulated to evaluate their own observations and conclusions about the psychology of aging.

Understanding the psychodynamics of older persons has proven valuable to psychotherapists, social workers, and physicians in general. Increasingly it has been incorporated into the thinking of human service planners and providers ranging from government agencies and business executives to dieticians and recreational workers in institutions for the elderly. Each person who utilizes psychodynamic principles will necessarily select and adapt them. This volume provides some of the groundwork for such applications in a series of structured papers and formal discussions. The resulting dialogue between experts features a variety of experiences and viewpoints, expressed through the interplay of observation, psychoanalytic theory, and clinical practice.

PART ONE

Normal Psychology
of the
Aging Process

Foreword

MARTIN A. BEREZIN, M.D.

THIS PART CONTAINS the proceedings of the First Annual Scientific Meeting of the Boston Society for Gerontologic Psychiatry. The Society is the first of its kind in the United States.

Some may question the wisdom of organizing a new society in an era when so many medical and scientific societies exist. Some may question the wisdom of suggesting a new medical speciality, i.e., gerontologic psychiatry, in an era when medicine has been criticized for having too many specialties already. These were questions with which we had to deal initially. The answers have come in the response, which has already shown itself in a number of ways in this community. We discovered a rather considerable number of professional people who felt the need for a group of the kind we have organized. A vacuum in the community demanded to be filled.

Response was forthcoming, especially from the field of social work. Clients being managed by various social service agencies have increased not only in numbers but in age, and the percentage of older people has increased remarkably. In some agencies the number of clients over 65 is close to 50 percent, and statistical extrapolations indicate that the relative and absolute numbers will continue to rise. Under this mounting pressure for service to the aged, social service agencies sought guidance from psychiatrists. The various agencies

[3]

quickly discovered that not many psychiatrists were trained and experienced in gerontological problems, and that the demand far exceeded the supply. A number of psychiatrists were drafted, so to speak, who, while not specifically trained, nevertheless undertook to help as best they could. Together the social workers and the psychiatrists learned by experience as they worked out various geriatric problems, and both developed certain skills. What was more significant, those psychiatrists who were willing to undertake consultations and supervisory work found themselves becoming quite interested, some to the point of enthusiasm. What is especially gratifying is that well-trained and qualified people from ancillary professions have joined to help explore and to help provide service — not only social workers, but psychologists, anthropologists, social scientists, educators, statisticians as well.

The problems encountered by social service agencies were simultaneously being encountered in mental hospitals, in old-age homes, in private practice. Gradually, increasing numbers not only of psychiatrists, but of allied professionals, have become interested "geriatricians." The numbers inevitably will increase because the aged population will increase, and similar groups in other cities will soon organize societies such as this one.

Historically, professional interest in the aged has concentrated essentially on economic matters, such as providing money, food, clothing, and shelter. Beginning with President Roosevelt, the far-sighted Social Security plan was established. Such matters were and are essential and basic. However, at this point in the twentieth century, it has become well recognized that food and clothing are not enough. Increasing attention has been directed to emotional and psychological problems, accompanied by a variety of efforts to manage them. The increased incidence of psychiatric disorders among our aged population, based on the absolute increase in the number of aged, has deluged us and has found us lacking in facilities and manpower to cope with it. In 1900 there were three million people in the United States over 65; today, there are five times as many. In ten years there will be 21 million. Each day more than one thousand people reach the age of 65.

It is significant that only five percent of the aged population require custodial care — but five percent of 15 million means that we now have 750 thousand people in this country who require custodial care. The yardstick of custodial care is, however, very crude and quite inaccurate in determining the need for psychiatric assistance. The real demand and the significant need come from a large segment of the 95 percent of aged who are not locked up.

Prophylactically, early prediction, early detection, and early management are important goals in order that our best efforts may be the more valuable. For these reasons, this Society has dedicated itself to the study of the aged in terms of dynamic psychiatry. It is not our intention to underemphasize or neglect all the external conditions impinging on the aged. We are, however, more interested in the psychological makeup of the aged in whatever ways it may differ from the younger age groups. We are interested in studying those variables which determine what is called successful or adaptive old age versus unsuccessful or psychological failure in old age. We feel much is still to be learned about the aged. Whereas there is a considerable literature dealing with external realities and with certain aspects of psychopathology, the literature dealing with the nature of the aged in our society is scanty. At this stage it is our aim to explore the intrapsychic life of the aged person.

For this reason, we have chosen as the subject of our First Annual Scientific Meeting what is after all a very broad topic, the "Normal Psychology of the Aging Process." It is much easier to define states of disease than to define what is healthy or normal. Our subject is, therefore, a difficult one. What emerges from this symposium will play a role in steering our course for the future.

[5]

Cultural and Personality Factors Associated with Aging: An Introduction

NORMAN E. ZINBERG, M.D.

AND

IRVING KAUFMAN, M.D.

THE TASK WE ARE ATTEMPTING in this introduction is a puzzling and difficult, but heartening one. A panel of psychiatrists has addressed itself in various ways to the topic, "The Normal Psychology of the Aging Process." The symposium, designed to represent the field of gerontologic psychiatry, reflects the variety of training, background, and interests in the field. A frame of reference to put these contributions into seemed indicated.

The puzzling nature of the job is clear in the attempt at definition. One could easily define gerontologic psychiatry as the treatment of the emotional disorders of the aged, but if it is a specialty, where are its full-time practitioners? It is true that many psychiatrists see older patients occasionally, or spend a fraction of their time as consultants to an old-age home or ward, but no one makes it his total commitment. To go a controversial step further, although much has been written of value about old people, is there a book that could be considered a recognized text? In fact, who is bold enough to specify exactly when a patient becomes a subject for gerontology? The delineation of the depth, breadth, and scope of the field is the difficult part, and obviously we can only make a beginning.

What is heartening is that psychiatry has become interested in aging. For this to have happened means that there are many more old people than there used to be. It also means that psychiatry is enlarging its horizons. For the sponsoring organization — The Boston Society for Gerontologic Psychiatry, Inc. — to have chosen the topic of the *normal* psychology of aging seems part of the present trend in all of psychiatry toward an interest in the process of personality development. To understand people, what is health as well as what is sickness must be understood. We must delineate ontogeny before attempting to determine deviation. That the panel of psychiatrists should have so faithfully adhered to the topic and given so relatively little consideration to emotional disorders is also worthy of note. Psychiatrists have long been notorious for illustrating so-called normal development by means of contrasting it with the abnormal.

The papers that follow embody discussions of fundamental theoretical and clinical aspects of the aging process. We have chosen, arbitrarily, six general headings to outline a structure for these various aspects.

First, the relationship of the physiology to the psychology of aging is considered under the heading of the physical phenomena of aging. This enormous subject is treated separately but briefly. Everything that follows returns to this topic and is based on it. Second, as all of the contributors essentially subscribed to a psychoanalytic point of view, the changes in the id, ego, and superego due to aging are considered. Although it is arbitrary to separate the next three topics — the vicissitudes of the sexual and aggressive instincts, interaction with other people, and the social and cultural implications of aging — from

[8]

each other, we have made the attempt. The last category, psychopathology of the aged, has been studied by many psychiatrists and will undoubtedly be the focus of future symposia; therefore, we have attempted only the barest outline to complete our sketch.

PHYSICAL PHENOMENA OF AGING

Aging as virtually synonymous with physical deterioration is a frequently expressed point of view. Among the concepts of aging as a process leading to death is the thesis that people die of disease. The proponents of this theory point out that over the years the capacity to re-establish homeostasis is reduced and basic body functions gradually deteriorate. For example, after an injection of sodium bicarbonate, PH and acid-base equilibrium return to normal in about eight hours in a young person, whereas it takes two to three days for a return to normal in a person 60 to 70 years old. Blood flow through the kidney in the 80-year-old man is about half that in the 20-year-old. It is further postulated that such changes are the result of a loss of cells (Shock, 1960).

A consideration of the physical phenomena of aging must include an evaluation of the necessity for the older person to adapt both physically and psychologically to generally impaired physical function that may include all of the body as well as specific disease of an organ or group of organs (Goldfarb and Turner, 1953; Goldfarb, 1955). The fact that organ changes mean an end to the capacity for reproduction may have a special significance, especially for women. The psychological reaction to this physical change has little to do with a realistic desire to have children, but a great deal to do with the person's basic identity. These physical changes lead to a different concept of the self and are of necessity associated with a different estimate of the amount and nature of available energy (Kahn, Zeman, and Goldfarb, 1958).

[9]

The self-image is established at the beginning of life and thereafter bears an important relationship to the concept of the body. The physical and energic changes that accompany aging require a shift in the "body image." Psychologically, it may be difficult to integrate this change, and the aged person's self-esteem may diminish. He may then mobilize a wide variety of defenses to cope with this threat; for example, some patients insist that nothing is wrong with them. Others insist that the valid physical finding represents only "nerves." Still others say that their increased and unending complaints are purely physical and deny the bitterness and uncertainty that accompany bodily changes.

The following case vignette illustrates how even a serious physical insult may seem preferable to an acknowledgment of growing old. A 66-year-old man, who, after work, drove a tractor on a small farm as a beloved hobby, was seized with severe pains up both arms to his shoulders and back. He went home, called his doctor, and announced that he thought he had had a heart attack. He was hospitalized and a thorough examination indicated that his heart was in good condition. A careful history revealed that whenever he had driven the tractor in recent months he had experienced discomfort in his arms and shoulders. It turned out that the tractor was an old one and in reality his arms and shoulders were no longer able to sustain the stress without complaint. But for this man to acknowledge the limitations of aging, and its associated weakness and helplessness, was harder to face than a serious but specific illness that afforded secondary gain and the promise of resolution.

In the aging, it is often difficult to separate physical disability from the effects of prolonged or intense unresolved emotional conflict. The assumption that aging is more or less synonymous with physical deterioration is not universally shared (Dunbar, 1957). Those who stress the role of emotional factors maintain that if certain emotional conflicts are resolved, then

[10]

many physical symptoms improve or are easier to bear. A significant portion of physical deterioration may then be viewed as caused by mental illness, and should and could be treated psychiatrically. This optimistic view is seductive to many psychiatrists. To the extent that a major factor in the effect of physical changes is a neurotic reaction, a wider use of mental health approaches would be indicated. The value of this point of view in encouraging the interest of psychiatrists and the development of mental health facilities for the aged cannot be underestimated. On the other hand, if false optimism is encouraged, the risk is run of disappointing both the older people and the professionals interested in geriatrics when, even in the absence of specific disease, loss of physical reserve leads to a general restriction of functions and proneness to a greater possibility of trauma, infection, and degenerative and chronic illness.

Structural Components of the Psyche

The Id

In aging, as in other stages of life, there is no direct representation of the id. The id remains an abstraction necessary for a theory based on biological drives. It is in the id that the instinctual drives and associated repressed conflicts remain in an unchanging, timeless state. The contradictory emotions of love and hate exist side by side. Since the impulses contained in the id are timeless, the process of aging does not change them (Schuster, 1952). What changes are the psychic structures through which the impulses reach consciousness, the physical apparatus available for the discharge of the impulses, and the reaction of the external world to the organism. While this last has no direct relation to the basic, primitive, instinctual responses, it certainly has bearing on the vicissitudes of the sexual and aggressive drives. For purposes of clarity, and especially

[11]

because of misunderstandings about sexuality in the aged, the vicissitudes of these id drives will be discussed in a separate section.

At the beginning of the twentieth century, when psychoanalysis was codifying its great discoveries, Freud and others who were influenced by him, notably Groddeck, were busy speculating about the contents of this reservoir of basic psychic energy. Because any representation of the id has to reach consciousness and expression in behavior by way of the ego, psychoanalytic interest slowly shifted to the ego. As modification of the ego was necessary to bring about therapeutic change, and as it was recognized that therapy had no effect on the id impulses, interest in the id became increasingly theoretical.

It is possible that interest in the alignment of psychic structures in the aging may reawaken interest in the id. A prominent clinical phenomenon of aging concerns the direct expression of impulses. With aging, the expression of a sexual or aggressive impulse is less likely to be surrounded by derivative motivations. The aim of the impulse may be somewhat altered, but inhibitions about its expression are fewer. An elderly patient who wishes total care from the hospital is much less likely to be nice to the nurses to get what he desires than is a young person. The aged patient is more likely to scream, or even soil the bed, if care is withheld. The screaming or soiling represents an almost direct expression of impulse without the delay, inhibition, substitution, or use of rational processes that one sees when the ego is integrated and in control of the impulses. A prominent concept in psychoanalytic theory is that primitive impulses are in part tamed by the gradual fusion of libidinal and aggressive components as they appear in the ego. The possibility that in aging there is a progressive defusion of these libidinal and aggressive elements, which permits greater direct expression, raises important theoretical and clinical issues.

Another problem directly related to the id is the avenue by

[12]

which an impulse arrives at discharge. For example, an elderly husband and wife each evening had a heated spat about inconsequentialitites and then, apparently satisfied, sat down to dinner. Upon questioning, there was no evidence of a long-standing sadomasochistic relationship; rather, they had developed this pattern late in life. Could it be that direct aggressive discharge was needed before they could tolerate the libidinal excitation of dinner? Such an example indicates that careful consideration should be given to what reaches the ego, and in what form, at each developmental stage of life.

Certainly the possibilities of substitute drive gratification in the aging are much discussed, especially regressive sexuality and the secret tyranny of the weak. The discussion usually concerns the controls of the ego and not the state of the impulse. If neutralization of aggressive and libidinal energies is considered part of maturation, it is certainly possible that in aging there is not only deneutralization but also change in what reaches the ego because of defusion.

The Ego

A hypothesis of ego psychology is that the ego undergoes development throughout life. Therefore, the fate of the ego is of necessity of paramount importance in a discussion of the normal psychology of aging. The form this development takes is extremely variable, although not infinitely so. As we have indicated, the instincts too undergo vicissitudes, but in a different way: the instincts need a mode of expression and, if one avenue is denied by the culture, then another is found. Finding acceptable modes of expression for the instincts, meeting the demands of the environment, satisfying the superego, and giving itself the opportunity for growth are the multiple functions of the ego (Waelder, 1936). The last, which represents the subtle problem of an identity and the satisfaction of the ego instincts, is the most complex and most individual.

Modern psychoanalytic theory allows for three sources of

[13]

energy in the psychic apparatus (Rapaport, 1951). The ego instincts, which roughly are self-preservative in the sense that their aim is man's coming to terms with his environment, now stand beside the libidinal and aggressive strivings as prime motivations of behavior. It is assumed that the ego is the origin of the force for the essential task of preserving the individual and maintaining the optimum balance between inner and outer strivings.

The specific problems associated with aging with which the ego must cope are the internal and external bodily changes, the loss of status characteristic of our future-oriented culture, the loss of significant people, the modification in the range of available activities, and, more philosophically, whatever it means to prepare for death. As each other developmental phase prepares for the next, so this period before the end of life is under the aegis of what is anticipated.

It is a truism that all ego functions are dependent on the person's situation. Perceptual thresholds are maintained by the values, special interests, and anxiety level of each person, and what the aged person permits himself to notice and his interpretation of what he sees are affected by his concept of himself (Leeds, 1960). Differences in perception are frequently illustrated by what a tree may mean: to a soldier—cover, to an artist—a model, to a tired wanderer—shade for a rest, to an ecologist—a statistic, etc. It was noted in a rest home how frequently geriatric patients asked the age of a tree and commented on its longevity. The question was never raised by the young patients, no matter how ill.

All of the defense mechanisms (A. Freud, 1936) and other ego functions that were available to the person in his youth for the purpose of coping with stress are still potentially available, but the life situation may be so altered that the original purpose of a defense mechanism cannot be achieved. For example, a man who utilized the defense mechanism of displacement and expressed forbidden hostile feelings toward au-

[14]

thority figures by kicking dogs cannot obtain the same relief in an old-age home where dogs are forbidden.

It is in the system of defenses that observations have been made which seem to indicate that different mechanisms come to the fore because they specifically serve the personality at this stage of development. The specificity of defenses in the individual is so great that some writers feel that, besides the plastic response to environmental pressures, a congenital preference for defense mechanisms is likely (Gill and Brenman, 1959), and it is understood that in any discussion of changes of defenses during aging we are discussing only relative shifts. Difficult as it is to generalize, the defenses most applicable to the aging seem to be regression, isolation, compartmentalization, and denial. There is some evidence that certain other defenses, such as repression and projection, play a different role in normal aging than in early stages of development.

Regression may serve the same basic function in the aged that repression does in youth. Our use of regression is an extension of Ernst Kris's (1952) concept of "regression in the service of the ego," and is to be differentiated from regression proper or regression as a component of pathological processes. Just as an appropriate degree of repression is necessary in youth to establish a balance between the id, the ego, and the environment, so may a degree of regression be necessary to maintain homeostatic balance in old age. In aging, the person may shift the balance between id, ego, and environment by a diminution of repression (Gitelson, 1948). Relative regression occurs in order for the person to maintain the homeostasis altered by the changes in the instincts and in environmental forces. A massive return of the repressed or an inability to permit the weakening of repression would occasion a pathological regression or symptom formation.

When physical and psychological capacities are impaired in aging — and some such modification is universal — regression as a defense may activate modes of adaptation that have been previously available. This is frequently exemplified in relationships with important people in the aged person's life. If there is a specific physical impairment, the ego is confronted with the task of finding a relatively conflict-free dependency relationship which is acceptable and thus adaptive. When this occurs, it may permit a smoother relationship with, for example, a son, daughter, or physician. If the regression entails the reinstatement of earlier stages of libidinal development, including character traits of this earlier phase, this too may be part of an adaptation that redirects the person's activities and wishes. For instance, even miserliness in someone who had been reasonably generous when younger may conserve financial resources, and, within the context of turning inward and not being part of the future-oriented culture, not push the person toward acquiring money, position, or power which may no longer have the same importance to him.

On the other hand, if the regressive reactions are not relatively conflict-free, the character traits or object relations characteristic of the regressed state may be unacceptable either to the ego or to the external environment. In such cases the regression is unlikely to remain transient and limited, and may create a cumulative problem, feeding on its own increased anxiety. Clinically this appears as a fixation, and mentally produces either an intrapsychic conflict manifested by symptoms or a struggle with the outside world.

Reference to the concept "conflict-free" is in terms of the ego-adaptive implications. For example, an oldster may complain about his dependence on someone else for accurate current memory without having the kind of conflict about dependency that would lead to maladaptive regression. This is in contrast to the person who says, "Take care of me" and accepts regression in a way that makes for inevitable conflict with an environment which can never satisfy such a wish.

Generally speaking, when a person regresses, the pattern of the regression follows patterns already established in him, although the particular stress of the environment may make for some selectiveness. This is generally accepted, but should be noted because a careful history of previous personality traits may clarify the patterns of adaptation and the problems that have resulted from personality changes in an older patient.

Isolation as a defense mechanism enables the older person to deal with concepts and affects that he could not tolerate otherwise. Conversations about death and infirmity could probably not take place without a high degree of isolation, and (clinically) many physicians feel that such conversations can be helpful if not permitted to become a morbid obsession. The equanimity with which older people can sometimes accept the death of old friends and relatives is remarkable. No doubt part of their grief is dispelled by the pleasure they feel in the awareness of their own continued existence, but that does not seem to be a sufficient explanation for the successful management of such a potentially anxiety-provoking subject; an increased capacity to isolate affect seems a necessary hypothesis.

This increased capacity is not within the voluntary control of the person and may spread into many areas of his life. As a result, the separation from feelings may convey to friends and family an icy distance that further interferes with the older person's maintaining close relationships. This may produce a vicious circle of retaliation and further withdrawal.

It is possible that the isolation of awareness of sequences and their causal relations observed so frequently in younger patients is less frequent in older people. The younger person may say that he has a headache and does not know why. A little later in the interview he may inadvertently mention a disagreement with his boss just preceding the headache and not make a conscious connection between the two phenomena. The observer, knowing the character structure of the patient, may feel certain that the headache resulted from the trouble with the boss, especially if it is a recurring pattern. The older patient is far less likely to "kid himself." His awareness of being

[17]

stirred up by disagreements may be accompanied by a cynical disregard for his own feelings, because he understands himself in a sense too well, but he is more likely to know where the feelings come from and why he is upset.

Compartmentalization, aided by the narrowing of consciousness, plays an important role in the aged. All of the factors such as physical disability, memory changes, reduced learning capacity, etc., put a premium on the person's dealing with one thing at a time, both internally and externally. Repetitiveness, rigidity, even what seems to be negativism, may be representations of compartmentalization. The aged person may experience a rigid necessity to repeat an old memory to a younger person even when he knows that it is boring or irritating. This may be an attempt to deal with the physical and emotional stress of maintaining contact with other people, and thus may be a necessary adaptive ego process enabling the older person to more effectively hold on to reality by holding on to what he knows, even at the expense of being pleasing.

The older person seems to be selective in the use of denial, especially against fantasies (Weinberg, 1959). Many feelings strongly resisted by younger people are accepted by the aged. The fact that people have destructive and envious urges is often admitted to consciousness without the anxiety and accompanying disorganization that might have occurred if the same feelings had reached awareness earlier in life. Older people seem to show greater acceptance of aggressive feelings than of sexual; perhaps there are more irritating than enjoyable events in their lives. When this awareness is commented on to older patients, they seem to agree that at least part of it is gained by their feeling that they have nothing to lose. They fear the judgment of others less because they see the future as unimportant. They also feel more put upon, and have less reserves of gratification to tolerate frustrations. On the other hand, when it comes to sexual feelings or aspects of physical deterioration, denial may be a necessary and useful defense

[18]

mechanism. At times denial and isolation are integrally linked. The apparent resignation of some older patients clearly indicates the use of both defenses.

Certainly the restrictions of the ego evidenced as avoidance of discomfort, whether intrapsychic, interpersonal, or environmental, are forms of denial. Stress such as illness or loss is painful. Anything that stirs up the threat of an event, such as travel or stimulation of memories, may cause painful affect. The aim is to narrow the field of awareness so as to avoid painful affect, and this is accomplished by denial of affect or the attempt to deny the existence of that which may be painful.

A weakening of repressive forces may be necessary to maintain a homeostatic balance in the personality of the aged. Thus we see selective denial, in which certain memories are admitted and others are excluded from consciousness. This is intensified by the freshness of the available past to the older person, even some aspects which are usually forbidden to consciousness. Some of this availability of past memory may be used to fill in the emptiness and crowd out more unpleasant thoughts. However, the accessibility to consciousness of unconscious primitive material which accompanies the early memories is hard to disregard and, at times, results in confusion and depression. On the positive side, this greater capacity for the aging person to dip into his unconscious may also account for the occasional flowering of creativeness in the later years of life (Grotjahn, 1951, 1955; Meerloo, 1955, 1961).

Although a physiologically determined diminution of sensory functioning often occurs, this appears to be a selective process. Many old people, for example, seem to see or hear what they wish to see or hear. It has been suggested that this selective process is further determined by the ego, as a means of reducing the intensity and quantity of external stimuli which may threaten to upset the psychic equilibrium (Swartz, 1960).

Although projection as a pathological defense is seen in

[19]

paranoia and other severe pathological responses in aging, in general the capacity of the older person to know his own feelings and motivations, even the less palatable ones, results in less frequent use of this defense mechanism than would be expected. Younger patients who are unsure of their boundaries often expect the outside world's response to them to be directly in terms of their own feelings. In the middle years, when so much energy is directed to the competitive acquisition of power, the use of projection is intensified. In the later years this trend tends to diminish, with a greater awareness of motives, feelings of cynicism, and even despair.

The Superego

The reorganization of the superego in aging has many of the same characteristics as the riddle of the Sphinx; in many ways, it ends up the way it began. We conceive of the earliest form of development of the superego as the global identification with a parental figure. Its growth is accomplished by the inclusion of more and more identifications with people and components of the social structure. If sufficient successful identifications are accompanied with a wide enough range, then an ordering of a system of values and the development of a flexible, reality-oriented conscience takes place.

It seems possible that in the aged this process is reversed. Although still expressed in the terms and the likenesses of people from adult life, the interchanges desired in relationships with people resemble those acceptable to the ego ideal early in life. The necessity for direct narcissistic supplies seems to be the overriding consideration in this return to an early pattern of ego-ideal relationship. The important difference between this development in the aged and a regressive move in a young adult is the appropriateness of the pattern for the needs of this stage of development. As in the young child, the consideration of ego ideal overrides and may conflict with the conscience. Correctness is often determined in relation to

[20]

important people and their responses, not by an inner system of mores. There is a shift away from more abstract representations of the ego ideal, and greater dependence on definite available figures. These figures, in their imagery, become very close to mother and father. Even if relatively abstract principles such as religion or patriotism are used, these become personalized rather than abstract; to the aged person, God becomes closer to "De Lawd" of *The Green Pastures* (Connelly, 1929) than to the intellectual god of modern religion (Goldfarb, 1955).

The older person's ego state, depleted by physical change and loss, probably could not tolerate a superego whose conscience was unmodified. Successful adaptation to the lessening capacity to appear always immaculate, clean-shaven, or with evenly applied mascara requires a weakening of conscience. A strict conscience would deny the person his necessary narcissistic supplies in the form of love and help from the external world.

Vicissitudes of Sexuality and Aggression

The libidinal and aggressive drives have to be dealt with by the aged while they are coping with shifts in their physical and emotional structure. Many sexual and aggressive characteristics of earlier stages of development persist into the advanced years of a person's life. The expression of these characteristics is influenced by an adaptive process relating instinctual drives, ego structure, and the culture.

The overt expression of sexuality in the aged is one area in which research is needed. We find that sexual interest and often sexual activity survive in the aged to a much greater extent than has been generally accepted by our culture (Newman and Nichols, 1960; N. Cameron, 1945). Only in recent times have we begun to study the sexual habits, capacities, and interests of people of all ages. Nowhere is there less true knowl-

[21]

edge and more myth than in the discussion of sexuality in the aged (Clow and Allen, 1951).

This lack of knowledge can be illustrated by the following occurrence on the teaching wards of a geriatric unit in a general hospital. Several groups of medical students from all four years of study were asked what they knew about the sexual habits and interests of the aged. Without exception they were embarrassed both by the question and by their lack of knowledge about the subject. When asked at last to guess, they all tended to the belief that, with rare exceptions, sexual interests and the expression of these interests slowly diminish to the vanishing point during and after the middle years. The more psychologically sophisticated students mentioned regressive manifestations of sexuality. What was most remarkable was the fact that this subject had never been mentioned by any instructor throughout the medical school career of these students. Even the socially acquired knowledge potentially available to both students and instructors by way of observation and innuendo seemed to be difficult for them to maintain in consciousness.

Anna Freud, in *The Ego and the Mechanisms of Defense* (1936), points out that the defense mechanism of repression is particularly utilized with the sexual drives and has a special relationship to the vicissitudes of the oedipal conflict. At some time in childhood the direct sexual wishes of the oedipal stage connected to parents or parent surrogates succumb to repression. This psychological milestone is viewed as important, and accorded due regard in the development of a balanced personality, or, when unresolved, in the production of psychopathology. Our experience with the medical students seems to show that not enough importance has been attached to the persistence of oedipal concerns and the defenses against them within the personality structure of professional people unimpaired by obvious neurosis. It is, of course, only speculation that ignorance in the young about the presence of hetero-

[22]

sexual urges and their expression in the older person is a derivative of the oedipal conflict. However, there is sufficient evidence of such attitudes to warrant further investigation. The assumption is that this repression is a further vicissitude of the oedipal conflict, is general, applies to everyone, and is not connected with neurosis. If correct, its implications for the medical management of many of the problems of the aged are enormous. Many old-age homes are divided into separate male and female sections, representing a morality reminiscent of early adolescence. The unquestioning acceptance of this division by physicians, both medical and psychiatric, is a powerful indication of the strength of the cultural wish to deny the existence of sexual expression by the aged.

The conflicts concerning sexual thoughts and behavior that are so clearly seen in younger people also survive. In many of the aged, conflicts concerning sexual expression are longstanding. However, many people who, during their youth and middle years, were able to achieve relative comfort about sexuality become uncomfortable with their erotic desires in a culture that in effect prohibits or ridicules the expression of such desire in the older person.

The fact that the idealized sexual standard of this culture emphasizes the firm bodies of youth may also reactivate oedipal conflicts in the aged. The passage of years has not made forbidden sexual interests any easier for the person to tolerate. In our example of the medical students we stressed the usual view of how oedipal conflicts affect the developing person. We know full well from our patients that it is not only children, but also parents, whose sexual interests and defenses against them are activated by the process of development. This *ronde* does not stop until death. The shame experienced by the older person as the result of a forbidden sexual impulse that may or may not be repressed sets up reverberations in his younger physician or family. The physicians in turn have the problem of struggling not only with their own more or less resolved oedipal

[23]

NORMAN E. ZINBERG — IRVING KAUFMAN

strivings, but also with the stimulus provided by the inhibited sexual reactions of their older patients, family, or friends. This rondelay of point and counterpoint is complicated by the cultural attitude which makes it extremely necessary for both sides to deny that it is taking place. When feelings are so urgently repressed, the result is often more rather than less activity, whether in covert expression or defensive reactions.

The situation, then, is that of the younger physician, who unknowingly has had his own ego balance somewhat disturbed, dealing with an aged patient, who needs help to accept and resolve feelings that he fears are forbidden. All too often this situation results in poor communication and agreement by both physician and patient to divert attention to body functions other than the directly sexual.

The most obvious increased concern in the aged is the great interest in bowel and eating difficulties. In the physical deterioration that so often accompanies aging, there usually are gastrointestinal difficulties. Particularly in the general hospital, where such malfunction is the rule rather than the exception, the gastrointestinal tract tends to be libidinized. We are keenly aware of the regressive sexual interests in the aged that take the form of concern with food and feces. We do not mean to deny these obvious complaints and their significance in the psychic economy of the aged; rather, we call attention to the fact that these pregenital interests may also serve as a covert expression of more direct genital concerns. If this indirect expression is accepted too readily at face value by the physician, then an opportunity to relieve anxiety may be lost. Reassurance is reassurance only if it deals with what the patient is anxious about. To give a laxative and to explain to the patient how his bowel difficulty will be relieved does not result in fewer questions about his constipation if the basic anxiety is about genital stimulation.

It would be inaccurate for us to give the impression that it is only in direct genital vigor that the physical changes of aging conflict with a cultural view. Particularly in the United States, the heritage of a pioneer culture seems to have culminated in enormous value being placed on youth, muscular capacity, and physical well-being of all sorts. When the older person becomes aware of physical changes of a deteriorating nature, whether for physiological or psychological reasons, a diminution of interest in any genital activity often occurs. It is in these people that we so often see a preoccupation with bowel and stomach functioning.

A clinical example will illustrate the point. A 71-year-old woman was admitted to the hospital with low-grade fever and multiple complaints of pain, anorexia, fatigue, and constipation. It was suspected that she had a simple viral infection, but her difficulties had been both great enough and of long enough duration to warrant hospitalization and study. Her medical examination was thorough, with careful attention paid to the areas of all of her complaints. The taking of the history had been somewhat difficult because she was garrulous, and her mind wandered when she was asked about details. Shortly after admission an enema was ordered. The patient militantly refused the enema, became disoriented, thrashed about in her bed, and was thoroughly refractory to any therapeutic intervention. A psychiatrist was summoned. He could not make any direct verbal contact with the patient, so he simply sat with her for a time and tried to listen to what she was muttering. He finally made out that the phrase repeated almost continuously was "if I was a *junge madluch* [young woman]." He began to question her, asking her, "What if you were a young woman?" She answered, "If I was a young woman I would understand it." The psychiatrist realized that she was trying to tell him that something had happened to her that would be understandable if she were a young woman. He questioned her carefully about her initial physical examination, explaining to her all the time that he was a physician and that this was a hospital. As she began to comprehend the

[25]

direction of his questions, she was able to convey that she had been, in her eyes, attacked genitally. It was ascertained that her initial workup had included both genital and rectal examinations which were entirely necessary to eliminate any possibility of a malignancy. When it was clear what the patient felt had happened to her, it was possible to relieve her anxiety, and she quieted down. It was not that the examining doctor had been negligent, but it was true that some of the usual preliminary preparations for such an examination had been omitted because of the difficulty in thinking of this sick, 71-year-old woman in sexual terms.

Not only the libidinal but also the aggressive drives are affected by the aging process. In fact, the diminution of overt libidinal expression may intensify the more direct expression of annoyance. While some people "mellow" with age, more become "crotchety" (Sheps, 1959). In regard to the expression of aggressive impulses, none of the aged are unaffected. For some, aging permits them to say what they think with the simple directness of childhood. For others, lifelong traits of generality, circumstantiality, and subterfuge become exaggerated. These opposites of directness and subterfuge are used so that each may experience his form of expression as a way to discharge his angry feelings.

Angry reactions in the aged are often better tolerated by the culture than are such reactions in younger people. Because of physical handicaps and the fact that everyday life is geared to the demands of the culture, the older patient has more than enough frustration and difficulty to allow him to rationalize and justify the expression of considerable aggression (Goldfarb, 1955).

For instance, in the roentgenological department of a general hospital, the patient may of necessity be kept waiting for a time between X-rays that require serial viewing. An old man of 78, whose stomach was under such surveillance, became enraged when he saw people being X-rayed who had arrived in

[26]

the department after he had. Although not in any physical discomfort, he was frustrated at being kept waiting, and further bothered when, as he saw it, others were taken ahead of him out of turn. This resulted in an outburst of such ferocity that orderlies had to be summoned to keep the peace. While this may be an extreme example, the older person is notoriously finicky about hotel accommodations or limit-setting rules such as traffic regulations.

With the blocking, fusion or defusion, and changes in expression of sexual and aggressive drives, especially under the impact of physical changes, there is a tendency for the aging to regress to manners and subjects associated with earlier stages of development. For example, the women in old-age homes sit in rockers and are all too willing to discuss only their operations, diets, or laxatives. A woman who was known by her associates to be friendly, outgoing, and generous became irritable, reclusive, and stingy during her later years. A man who had been a source of strength and support to much of his family became childish, peevish, and demanding in his old age. These were people who, because of loss, change in financial status, and physical deterioration, were especially hard-hit and responded severely.

These sexual and aggressive phenomena cannot be separated from the physical and cultural phenomena of aging. Neither can they be separated from the changes in the defense system and in other aspects of the ego's functioning with aging.

Interpersonal Relationships

Like people at all stages of development, the aging need interpersonal relationships to sustain emotional life. The aging person's interpersonal relationships are influenced by previous personality patterns, the presence or degree of organic difficulty, and the ego structure.

The most obvious change in the older person's relationship

[27]

with people close to him is his tendency to reinstate early patterns of behavior. The older person frequently casts important family members or others, especially doctors, in the role of parent surrogates. This is difficult for everyone. It is erratic. Sometimes the older person will expect or demand that others take over, make decisions, and supply all his needs; at other times he will zealously guard every bit of prerogative, status, or position. Often an excess in either direction results in remorse and loss of self-esteem. Careful management by family and doctors is necessary, and this necessity is hard for both. Some flexibility is necessary to sustain successful object relations, and the personality changes of aging limit this range (Rosen and Neugarten, 1960).

Although it is not possible to define one single type of older person, certain characteristics emerge with sufficient frequency to make them worthy of consideration. Interactions with people are related to the tasks of the ego, which, at this stage, seem to be, even more than at other stages, the obtaining of narcissistic supplies. These supplies are obtained by means of a reinstatement of methods of gaining direct response from the outside that were prominent early in life. Although a desire for material things by the old person may be great, it is probable that what he desires primarily is the love, succor, respect, and gratification that comes from people. What is accentuated is the need, and the awareness of the need, for these supplies at a time when, for many reasons, fewer responses and fewer substitutes for responses from people are available. For example, a bedridden grandmother would give her young grandson 25 cents after he talked with her for a half-hour. The importance of these narcissistic supplies cannot be overestimated. Their loss, whether it be the "hello" from the grocer or the weekly telephone call from the daughter, can result in repressive or depressive reactions.

In a way, the older person is confronted with conflicting and often opposite choices. Because of both internal and cultural pressures, he is in the process of disengaging himself

[28]

from many ties. These include ties to friends and relatives who die, to jobs, and often to housing. At the same time, there is an urgency to live in the present and not look forward to the friends he might make next summer or even next week. Moreover, although internal pressures of physical infirmity or decreased capacity make for a narcissistic orientation, at the same time there is a new desire to live vicariously through the younger generation. The result of these forces is often a person who at times is remarkably direct, forthright, and open in his thoughts, desires, wishes, and expressions of dissatisfaction, but at other times, and in other areas of his life, may appear to be quite apathetic. Some persons become so apathetic, narcissistic, or self-centered that they are unable to respond beyond themselves and may require institutional or nursing care. Sometimes, with increased attention, such people can be helped to be more responsive.

As a part of the need to hold on to people, older persons often become "sticky," loquacious, and repetitious. This at times results in the younger person wishing to rid himself of the older one, and can produce a vicious circle of increased demand and increased rejection (Linden, 1957).

Preoccupation with the body, whether with food intake, bowel functioning, accidents, or operations, is a not infrequent baseline of the conversation of older persons. These preoccupations are generally most acceptable to other older persons, who tend to respond in kind. But in many ways this behavior is analogous to the parallel play patterns of prenursery school children, where the presence of the other person and his activities give some justification for narcissistic interests. Neither older person seems disappointed that the other does not become involved in a real interchange. In fact, such a direct focus may even be threatening, as part of the unconscious motivation for talking about the body is an attempt magically to relieve anxiety about what is happening. The young child who has been to the doctor for an inoculation will repeatedly play doctor and inoculate his teddy bear. The older

[29]

person who is confronted with infirmity or diminished capacity to use his body also utilizes the repetition compulsion, talking about his body and its functions in the hope that he will feel better and do better.

Since the above pattern is alien and anxiety-stimulating to younger persons, they tend to avoid participating in such conversations or to stop them. This action thwarts the emotional needs of the older person and leads to conflict between generations in terms of the defense patterns they use in relating to each other. Perhaps greater understanding of the needs of the old would lead to greater tolerance in the young.

Two opposite extremes of behavior, already mentioned in the discussion on sexuality and aggression, warrant special mention here. Some older persons mellow and become more tolerant, while others become cantankerous and irritable. A variety of factors apparently determines the direction the older persons will take. Those who have both experienced gratifications and successfully mastered disappointments tend to mellow. Those who, like "the spoiled child," have tended to be orally demanding and have little tolerance for frustration, tend to become increasingly bitter and irritable about the numerous frustrations associated with aging.

The use of isolation and compartmentalization, particularly in relation to the loss of friends, etc., is significant for the interpersonal relationships of the older person. These necessary defense mechanisms may give an erroneous impression that the person does not care, or no longer has any "feelings." This is far from true; but temporarily or in relation to a specific person or event, he may need to withdraw or be less responsive.

SOCIAL AND CULTURAL IMPLICATIONS OF AGING

A consideration of the influence of the environment on the aging person must include an evaluation of Western culture and its values and the major institutions that affect the aging persons. The physician, the psychiatrist, and the general community agencies have primary contributions to make to the well-being, therapy, and management of the aging population. In this group the need for direct treatment is usually less than the need for consistent realistic management of their lives. For the optimum care of these patients, as with other segments of the population whose condition induces dependency—the chronically ill or children, for instance—it is necessary to involve the essential family figures and such community resources as public health nurses, social agencies, hospital and rehabilitation facilities, etc. (Cohen, 1960).

Let us turn to a consideration of the influence of Western culture and its values upon the aging person.

In Western civilization, the Protestant ethic stresses the necessity for independence and the overcoming of instinctual drives and unconscious wishes. In many ways the emphasis remains on the "will" rather than on the "reason." Strength is measured by the capacity to achieve, and to combat and resist incapacity. Immorality of thought and deed as well as dependency are seen as weaknesses of the physical or moral fiber. Moreover, the culture retains a heritage of pioneer days and rugged individualism, even if, in fact, individualism has been in abeyance for many years. People try to look young and act young. An example of this phenomenon is the current "star" situation in motion pictures. Many of the most important actors and actresses who are into their fifties and older play romantic heroes and heroines opposite quite young men and women. They attempt to perpetuate a fiction of youth because, if they should leave such parts, the only place to go would be to elderly character roles. There is no middle ground, so they put off the transition as long as possible.

This situation reflects the American worship of youth, physical fitness, and strength, which leaves little for the older person. In the young the dream is to "succeed," and there is a constant forging ahead, until suddenly one is old and slipping back with little opportunity for a meaningful goal or way of life. There is no plateau or level ground. This situation is further reinforced by the general policies, in this country, of not hiring people over a certain age, and of compulsory retirement. In these ways the culture further contributes to the aging person's difficulty in finding channels for self-expression or self-esteem. Our commercial, industrial, and even educational institutions pay little heed to their "counselors." Whether it is a kick upstairs to Chairman of the Board, or simply retirement at half pay, the culture usually forces retirement on older people at a specific age, regardless of their physical and emotional condition.

In many people, the retirement syndrome begins before retirement. Obsolescence is so much a part of everyday life that the older worker senses long before retirement that he is not the shiny new model that everyone in the advertisements wants. The older man becomes concerned with his work performance and insecure about his position. If he should leave his current job, at his age it will be hard to get another that is equivalent. If he becomes unemployed, he must often take what he can get. The accompanying insecurity does not help his work performance or mood at work, and we have the beginning of a vicious circle. The idea of forced retirement is a painful one; older people see retirement as the first step away from vigor. Their perception of themselves changes more than they themselves do, but the result can be a self-fulfilling prophecy, particularly as the perception is buttressed by the view of society.

Three personality types have special difficulty with retirement. The true obsessive, who needs work to structure his life, who has always found vacations and even Sundays a little unsettling, upon retirement finds himself with a perpetual "Sunday neurosis." For him a threat to his ability to be active seems total and disorganizing, and leaves him passive and weak in his own eyes. Those who have made an excessive libid-inal investment in the subject of their work find that separa-tion results in the same kind of depression that results from the loss of a loved person. The work had become the satisfaction itself, not a means to that end. The third type is the person who has used work as a way of feeling that he is useful and has something of value to give. He is haunted by the feelings of worthlessness and emptiness that he has spent a lifetime hold-ing at bay.

The problems associated with retirement seem to be, in part, culturally determined. For example, the suicide rate of old people in this country is higher than that of old people in Japan. In this country there seems to be no comfortable natu-ral position, no plan for aging, that satisfies the needs of the old people and of the culture. The Japanese revere their aged, and the concern for and even worship of ancestors provides a firm base in faith and even worship for both the older and younger generations. The Eskimos, on the other hand, leave the oldest and most infirm out to freeze when the hunting and fishing are inadequate to support life for all. It is a harsh plan, but one that satisfies the need and is clear to all.

It is probable that, in the general homogenization of cul-tures that is taking place in the world, these specific ways of dealing with the aged will disappear. It is also probable that if as a race we survive our knowledge of nucleonics, the problem of the aged will be only one aspect of the population explosion. However, it is obvious that other groups have found ways of meeting the problem that are different from ours even if a so-lution such as that of the Eskimos would be wholly unaccept-able to us.

Enforced retirement has created a number of interesting phenomena whose effect has yet to be totally evaluated. There has been an enormous growth of old-age "towns," particularly in Florida, Texas, Arizona, and California. Here the older person tries to redeem the promise that after a lifetime of work he will have leisure for relaxation and a good time. In many instances it seems to have worked well. Careful planning architecturally, medically, and socially has contributed to a way of life that many retired people find acceptable and pleasant. The concentration of old people in states with a good climate is not limited to the winter months, although it is heaviest then. So many retired people have moved to California, for instance, that the state has passed laws to prevent the older person from practicing a trade or profession on a part-time basis. The state legislature feared that the older person who wished to work only to the extent of not endangering his Social Security income would work more cheaply than a younger person, and thus hamper the laborer or professional on whom the industrial growth of the state depended. Here too a major change may be in the offing as the ever-increasing number of older people represents a greater political force. This is not a new phenomenon, for it is several decades since the Townsend plan attracted political attention to the geriatric population as a political bloc. An attempt to protect their interests led the aged to cut across party lines and old ties. Politicians who had depended on older people as party regulars who were "set in their ways" increasingly found that there was a new "union" which had to be considered as a unit. In the states where older people have settled in significant numbers they are considered by some politicians as the decisive political force when an issue is in doubt, and are courted accordingly.

Many of the problems we have mentioned make the way hard for the politician. He finds the older voter often embittered by a feeling of a lifetime of work not sufficiently appreciated, and his vote may seem one of the few ways he can show his displeasure. He is suspicious of false promises and yet wants, even demands, guarantees of security that are fiscally unreasonable. This mixture in the aging of conservatism and a reckless wish to be gratified is observable in other areas of their lives as well.

[34]

Another important fact in political and economic life is that women are increasingly outliving men. As a result, more and more of the wealth of this country is controlled by women, and a greater percentage of the voters are women, and old women at that. Generally speaking, older women seem to have a more secure place in the culture than do older men. When the men are alive and retired, the women's traditional duties of shopping, cooking, and cleaning house are augmented by having the men at home. This situation is a shift from the middle years when the man is at the height of his productivity, the children are about grown, and the woman seems to have the most difficult time finding a satisfactory niche for herself.

In areas other than child rearing, such as general management, care of a house and a kitchen, a more secure position of teacher and purveyor of tradition seems to remain with women. The day when the father taught his skills to his son is past, and in our modern industrial society the position of the older man seems the more difficult one. However, whether the husband is alive or not, the role of grandmother may be an important and even essential one. Many pediatricians and child psychiatrists comment on the importance of the grandmother in child rearing. Recently, a young pediatrician said that as a medical student and intern he learned almost exclusively about children, which was what attracted him to pediatrics. He said that he had dimly known that the problem in the practice of pediatrics was the anxious or nervous mother, and he was more or less prepared for her. However, he was not prepared for the formidable, often knowledgeable, and always opinionated grandmother who interviewed him with each house call as if he were a job applicant. Had he known about the grandmothers, he said, he would have gone into pathology.

The physician may play a crucial role in maximizing the effective functioning of the older person. In all persons, of course, total functioning is dependent on the relation between

[35]

physical and psychological well-being, but this balance is infinitely more precarious in the aged, and the general physician is becoming increasingly aware of the responsibility this fact puts upon him. Relatively minor physical ailments that could be shrugged off by the younger patient have to be treated in the aged so as not to alter the homeostasis and institute a regression.

The problems faced by the geriatrician are many, and chief among them is that of communication. As we have already noted, enduring personality traits tend to become accentuated and more poorly controlled. A taciturn or a garrulous person tends to be more so, and problems of control and dominance and submission are common and very much affect the doctor-patient relationship. For instance, frequently a patient who has been uncomfortable and complaining bitterly to his family will, when he goes to the doctor, with great effort pull himself together and tell the doctor that things aren't so bad. The motivation for this change in attitude may be a fear of the doctor or the implications of illness, a wish to please the doctor and win his regard, or many other complex feelings. It is important for the physician to be aware of possible subterfuge in order to determine accurately the extent of the disturbance. Moreover, the family will be bewildered by the patient's change of mood, and one of the physician's jobs, and a difficult one, is to explain it to the family to prevent their being angry at the patient. The reverse situation—the patient who says little or nothing to the family, but opens up to the physician—presents equally difficult problems of diagnosis and help for the family.

Such fluctuations in mood and patterns of relating to others in older people make for difficulty in obtaining a medical history. Matters are further complicated by the erratic nature of effective functioning in many older people. Confusion can result because some areas of functioning endure better than others for no apparent reason. For instance, an older man who retains a "head for figures" may give a medical history that is

[36]

accurate about dates and temporal relationships, but distorted in descriptions of symptoms connected with pain. The patient who is friendly with one member of the family and paranoid about another presents a problem in diagnosis and communication. Discussion of physical functions can be equally erratic and confusing.

A physician who has known the patient for a long time and has some idea of his baseline of functioning is the best person to make any judgments about the patient's physical and social well-being. This is because many decisions concerning the social reality of the patient are based on the assessment of his physical capacities. But even in this professional relationship, the nature of prolonged interactions between two people may result in difficulty. It is easy to minimize or overlook early signs of decompensation. The physician, especially the older physician, may, because of old ties to the patient, hesitate to take a strong stand when he notices difficulties. The physician is "used to" seeing the patient in a certain way and hopes that this image can be retained.

The physician's problems are increased by the difficulties of diagnosis. Disorientation and depression play a significant role in many diseases that affect the aged — cardiac and muscular disorders, anemia, rheumatism, and avitaminosis being only a few. What comes first is very hard to determine. An older person who gets depressed may eat poorly and develop a secondary anemia. The physician who treats the anemia alone may find himself getting poor results and becoming confused about diagnosis. On the other hand, an older person may be admitted to the hospital in cardiac decompensation with a high degree of disorientation. What appears at first to be a psychological disturbance of some severity clears completely within 24 hours with the administration of digitalis. Such situations are constantly complicated by the fact that it is almost always desirable to reduce bed rest and invalidism in the older patient to a minimum. Often the geriatrician wishes

[37]

to avoid hospitalization and not to interfere with the patient's capacity to manage himself. Therefore, a diagnosis must include an understanding of the physiological and psychological fragility of the older person and a clear awareness of the extent of regression he has already experienced and can tolerate. The family's uncertainty, which often includes considerable annoyance and guilt, leads them to react excessively. The alternatives of "Well, let's send him to an old-age home now, or "Anything at all, Doctor; don't spare any expense," or "We will find the money somehow" are extreme attitudes that the geriatrician frequently hears expressed. Such reactions are usually inappropriate. However, it is necessary to prevent the family from shipping off an older person because they are angry, and to prevent the family or the patient from unnecessarily spending life savings when a home or a clinic is indicated. This requires tact, certainty, and the expenditure of time by the physician.

Another difficulty for the physician treating the older patient is philosophical. Everyone, including doctors, has an idea about how he wishes to be treated in relation to chronic illness and impending death. It is essential that the physician be aware of his own philosophy of life, since he does communicate it. Nevertheless, he should not impose his principles and ethics on the patient. The 78-year-old man with a cardiac condition could prolong his life by inactivity, but he wishes to visit his grandchildren whom he has never seen. The way in which the physician tells this man about his condition will greatly affect his decision. Such problems in the practice of a busy physician are numberless.

The role of the psychiatrist in managing geriatric problems is complicated because relatively few geriatric patients are referred to psychiatrists, especially dynamic psychiatrists. Psychiatrists are usually assumed to be primarily interested in helping people to do better in the future. With the older patient, doing better in some hypothetical future is of little interest, while obtaining some relief in the present is what counts. The psychiatrist has had little interest in the aged because there is little use of insight therapy and verbal communication is often difficult (Cutner, 1950).

The psychiatrist's difficulties in treating the geriatric population are easily as many as those of the general physician. As general planning for the aged includes vocational, recreational, and architectural as well as medical planning, the psychiatrist finds himself acting as an advisor in specialties with which he is largely unfamiliar. He has to become a student of these specialties in order to be an effective advisor, and this is time-consuming and demanding.

As will be discussed later, the full range of psychopathology occurs in the aged. Specific indications for drug and shock therapy for aged patients arise more frequently. The somatic therapies require extensive knowledge of the physiological and biochemical reactions and skill in administration, so that close cooperation with a general physician is essential. Drug intoxication occurs easily and is common in the older patient. It is often difficult to predict what dosage of drugs will cause complications, so the recognition of the early clinical or laboratory findings of a toxic reaction depends on careful observation of the patient, with close communication between the psychiatrist and the internist.

Communication between the psychiatrist and his older patient is potentially as difficult as it is between the general physician and the older patient. An understanding of the change in the defense systems of the older person is basic (Hollander, 1952). The change in the use of isolation, compartmentalization, and especially regression has to be understood and accepted by the therapist. If the therapist expects the older patient to present things or, in a sense, even to think like his younger patients, he will find himself in a struggle rather than a therapeutic relationship. The older person's values are different, too. The conflict of generations may take many forms.

[39]

Persons whose adolescence and young adulthood took place before the First World War tend to yearn, when old, for the time when things were slower and families closer. They remember the songs and the literature of that era and, for them, the psychiatrist represents a different generation who can never share their appreciation and pleasure in a memory of Teddy Roosevelt or the incomparable Lily Langtry. It is hard to help them feel that it is worthwhile talking to someone who may not have experienced the content of their musings. Persistent rumination may imply the existence of an organic component or physical problems. Often the actual rate of speech changes and can make an understanding of frequent circumstantiality even more difficult. With the interest in the past, the patient may also dredge up archaic ways of expressing himself that are ambiguous. If the psychiatrist has to ask for clarification, it emphasizes for the patient that he does not understand. This is especially a problem if the patient's early experience was with a different language. Sometimes the patient seems not to focus at all on the psychiatrist. It is clear that he is talking because he is lonely, and the conversation is actually directed to someone who exists in his own past, not to the therapist at all.

In general, older people tend to identify the psychiatrist with someone with whom they are familiar (Meerloo, 1955, 1961). They can relate better when they can make a concrete identification of the psychiatrist with someone like their mother, brother, old friend, previous doctor, etc. This identification bridges a gap and is often unshaken by an awareness that it is not so. The older patient may know that it is not so, but may not want to have it mentioned. An acceptance of being called by someone else's name, or having his hand wrung or even kissed, is unusual in the psychiatrist who deals only with younger patients, and he may find it difficult to tolerate both personally and professionally. It is possible that the psychiatrist is uncomfortable because such labile emotions stir up many of his own embarrassed feelings related to parents, as well as his own more general concern about keeping out of the treatment feelings he believes do not belong there. Professionally he is used to certain routines and standard patterns of exchange with patients which support a psychiatric objectivity. The direct assault on the defenses that so often occurs with the older patient requires an understanding that this stage of development decreases repression in thought and suppression in act.

Psychiatric treatment of the aged may also entail temporal and geographical difficulties. Often the patient either cannot come to the psychiatrist's office at all or has to be brought by someone else. Making an appointment in itself can become a complicated operation. Also, the older patient may want to have someone else present during the interview to fill in memory gaps or to supply the support of the familiar. This may complicate the interview for the psychiatrist as well as present problems of scheduling. The 50-minute hour was not necessarily designed for the attention span of the older patient, and he is not necessarily consistent. The psychiatrist has to judge when he requires more time and when he is too anxious to stay more than a few minutes. This wreaks havoc with a psychiatrist's precious schedule. The inevitability of involvement with family members, who often have disagreements among themselves, requires a large commitment of time to seeing and talking to them.

Perhaps the single greatest difficulty in treating the older patient, from which many of the other difficulties stem, is that the patient often has no conscious idea why he comes or is brought to the psychiatrist. The psychiatrist cannot ask his favorite question, "What do you see as the problem or difficulty?" and expect an answer. One of the primary rules of all medicine is that, before instituting treatment, it is necessary to know what the problem is. With a young neurotic, the first step toward cure is often the recognition of the problem, and psychiatrists are used to thinking in these terms. The vagueness and diffuseness of the older person's reasons for psychiatric treatment often have to be accepted by the psychiatrist, at least initially, but, as could be expected, not without considerable anxiety.

So much of dynamic psychiatry has been oriented to long-term treatment aimed at increasing the patient's understanding, that treatment aimed at strengthening ego functioning, or simply at helping the patient feel better, seems alien. Although much of the treatment of the older patient results from situations which are more or less emergencies, after the initial crisis more long-standing psychiatric difficulties are found to be involved (Goldfarb, 1955). The patient frequently requires a definite period of treatment, not just an hour or two, to handle a crisis. The older person on his own would not have sought out a psychiatrist. However, his apparent lack of conscious motivation for treatment is not the problem, but reflects in part the way the older patient looks at the world (Grotjahn, 1951, 1955).

The spread of psychiatric interest in treating the aged is part of a general extension of dynamic psychology into areas other than psychoanalysis. When psychoanalytic psychiatrists began to treat psychotics, they became interested in the patients' lives other than the time they spent in therapy. For instance, when the hospitalized patient went to occupational or recreational therapy, the psychiatrist prescribed what task would be of greatest value in furthering his therapy or general emotional well-being. With the treatment of the aged, this trend reaches its zenith, because, much more than the general physician or the community agency, the psychiatrist who treats an aged person is consulted about every aspect of his patient's life. The room the patient should have, the number of steps, the amount of company, the amount of exercise, the amount of rest, the extent of work, his diet, his bowels, and even his sexual interests are discussed with the psychiatrist. The psychiatrist is even called in for consultation in the planning of large architectural developments devoted exclusively to the aged. He is asked what rest, play, and work facilities are necessary to ensure the tenants of these developments the ways to gain self-esteem and maintain narcissistic supplies. Some architects, physiotherapists, occupational therapists, etc., now have a sophisticated view of psychodynamic concepts.

With this enormous demand on the psychoanalyst to devise whole new sets of approaches, he can no longer depend on insight as his chief therapeutic lever. Many of the therapies require a relatively short-term contact that permits or requires little interpretive intervention. However, once the relationship is established, there is a need for continuity, even if the appointments are infrequent. In the older patient's ecology, instability because of loss and death is so frequent that a concrete and stable relationship with the psychiatrist must be maintained. All of these deviations from classical techniques may affect the psychiatrist's self-image and arouse his concern about what his colleagues think of him. He fears he will be seen as controlling and manipulative by behaving so actively, and that he will be accused of living out omnipotent fantasies. As work with older people invariably stirs up the psychiatrist's early fantasies of controlling his own parents, he is peculiarly susceptible to such accusations, particularly by his colleagues. What is worse is that, with all of the activity and thoughtful attention, the therapeutic goals remain limited and often discouraging. The narcissism of the psychiatrist is offended in both directions. He is guilty because of old wishes to control his parents, and impotent because he can do so little beneficially at a pace that would gratify him.

By stressing so heavily the dependence of psychotherapy with the aged on principles other than those of greater understanding of individual dynamics, we do not mean that the more usual clarification of less conscious conflict is not very important. While the psychotherapeutic technique must remain flexible, people at all ages have an id, an ego, and unconscious and preconscious conflicts that, if aroused, can cause difficulty and can yield to understanding. It is widely unrecognized how much the regressed ego in the later stages of development is dependent for homeostasis and balance on outside nutriment. A young adult can draw on his internalized ego ideal for sustenance if things do not go well for him in the external world. The aged person is less likely to have this recourse, and the therapist must always consider his greater susceptibility to narcissistic injury.

From all of the difficulties mentioned for both psychiatrist and patient, it is obvious that psychiatric treatment is expensive in terms of time and energy. By those measures it must also be expensive financially (Gordon, 1960). This, of course, brings up the whole problem of medical care for the aged. Many old people live on Social Security benefits, the remnants of savings, or the bounty of their families. Relatively few have accumulated a large sum of money or own something that will provide a continuing adequate income. Most of the psychiatric measures we have discussed require extensive financing by some agency, usually the local, state, or federal government. The problem of financing is basic because, although we have stressed the difficulties of working psychiatrically with the old, we suspect that much can be done that is helpful. Probably much more can be done than has been until now. The community as well as the psychiatrists have not as yet exhausted all the available knowledge and resources, in large part because of inadequate financing.

Social agencies of various kinds can be of great help with many of the problems of physical impairment and emotional difficulties of the aged. Physicians interested in geriatrics find it of value to maintain a close liason with the rehabilitation and family services of the community (Hollander, 1951). The agencies, of course, are constantly turning to the physicians of their clients for help in decisions of a psychological nature

[44]

which are to some extent dependent on the patients' physical status. Gradually, the medical profession is accepting and even welcoming this interaction, but until recently many physicians felt that the requests of the community agencies were excessive and frightening. The agencies themselves have learned that the doctor cannot be expected to be omniscient about the older patient, whose condition can change rapidly.

The community's problems with the older patient are essentially the same as those of the geriatrician and the psychiatrist. Proper housing, recreational facilities, work opportunities, counseling, and medical care for the aged are the responsibility of the community (Rosenbaum, 1959; Cohen, 1960). As physicians have to make a diagnosis before they can treat a problem, the community must first be aware of what is needed before it can supply it. The community also needs to be educated about what is already available so that, when a need arises, the best use can be made of what is there. All too often, resources thought of as unlikely or unavailable are actually available and can be tapped. For example, untrained volunteers were introduced into the old-age section of a local hospital. These volunteers had not yet learned that the old people were "hopeless"; they spent time with them and were able to revitalize many and return them to the community. Even those who were less spectacularly helped benefited from the increased brightness of this entire division of the hospital.

The integration of community services for the aged requires thoughtful and specialized administration which is available in very few communities. It has been demonstrated that, when multiple community resources are mobilized, more of the old may be maintained outside of institutions. In the long run this saves not only money but people. The difference between the well and the sick in this group is not a sharp one. Prevention of severe difficulty requires organization. The older people themselves find it hard to recognize many important changes. A man may leave his home less and less frequently, but withdraws so gradually that no one takes notice until he does not appear at all for a long period. A case-finding agency might pick up such a case and offer help. Such an agency would have to be prepared to deal with a number of complex legal problems: for instance, the aged woman with no family who is not overtly psychotic but is starving herself, and is usually discovered, if at all, when she develops pneumonia or some fulminating condition secondary to her malnutrition. What would be the legal position of an agency that tried to step in before something drastic occurred? The legal problems posed by trying to protect the person's civil liberties as well as looking after his well-being are not easy ones.

Until now, many programs have emphasized improved institutional facilities rather than overall planning. Sometimes there are misunderstandings based on stereotypes of what old people can or should do. Moving to even a good old-age home or to a nice home in the suburbs with relatives, which is intended to make the old people more comfortable, often has the reverse effect. They miss their old neighborhoods and their old cronies. The better fixtures do not supply the human ties that are required.

A stable community, hopefully, would include all age ranges. A proper proportion of old people is needed to add balance and a sense of continuity to the community. For children, the observance of various phases of life gives a different meaning to their own growing up. A community without older people is almost as sterile as one without children.

When we speak of education about aging and the aged, we find that what we want to teach primarily are attitudes. These are hard to teach because they are not concrete and specific and because certain cultural and psychological values stand against teaching appreciation of aging and the aged (Rosenbaum, 1959). It would be an interesting experiment to unleash the full-fledged Madison Avenue force that sells autos, eggbeaters, and ice to the Eskimos to educate the public about what could be done for the aged. But before we could turn to the advertising business we would have to be clearer in our own minds about what we want to convey. Research about the process of aging is needed at all levels, but much that should be known about aging may not be as complex as much of the work in the social sciences is. For instance, we know comparatively little about the current range of attitudes in different-sized communities, in different parts of the country, toward the older person. In some ways we are not sufficiently aware of what our older population wants from the community. The President's Commission on Aging and the generally greater interest of the federal government may make possible the gathering of this information either locally or nationally. It is probable that action and interest on both levels will be necessary before we can "sell" a better understanding of aging.

PSYCHOPATHOLOGY

Psychopathology in the aging person includes the full spectrum of neurotic, psychosomatic, behavioral, psychotic, and organic disturbances (N. Cameron, 1945). However, the clinical evaluation of these conditions is complicated by two common characteristics of aging. The first is the emotional reactions to this stage of development which tend to produce a syndrome characterized by regression, hostile-dependent patterns of behavior, and childishness. This somewhat depressed and apathetic functional syndrome is often difficult to differentiate from the second, the more specific organic deterioration (Gitelson, 1948). An example is the frequency of the "small stroke" syndrome, in which the person has a relatively minor brain lesion from which he recovers, but begins to show some deterioration in habits, dress, and general capacity to function. In addition, organic brain damage from infection, degeneration, arteriosclerosis, etc., may imitate psychopathology

[47]

or may liberate underlying psychopathology which clinically is extremely difficult to differentiate from depression, schizophrenia, manic state, or impulse-ridden character disorder.

It is only by the traditional combinations of careful medical and psychiatric history, thorough physical examination and equally thorough psychiatric evaluation, and observation over a period of time that one can begin to make the differential diagnosis necessary in order to institute management and treatment procedures.

Perhaps the pathologic phenomena most distressing to the community are the behavioral disturbances which sometimes occur in the aging (Rockwell, 1946). These can be the continuation of a life-long pattern of psychopathic behavior, or be secondary to emotional or organic impairment of cerebral functioning. Etiology is important not only for the benefit of the patient, but because the community has to be protected as well. For example, if the patient clearly has an organic syndrome, he may require indefinite custodial care; but the person whose disturbed behavior is secondary to the emotional response to aging may or may not need inpatient care.

Exhibitionism, voyeurism, sadism, perverse preoccupation, and masturbation are relatively common among the psychopathological manifestations of aging. All too often police blotters register the fact that an older man of previous unblemished reputation is apprehended for attempted molestation of a child. This molesting frequently consists of the man's attempt to expose his genitalia rather than to perform a physical act on the child, and the principal motivation seems to be a need for reassurance about his retention of maleness. Such an act nonetheless frightens the victim and leads to police action. Unfortunately, as far as entanglement with the law is concerned, this is much like similar phenomena in the child or adolescent who chooses a victim who can be impressed and frightened. An older woman might just remind the man to zip his fly.

[48]

Some psychotic manifestations of aging are unquestionably and directly related to organic changes. However, autopsy findings indicate that frequently there is no direct correlation between the psychopathological manifestation and the arteriosclerotic or senile changes in the brain. The disturbed thinking or behavior of patients who exhibit focal neurological changes is more often correlated with specific brain damage. In the reactions that are undeniably organic in etiology, the form the psychological reactions take is determined by underlying personality characteristics which are liberated by the organic changes. Brain damage cannot produce a new personality; it can only release that which is already there.

The most common psychotic manifestation of aging is the senile psychosis which also does not, on microscopic examination of the pathological section, correlate with a degree of brain damage, although there are important organic components in this disturbance (Leeds, 1960). The most frequent precipitating factors in these conditions are interruptions of customary patterns of life, such as the death of a person close to the patient or a major dislocation of milieu. At first, the verbalizations of a senile psychotic seem to make no sense, but on more careful consideration it is often possible to understand some of what is being expressed. Apparently there has been a breakdown in the complex process of psychic integration that maintains the usual contact between instinctual derivatives and external reality, including the regular sequence of temporal and spatial relations. The frequently observed relating of people in the person's current life with previous important persons such as a friend or a mother becomes intensified. For the senile patient, these people become truly interchangeable or fused, and all of them seem to exist in the present.

Psychosomatic symptoms or organic disorders unquestionably occur in the aged. The problem of diagnosis becomes paramount because of the difficulty in differentiating a functional symptom, or a functional exacerbation of an existing

[49]

physiological condition, from the usual physical disabilities of aging. For example, preoccupation with cancer in some persons may be a type of phobia. Other persons seem to be aware of the physical changes associated with the developing cancer long before physical examination, X-ray, or laboratory tests can make the diagnosis.

Depression is the most frequent psychological difficulty encountered in the aged and the one for which they are most likely to come to psychiatric treatment. It may be stated that at least one basic concomitant of successful aging is the ability to tolerate depression. Such vicissitudes of aging as physical incapacity, loss, little future orientation, and changes in status all contribute to depression. It is essential to differentiate between those aspects of the philosophy of aging which regularly include these vicissitudes, and the psychopathological entity which can be very severe in this age group. The capacity to withstand even severe depressions for relatively brief periods without total despair is part of the person's acceptance of the chronic depressive circumstance of aging. Increasingly, writers are concerned with the capacity to bear depression at all developmental stages as part of relative mental health, so that concern with the older person's acceptance of chronic depression does not imply pessimism about successful aging in general. Rather, the concern is about initiating a dangerous cycle where a new minor loss of capacity in an aged person, with an accompanying appropriate depressive reaction, results in excessive anxiety from the younger external world about this depression. The excessive response, in turn, frightens the older person and increases his depression.

We do not mean to suggest that the initial depressive reaction should be ignored, but we do wish to convey that when trauma occurs, many older patients will get depressed. They know and accept this depression as a transient, necessary discharge that has occurred before and from which they will recover. If the outside world becomes overanxious, the patient's

[50]

ever-present fantasies that the minor change presages major ones become active and the depression deepens. To point out the danger of excessive reaction to an aged patient's emotional response may seem overcautious in view of the fact that the great problem is unawareness or lack of reaction to the aged person's emotional state. However, it is worthwhile to consider both dangers. Often, if no effective support is tendered from the external environment during a transient depression, the reaction intensifies, the person's defenses weaken, and a pathological state results.

Depression as a pathological entity, with the frank admission into consciousness of primitive self-destructive urges, is frequently encountered and difficult to treat in the aged. Many hospitals report with awe the patient who is moderately ill, becomes depressed, loses "the will to live," and dies. In state hospitals, despite the wild, frenzied behavior of the manic phase, it is during the depressed phase that manic-depressive psychotics die from intercurrent infections. No area of gerontologic psychiatry requires more careful investigation than depression, but an intensive consideration of this phenomenon lies outside the scope of this survey.

Almost all of the other psychopathological states that permit more direct representation of id derivatives can occur in the older patient. Paranoid schizophrenia, obsessive states, hysterical conversions, etc., may make their appearance in the aging. It is hoped that future symposia will consider in detail the entire range of psychopathology in the aged and the differentiation of psychopathology from more or less normal psychological changes which occur as a result of or reaction to this developmental stage.

Summary

Our objective in this introduction has been twofold: first, to develop a frame of reference for the papers that follow, and second, to present briefly the basic concepts necessary for an understanding of the aging process. Some of these concepts will be developed in greater detail in the following papers.

Our orientation is to consider aging as a developmental stage of the human organism. Often in the past "normal" aging was applied only to those persons who by rare good fortune avoided certain physical, emotional, and social upheavals that usually accompany aging. Normal aging was viewed as the least amount of aging rather than as a developmental stage with its own characteristics. Each life stage poses different problems, and it is possible that the aging person, besides having to master his own set of difficulties, is also faced with the precipitates and unresolved residues of other developmental phases.

It is necessary to consider the complex interaction between the ego and superego as these psychic structures adapt both to the internal physical and psychical changes of aging and to external cultural forces. There are normal adaptive patterns as well as physical and emotional disturbances.

Successful medical and psychological management at this stage of development does not and should not imply a prolongation of previous stages of development, but regression is a necessary adaptive mechanism which the person and the environment must accept. For example, a diminished capacity to remember recent events can often be handled by the use of a notebook to list appointments or telephone numbers. The slowing down that results from physical changes can be dealt with by the allowance of enough time for keeping appointments or getting dressed for dinner. In general, there needs to be some toleration for physical and emotional changes by the aged themselves and by those around them. Regression and lessened repression, which release instinctual energy, may enable the person to maintain the homeostatic balance of id, ego, and superego characteristic of and necessary for his sense of well-being. At times this balance may be uneven; id

[52]

impulses may break through, or the regression may go beyond the level tolerable to the ego ideal and the environment. Sometimes excessive regression can give the inaccurate impression of severe psychopathology. Actually, this form of unsuccessful aging may be handled by increasing the emotional supplies and does not necessarily require any other form of therapy.

Because this culture extols growth and progress, little value is given to the wisdom and experience of the aging. The process of enforced retirement further adds to the devaluation of the older person. Other cultures have built-in patterns and roles that supply a sense of worth to the older person. It would be highly desirable if something could be done within this culture to give greater value and acceptance to the aging person.

In our survey of the problems of the aged and in almost all of the papers to follow, the concept of regression as a defense mechanism and as a central explanatory construct has been considered vital. More specifically, the capacity to tolerate the physical and emotional changes that we refer to as regression can be used as a definition of "successful aging," whatever that is. It is implicit that the regression of aging and the establishment of a new homeostatic level do not take place in one leap. Rather, there is a gradual shift in which the regressive processes and the tolerance of them slowly amalgamate into new personality patterns.

Let us carry these thoughts about the slow rate of change in people a step further. How do we die? Do we really die all at once or do we die each time we go to sleep? Do we die a little each time we experience pain or are ill, frightened, or traumatized? In particular, do we die a little every time we lose someone who is significant for us? Perhaps all of these things are preparation; perhaps each time we see someone else die, we know death a bit more closely. If this is true, it might be another reason for the unpopularity of geriatrics as a specialty, although to specify any one reason for a person's making the highly complex choice of a life's work is foolish. Nevertheless, if there is any one psychological fact that seems to make life difficult for physicians it is to feel helpless. Not to be able to do, or to help, or to fix, or at least to explain is anathema. The physician has the closest struggle with the dying, and he has always hoped to learn how to win for his patients and also for himself. Never to learn about the process is very hard and leaves him helpless. On the other hand, the doctor may also hope, each time a patient dies, to come to terms with it, and by so doing hope to be better prepared for his own death.

In discussing that ultimate end product of aging, death, another point is important (Eissler, 1955). What is meant when someone speaks of dying? It can usually be shown that when an aged person considers his death, he is expressing fear about infirmity, illness, and the prospect of becoming incapacitated and unproductive. Once the fear of dying is translated into fear of these dread prospects, the patient feels relieved and is more susceptible to reassurance. This does not mean that there is no real concern about death. Rather, there is no language or concept to express this concern, and one falls back on the experience or partial experience with death that one has felt directly or through others. It is even possible that the difficulty in comprehending this unknown phenomenon intensifies the concerns about incapacity, etc., which may be, in addition to intrinsic sources of anxiety, screens for the basic fear.

There is no way to prevent death, but much can be done to maximize functioning and reduce physical and emotional disability in the aged. Existing resources have been inadequately used.

Earlier diagnosis of mental and physical illness, more effective use of community resources, and educational procedures for the community would do much to make this stage of development more meaningful and less painful to all concerned. Careful consideration should be given to how anxieties about aging and dying lead to the neglect of people in this period of

[54]

life. With the increased numbers of aging persons resulting from advances in medical knowledge, there is a need for more effective preventive measures, more effort to maximize the value of this stage of development, and more successful management of pathological features when they do occur.

A Psychosocial and Sociophysiological Approach to Aging

ALVIN I. GOLDFARB, M.D.

"OLD AGE" AND "CHRONIC ILLNESS" may for many purposes be regarded as synonyms. Illness not only accelerates aging but actually mimics the aged state; old age may be described or treated as a state of chronic illness. Cicero said: "So feeble are many old men that they cannot execute any task or duty or any functions of life whatever, but that in truth is not the peculiar fault of old age but belongs in common to bad health." In this way he made a distinction between chronological old age and the state of being aged which still holds true. The aged state, true old age, as contrasted to chronological old age, is a condition in which previous functional efficiency has been lost.

A morbid change appears to take place as the result of a number of failures or strains in reaction to stress. When these defects become irreversible, the organism has aged. How, where, and to what extent these strains occur is partly contingent on hereditary factors. Those processes of organismic and environmental interaction which can be lumped together under the general heading of illness and accidents, and which can occur at any time of life, are significant stresses which con-

[57]

tribute to aging. These processes may be, for a particular person, truly accidental—"We are all at the mercy of a falling tile"—or they may be partially determined by the person. Their occurrence and effect may or may not be contingent on genetic or otherwise acquired susceptibilities.

Some factors, which the individual can control to some extent, and which affect his longevity and possibly the speed with which he reaches the aged state, are, for example, obesity, smoking, and place of residence. A man 25 pounds overweight has in effect decreased his probable life span by about three and a half years; one who smokes a pack or two of cigarettes a day has decreased his probable life span by seven to 12 years. If he is a city dweller he sacrifices five years, and if he fails to marry or remain married he sacrifices another five years. I do not know whether these are cumulative factors, in contrast to determinants of life span which are out of one's control, such as the age of the mother at conception, the total life span of all the grandparents, and one's sex. Each of these appears to be related to the inherited life potential (Jones, 1959).

Whatever its causes, true old age is a state of the organism in which inefficient functioning decreases the capacity to compensate and recover from strain. The state is a dynamic one which contributes to its own acceleration. It is irreversible, although its progress may be slowed; it is inevitable; and it finally ends in death.

At present, for many fictive reasons, we choose to regard the chronological age of 65 years as the time a person enters old age. We do this because it is then that the majority of persons show the outward physical characteristics we associate with physical functional decline, and because before this age certain types of mental functional deficiencies are relatively rare. Although one of the commonest symptoms of functional inefficiency, fatigue, seems to appear much earlier, after 65 years of age most signs of functional inefficiency begin to appear with greater statistical frequency.

[58]

In sum, aging is best defined as a progressive, irreversible loss of functional efficiency, and we may arbitrarily declare that it begins in the sixty-fifth year of life because by this time, in our society, almost everyone evidences some signs or symptoms of aging.

The functional signs of the aged state include a loss of sensory, effector, homeostatic, and central nervous integrative efficiency and, to the person's dissatisfaction and further embarrassment, this may be complicated by alteration of appearance, role, and status, as well as by the loss of social and economic support. Old age, therefore, is not only a state of increasing functional inefficiency but occurs within a milieu that grows progressively more unfavorable for the person. Under such conditions, persons can be expected to have feelings of helplessness, anger, and depression.

As psychiatrists and workers interested in psychological medicine, we know that anxiety, anger, and depression may be expressed in a variety of ways. Noting differences in the prevalence of such symptoms may be a guide to what protects the person from the development of feelings of helplessness in these circumstances of personal loss with aging.

Institutionalization seems to be a protective measure for aged persons in certain circumstances. Tuckman, Lorge, Steinhardt, and Zeman (1953) compared the complaints of persons in the Home for the Aged and Infirm Hebrews of New York with aged persons living in their own homes, using the Cornell Medical Index as the measure. They found that the institutionalized men reported fewer symptoms of physical illness—fewer somatic complaints—than did those who lived in their own homes. This finding could not be attributed to actual differences in physical health. Rather, it seemed that institutional care and protection tended to reduce the number of compaints. Women, on the other hand, did not show this difference. The investigators speculated that it is less accepable for women in our society to enter an institution than for men, and that they therefore complained of illness as though to justify their residence there. Whatever the true explanation for the women, some aged men in institutions appear to suffer less than men in their own homes.

Shrut (1958a, 1958b), in a study of anxiety in terms of attitudes toward old age and death in the same institution, compared persons who lived in the large central house to those who lived in the apartment-house residence. He found that the apartment dwellers, who lived under conditions more like their former ones, evidenced less fear of and preoccupation with death. Also, those who lived in the more hospital-like building had a less realistic estimate of their own health and showed more obvious anxiety about their health than did the apartment dwellers. A continuation of old habits and ways of life together with relatively good health, or living as though it were good, appear to be protections against anxiety as evinced in fears of death.

We have also noted that feelings of helplessness and evidences of subsequent anxiety are less likely to develop in persons who have early acquired self-esteem, confidence, and an active problem-solving attitude toward life's challenges. Oberleder (1957), in a study of two groups of residents in the Home for Aged and Infirm Hebrews, showed that persons who appeared to be unable to accept and utilize the institution effectively, who were aggressive, demanding, and critical, tended to think about aging in unflattering and frightening generalizations. On the other hand, the group characterized by relatively good adjustment to institutional life, as shown by sociability, participation in group activities, and pursuit of individual interest, even though within the institution, tended to reject stereotyped thinking about aging. They thought of the old as capable, active, energetic, and flexible, even though some of their own physical and mental characteristics would seem to belie such a view.

A study by Kahn, Zeman, and Goldfarb (1958), using a

[60]

psychological test of ability to pick a figure out of an ambiguous ground, indicated that persons who are resourceful and who show an assertive approach to specific problems tend to have fewer somatic complaints, irrespective of thier true medical status. Such persons have fewer complaints than do persons who appear to be more passive in their orientation to the same test. Still another study by Pollack, Kahn, and Goldfarb (1958) suggests that a good early education is an important personality protection against the development of feelings of helplessness as one grows older, reflected in a loss of effectual social functioning.

Responses to the Bender face-hand test, the double simultaneous stimulation of cheek and hand, were used as a measure of the level of functing (Bender, Green, and Fink, 1954). Correct identification of both stimuli after a short teaching trial run was found to be more closely related to the amount of formal education than was age. We have found in our surveys of aged persons in various types of institutions that on this test physical status is more closely correlated with correct responses than with age. From this result we could draw a further inference—that good early opportunity or absence of deprivation in early years, which makes for good education, may also contribute to the individual's ability to protect his physical health. In an older person this is in turn related to mental-physical efficiency.

In institutions providing poor general care and permeated by an atmosphere of despair and futility, the responses of the residents to the face-hand test and to a mental status questionnaire were much poorer than those of residents in homes with an atmosphere of greater activity and hope. The residents in the more custodial type of institution were frequently apathetic and withdrawn (Goldfarb, Kahn, Pollack, and Gerber, 1960).

In sum, the early establishment of self-assertive trends, or at least the absence of early acquisition of paralyzing inhibi-

[61]

tions, a good early education to aid in the mastery of problems arising from within and from without, protection, a setting in keeping with one's past, and a social atmosphere of interest and hope in contrast to neglect and futility, have been demonstrated to preclude or minimize psychological elaborations of feelings of helplessness and of emotional overreaction in the aged.

The large group of persons who are 65 years of age or older in our country vary greatly in health, education, cultural and socioeconomic background, and, not least of all, in age. Within this varied group are found many kinds of mental disorder: some acquired or first noted in old age, many for which there is a clear history in earlier years.

The mental illnesses which develop or first come to attention in this heterogeneous group of elderly persons are now a prominent public health problem. We are at present more concerned with the special difficulties of adjustment, and how they affect the community, than we are with the nosology of these mental illnesses. My own thinking about dealing with the aged is somewhat along the lines of Caplan's (1961) concept of "crises," but is derived from Meyer's (1890-1945) conceptualization of the importance and meaning of the patient's complaint or of his milieu.

The complaint which calls the psychiatrist's attention to the problem may be that of the patient, of his family or community, or of his physician. It constitutes the focal point for treatment and the area from which we anamnestically and dynamically orient ourselves for diagnostic and treatment purposes. The complaints have both hidden and open, or conscious and unconscious, aspects, from the point of view of both the complainer and of the one complained to. Thus the complaint may incorporate a number of combinations of factors. Out of this welter of interacting variables the psychiatrist has to choose the factors at work which appear to be most significant in creating the disturbance and most susceptible to modification. The

[62]

aged persons who have had previous admissions to psychiatric hospitals or have grown old within them, or who have had obvious and disabling psychiatric disorders intermittently or continuously from their youth, are also a concern of psychiatry; however, our consideration of the aged as an area of subspecialization focuses on special individual, social, and health problems. On this basis, I think those with psychiatric illness since their youth can be separated from those presenting psychiatric illness in old age.

This distinction arbitrarily relieves us from attempting to deal here with the numerous aged schizophrenics, the manic-depressives, and the cases of so-called involutional psychoses whose onset was clearly in the middle rather than the later years, as well as certain other disorders which, statistically speaking, tend to occur before the late years of life.

This delimitation need not, however, exclude a number of persons who have suffered focal brain damage because of carotid or cerebral arterial occlusion. In their brain-damaged state and in their reactions to it, they may resemble persons who have suffered head injury or cerebral dysfunction on account of an expanding intracranial lesion more than they do the aged who have suffered multiple strokes or chronic cerebral dysfunction. However, their expectations, role, status, and the possible imminence of more diffuse and chronic cerebral dysfunction, whether it be because of malsupport due to systemic disease, or an intrinsic cerebral process, suggests that they should be part of our concern. It is possible, of course, for persons of any age to have reversible brain dysfunction on the basis of what seems to be diffuse damage. There are deliriums, states of acute brain syndrome, which can and do occur frequently in the aged, and are not truly special for them. What is special about such deliriums in the aged is that they often occur in a setting of previously unnoted chronic brain syndrome, and may lead to or mark further development of such disorders.

[63]

The disorders which we can regard as "special" to old age are those with that diffuse progressive decline in cerebral substance and function now called chronic brain syndrome, and also those disorders of behavior which appear to begin, or at least emerge, as significant pathological states for the first time in later life, whether because of a change of symptoms, in the person's general health, or in the socio-economic environment.

We can group aged patients with mental disorders as showing evidence of chronic brain syndromes or as being free of such signs, with or without behavior disturbances. Our categories are then: (1) those suffering with psychoses, psychoneuroses, and psychophysiologic or character disorders in the absence of chronic brain syndrome; (2) those with such disorders who also show evidence of chronic brain syndrome; and (3) those who become our patients almost entirely on the basis of defects of orientation, memory, and weakened intellectual powers, that is, because of the signs of their brain damage alone. It is the last two groups which now comprise the bulk of present-day geriatric psychiatric practice. However, I think that the first group, disordered but without chronic brain syndrome, will in time comprise more of our patients. Little by little, more and more of them are seen in our offices as well as in hospitals.

These three categories can, I think, be helpful in estimating the person's life expectancy, in predicting the course and outcome of his disorder, and in making decisions about living arrangements and the need for special care. However, these subdivisions should not encourage us to ignore strong cross-group similarities. As we focus on the crises that occur, or as we deal with the personal and environmental complaints that arise, we get the strong impression that the behavior displayed in all these conditions can be regarded as socially oriented and as motivated. All such behavior can be considered, for treatment purposes, to have the psychodynamic characteristics of a hysterical neurosis.

The mentally disordered aged whose disorders appear in later life are in many respects indistinguishable from those whose disorders were noted earlier, whether treated or not. The late development or discovery of their disorder may have been contingent on general health, economic resources, family protection, special skills, family or community tolerance, or simply a result of the fact that their specific symptoms failed to mobilize community or family action. There are considerable psychosocial differences between the person who is protected until his later years and the person who is revealed as disordered in earlier years in both the character of the person and the characteristics of his subculture and family group, even though in personality type and in general reaction type he may be indistinguishable from others.

Patients are not always aware of or capable of verbalizing their sufferings. Their families, communities, or physicians respond to their handling of distress according to their abilities to discern the disturbances. The emotional capacity to become aware of them, and the community's readiness, ability, or need to recognize and aid in their treatment in contrast to denying, ignoring, or defining the disorders as a variation of "normal," or as criminal behavior, are crucial. Mental health, like physical health, remains in part a matter of definition, and its definition depends very much indeed on general social and specific local community demands and tolerance. Mental ill-health is usually regarded less tolerantly than physical ill-health which may require very similar family or community action.

It is true that along with chronic brain syndrome we usually find physical functional inefficiency. Kahn, Goldfarb, Pollack, and Peck (1960) have demonstrated that poor physical functional status is more closely correlated with poor mental functioning than is chronological age in the older age population. Poor physical status and poor mental status, it seems to us, cannot be separated and compartmentalized for care of the aged; the existence of either one calls for careful appraisal and treatment of the other, which usually accompanies it. Nevertheless, there are tendencies to stress the organic, physical, or medical nature of certain disorders and to push aside their so-called mental, psychological, and emotional aspect, their impact on social functioning, and the social corrective action indicated by their development and persistence. Often we would like to forget the psychosocial aspects and try to treat them in a traditional, strictly medical, way.

In some places and times of the past, anxiety and mental disorder, although not recognized clearly as medical matters, were more readily ascribed to difficulties in psychosocial functioning than in some of our modern communities. Mental disorders were regarded as states of personal conflict and inner disturbances due to temptation, or guilt because of feelings of sin, and were considered by enlightened men as requiring individual guidance and social action of an educational nature, whether religious or secular. In contrast, at present there is a strong tendency to regard many disorders of thought, behavior, and emotion in aged persons either as "normal" phenomena or as neurological and "physical" phenomena, instead of as psychiatric, social, and psychological, and as adaptional maneuvers for survival and relief of tension, possibly rendered less efficient and more bizarre by brain damage or systemic disease.

The classification of these disorders as nonpsychiatric results in confused planning and implementation of care. Insistence on thinking of the state of these persons as a normal development makes for considerable administrative confusion. In New York City we find that over 80 percent of institutionalized aged persons suffer from the psychiatric disorder, *chronic brain syndrome*. Elsewhere the reported figure may be lower because of different or euphemistic diagnoses. Where little psychiatric disorder is reported in nursing and old-age homes, the behavioral disorders, which form so large a part of the medical problems of the aged but are not so identified, are then regarded helplessly. In such communities the sufferers may be medically neglected, or may not come to psychiatric attention until a crisis occurs, and possibly not even then. The failure to recognize disorders in the aged which may properly be regarded as psychiatric can be considered from many points of view. A most important reason for reluctance to deal with them is financial. I can give as an example the dilemma in New York City. There at least 70 percent of the aged residents of nursing homes, most of whom we found to have chronic brain syndrome in some degree, are supported by the Department of Welfare. This department allocates funds for individual support obtained from the city, state, and federal governments. The proportion of payment is approximately one half from the federal government, one quarter from the city, and one quarter from the state. Should the patient in a nursing home or an old-age home receive a diagnosis of mental disorder, regulations prescribe that he be transferred to the state hospital for care. This ruling is intended to prevent the development of unsupervised, improperly staffed "snake-pits"; unfortunately they tend to emerge because of the admission of aged, undiagnosed, mentally ill patients. If a psychiatric diagnosis is made, the patient legally must be removed to the state hospital and, in the absence of private funds or family contributions, his care becomes completely the financial burden of the state. Two forces tend to keep this diagnosis from being made: (1) the nursing home operator's natural desire to keep and care for his paying resident, or the old-age home's reluctance to part with its old friend; and (2) the state's desire to keep the patient from swelling the number of indigent in the already overcrowded psychiatric hospitals. Thus, on the one hand, we have seen nursing homes and old-age homes euphemistically and sometimes affectionately calling those mentally disordered persons "seniles," and, on the other hand, the state

[67]

ascribing normality and lack of need for hospital care to them by calling them "dotards." But the patient continues to suffer, and the sophisticated community is agitated by its burden.

Fortunately this state of affairs is now being improved in New York State by concerted action on the part of the Departments of Mental Hygiene and Social Welfare and through cooperation of these bureaus and the New York City Department of Hospitals and the New York City Community Mental Health Board. This activity cannot be detailed here (Hoch and Houston, 1958).

I would like to elaborate briefly on another aspect of our failure to recognize the needs of aged persons for psychotherapeutic types of care, because of its special pertinence to our interest in psychodynamics.

Those experienced in psychotherapy who have watched the selection of persons for psychotherapy in clinics, or have supervised psychiatric residents and therapists in training, are aware of the tendency to select young, attractive, articulate, well-educated patients who are well motivated toward conversational techniques and who have respect for psychoanalysis. The young male analyst in training sympathizes or empathizes with pretty young girls, especially the anxious, breathless, glamourous ones, and he also reacts somewhat similarly to nice-looking, intelligent young men, especially well-educated ones who show promise of making their mark and of being grateful disciples. Aged persons are not generally viewed with favor as candidates for psychotherapeutic techniques, or, for that matter, for any techniques which bring the doctor into a direct or sustained relationship with them. Kahn, Goldfarb, Pollack, and Peck (1961) have emphasized that the critical factor in selecting patients for psychotherapy may be the possible communicative interaction between therapist and patient. Better educated, native-born, and younger patients were most likely to receive psychotherapy, while electroshock therapy was given to the older, foreign-born, and more poorly educated patients.

A study at the Home for Aged and Infirm Hebrews, where elderly persons have for many years received individual psychotherapy, has shown that these same factors are at work in the choice of persons for individual care. It is understandable that persons who are better educated, functioning at a superior intellectual level (as measured by the mental status questionnaire), and more alert (as measured by the face-hand test) should be more appealing to the psychiatrists as candidates for psychotherapy.

Aged men and women do not find many doctors interested in them because they are far from physically attractive, they are neither sexually stimulating nor sexually gratifying to look at, they seem intellectually faded, and, although they may be verbal, they are not articulate; in addition, poverty, failing strength, and failing mental power combine against their ability to keep clean. Moreover, they do not offer promise of responding well; rather, they often tend to grow worse no matter how much we do. This poses a threat to psychotherapists' yearnings for omnipotence. Also, the biological "experience" of aging places the aged person in an informed position which threatens the younger therapists' yearnings for omniscience. It is interesting to follow psychiatrists' writing as they themselves age and learn. As Zeman has put it, it is not "something that happens just to the other fellow."

Another reason aged patients repel psychotherapeutically inclined psychiatrists is their rather obvious search to be helped, rather than to learn about how to help themselves. The very helpless, clinging, and demanding are frightening, as any new and untrained mother can attest. I need scarcely mention that aged persons can also remind us of our parents, and very likely of our own mortality, especially if we have lost a parent figure. In short, they defy our omnipotence, rip holes in our omniscience, show no promise of being grateful, do not stimulate or excite us, and constantly threaten to dirty our clean skins, clothing, bill of health, or our medical record of success in treatment.

[69]

Kahn, Zeman, and Goldfarb (1958) have called attention to a famous painting by Rubens which depicts an aged man being breast-fed by a woman, a pictorialization of a common legend and an even more common fantasy. Steinbeck (1939), in the climax of *The Grapes of Wrath*, a novel which emphasizes man's dependency on society for survival at any age, depicts a similar situation. Such allegories are useful clues to what may lie beneath the excessive compassion or irrational revulsion experienced for the aged by younger people. The fantasy, in the aged, caters to the need to be fed and cared for; in the young, the fantasy is of being strong and the parent figure. In the aged, this fantasy can also represent cannibalistic devouring rage; in the young it can evidence fear of being devoured and "used up," or be a reparative, defensive mastery of less welcome fantasies of being devoured and destroyed. The idea that strength and life are obtainable by the old from the young by incorporation—sucking, eating, cannibalism— as well as by way of body contact and absorption, or by passage of spirit from a distance, appears to be ancient and universal. Medicine men and witches, sorcerers and magicians, even evil or good spirits who can heal or harm by taking out of a person into themselves what is bad or what is good, are commonly gray, wrinkled, bent and gnarled, or have long white beards. This brings to mind, for example, the Old Testament story of how David, a weak old man, although king and with royal powers, found an "exceedingly fair" virgin maiden to beome an attendant to him and "to minister to him and to lie with him" in the hope that he would become stimulated, warm, lively.

We can easily understand how in a time when central heating was unknown and shelters were cold and drafty, a king or commander might choose a healthy young person with whom to huddle so as to preserve and gain heat. For the aged royal Israelites it might be a fair young virgin; for the Roman of Hadrian's time it might be a comely and athletic young man.

[70]

In each case the royal powerful elder person receives a service, takes it from the young. If, however, he gives very little direct or personal pleasure to his attendants because of age and impotence, and if the service required is felt as restricting, burdensome, or distasteful by the youth or maiden, then even if it is sanctioned or enforced by law and tradition, and even if it is given in the name of love (often a handy term for a mixture of fear, guilt, obligation, and submission), then fear and anger will be roused in the young. These emotions can be expected to lead to thoughts and behavior which arouse guilt and fear of retaliation, with consequent reinforcement of an unhealthy bond to aged persons consisting of reparative attempts to mask, to atone for, and to be forgiven the angry thoughts and fantasies.

The belief that when the old sleep with the young they become strengthened at the expense of the young was expressed by "mesmerists" as an argument to prove the reality of the passing of an invisible substance in mesmerism. For example, as late as 1893, Carl Sextus, a lay hypnotist, wrote, "An infirm old lady . . . was so aware of the benefit that she derived from sleeping with young people, that, with a sort of horrid vampirism she always obliged her maids to share her bed, thus successively destroying the health of several attendants. Even among animals it has been found that the young cannot be too closely associated with the old without suffering detriment. Young horses standing in a stable with old ones become less healthy." He also noted, "The celebrated German psysiologist, Hufeland, has remarked the longevity of schoolmasters, and he attributes it to their living so constantly amidst the healthy emanations of young persons." We now interpret such benefits obtained by the old from contact with the young differently. The fear and distrust of the aged by the young and healthy may often be not only a reluctance to assume a burden, but also resentment at the reversal of the roles considered more natural and fitting by younger persons who

[71]

have been used to parental care and protection and are loath to relinquish it.

In his younger patients, the apprentice psychotherapist may mistake superficially good rapport for "transference," and glibness and ingratiation for motivation toward self-help. He all too often forgets that the patient's initial respect for psychoanalytically oriented psychotherapy is frequently merely a special elaboration of a search for magic, or a variation on the theme of readiness to submit to authority in that condition of heightened suggestibility which is the basis of the hypnotic state. He may fail to recognize that the helplessness of an aged patient may make possible the same kind of relationship, differently expressed, which provides him with the greatest possible leverage for helping the patient—a delegation of the therapist to an influential parental role. What seems to be poor rapport and a reluctance or fear to deal with the doctor can be misunderstood as an absence of "transference," or if it is recognized as a so-called negative transference its great usefulness may not be fully appreciated. One of the most important factors making for reluctance to undertake psychotherapy with the aged is the feeling of helplessness and frustration experienced in the face of a process the person feels unable to control and to understand.

Adequate medical and neurological training of psychiatrists about the disorders of the aged can assist in providing at least an illusion of control, by furnishing explanatory theoretical structures. When we cannot control an organism-environmental process called disease, we gain great reassurance from our capacity to describe its mechanisms, origin, development, and probable outcome, as though obsessionally reassured that our manipulation of the words is somehow affecting their referents. Fortunately, we also have evidence that psychotherapeutic experiences can be repeated and reinforced, revealing unsuspected abilities of the aged person for healthy adaptation. This can bring great satisfaction to the psychiatrist.

[72]

In summary, it seems that the aged mentally ill patient may be disregarded, ignored, considered unworthy or too difficult for treatment because his techniques for gaining help are not sufficiently winning and his resources inadequately appreciated; thus an opportunity to ease his suffering and improve his functioning may be lost. Therapists should rationally view aged persons more optimistically.

Finally, mention must be made of the relation between individual and social dynamics. The decline in functional efficiency of aged persons may thrust a burden of care on family, friends, and community. Special reactions to this may be reflected in a number of ways. These ways are greatly influenced by the type of social economy and the way it developed, but all seem to have a common denominator, i.e., fear or anger elaborated as compassion or rationalized neglect, interwoven with guilt or with guilty fear of retaliation for resentful, angry, or rejecting thoughts. The elaboration of patterns or rituals of compassion and of care or neglect in different societies appears to have common roots.

Indoctrination with ideals of service to the sick, the weak, and the old is a part of socialization; it requires the inhibition of self-seeking and self-defensive trends, and people must be inculcated in the context of the society and in accordance with its needs. Not only failure to become socialized in this way, but also successful socialization may, in some societies, lead to behavior which appears cruel and strange when viewed from other social frames of reference. Probably nowhere, really, do the well-acculturated of the society mistreat or neglect all the old out of inhumanity toward old age. And probably nowhere, despite the claims of any culture, are all the old treated with complete deference, respect, and solicitude. We can in fact often presume that opposite thoughts may underlie protestations of respect and protection. The old are dealt with in accordance with the needs of the society; where food is scarce the old may be permitted or helped to die. Death is a gift the legendary Eskimo would have given his aged parent should conditions have required his execution, and both parent and child would have so regarded it. It is my impression that our society is neither cruel and neglectful, nor rejecting of the aged: the self-perpetuating society builds into the individual what society expects from him; the seemingly casual care for the aged by the root gatherers, hunters, nomadic herders, and agrarian societies was possibly less effective and their ritualized neglect probably more stringent than our own.

We are at a point where social and economic changes require revision of views about family responsibility and family care. Our present industrialized society requires organization on a community level if the aged are to be cared for because few small families today can support the burden of an aged relative, and the extended family as a functional unit appears to be a thing of the past. It is likely in any case that the extended family could scarcely deal with the problems of aged persons whose absolute and relative number is now increased so that too many, simultaneously, arrive at points requiring care for family efforts to be adequate to their needs. Each family unit has at least one and probably more than one aged parent to care for or to share in caring for — and this need for care often extends into the old age of the responsible child or children. This is a new and interesting social situation. The social institutions to which it gives rise should also be interesting.

Some Intrapsychic Aspects of Aging

Martin A. Berezin, m.d.

In our efforts to study and understand the process of aging, we begin with a problem of definition. What is old age, and when does it begin? Aside from philosophical and physiological considerations which state that aging begins at birth, we are faced with standardizing our communications by a more or less arbitrary decision in which it is declared that old age is reached at a certain chronological period. For years there has been no agreement on what age we should call old age. Many years ago, 40 was considered to be old age, e.g., "Life begins at 40," but this age has gradually been extended upward, and popular agreement now seems to be on 65, an age no doubt inspired by Social Security regulations.

Aside from this agreed-upon chronological consideration, a number of phenomena are unique to the period we call old age and in turn give definition to this period of life. These phenomena are both external and intraorganismic.

But first, I would like to raise two questions, which initially attracted me to the study of aging. These questions are: (1) Why is one person old at 50, while another is young at 70? — and (2) Why and how is it that a person who has lived a successful, adaptive life and maintained his psychic equilibrium, in old age manifests signs and symptoms of a psychiatric breakdown for the first time?

Efforts to answer these questions lead one into many fascinating avenues. Implied in the above questions is the problem of determining what is "healthy," "normal," or "successful" aging — an implication we may not be able to answer at all, but the effort to do so should not be blunted. In the consideration of these questions, my own inclination is toward a closer scrutiny of the intrapsychic phenomena. Extraorganismic conditions should not, however, be neglected, overlooked, or underemphasized, and I will describe briefly some of the external conditions which occur to and involve the aged intimately and sometimes quite uniquely.

To begin with, the aged person suffers from various losses. He loses members of his family and friends. Losses may occur through death or, in the case of children, marriages and moving away. Each succeeding loss results in grief and mourning, with a consequent sense of aloneness and loneliness with which the individual learns to cope.

Another condition which impinges on the aged person is loss of occupation, either by retirement or semiretirement, and this in turn results in a reduced income. Loss of occupation also may result in loss of status and prestige, especially in our achievement-oriented culture.

Of considerable significance to the aged are the somatic changes which inevitably accompany old age — diminished acuity in vision and hearing, loss of elasticity of the skin, degenerative changes in joints, generalized changes in body contours which occur as a result of loss or shift in fatty deposits, menopausal changes in women and prostatic changes in men, vascular changes throughout the body, significantly in the vessels which supply the brain and heart, etc. When these changes occur, a shift in the self-image must occur. Alterations in the self-image usually require considerable flexibility in ego management. All these occurrences are consistent with the "normal crisis" of aging, a term which I owe to Dr. Grete L. Bibring (personal communication) as she used it to refer to the normal crisis of pregnancy. In old age the crisis is much longer, more drawn-out; it is a crisis in slow motion, as it were.

These, then, are some of the conditions which impinge on a and affect the aging person. The focus of this presentation, however, is not on these conditions, but rather on the type of personality structure on which these conditions impinge. Each person in his own way manages, successfully or unsuccessfully as the case may be, these different categories by those modes of management, through those ego functions, which are part of his character, his habitual mode of functioning in his lifetime. He has no other way available to him.

An attempt to understand aging by focusing only on external conditions to the exclusion of the intrapsychic components is absurdly one-sided. Unfortunately, there are those who attribute disorders of aging essentially to external factors. This view, when reduced to its fundamentals, implies that all that is necessary is to rectify external conditions, provide the material necessities of life, and all old people will magically be well.

Obviously, it is essential to us to know as much as possible about the psyche in which events such as those mentioned above evoke responses. For instance, we know that there are a variety of responses to retirement. We hear of some retired people who die in six months, of others who become severely depressed, of still others who go on for years in a quite contented fashion. With this illustration as a simple model, we can explore certain phenomena of the intrapsychic life which, when understood, enable us to understand better the significance of external occurrences.

We are seriously handicapped in our efforts to study the psychodynamic aspects of aging because our usual clinical material, from which inevitably all theoretical considerations must be derived, is cross-sectional. Sometimes all that is available is an interview, perhaps several, with some filling in of the past history by others. From such sources we must attempt to understand a lifetime process, and our attempts often involve a certain amount of conjecture. What would be ideal, of course, would be longitudinal case studies. So far the only case we know of which has been studied longitudinally and reported is that of Freud's (1918) Wolf Man.

REGRESSION

Regression is probably the most commonly observable clinical phenomenon in the aging. It is the one most commonly alluded to and most easily understood, by psychiatrists and lay people alike. The intrapsychic significance in the process of aging is so obvious as to be axiomatic. Regression is the *sine qua non* of aging — there is no aging without it. However, there are at least two considerations which make discussion necessary: one is the value judgment so frequently connoted in the use of the term, and the other is that regression in the aged is not the same as regression in younger people. This last statement requires some clarification: as a movement or maneuver within the psyche, regression as a process may not differ at any age level, but the circumstances which bring it about may vary. In addition, regression in a young person may represent something much more pathological than the "normal" regressive processes of the aged one.

The recognition of regression by the lay person has come to us through the centuries with the recognition of the entity so commonly referred to as the "second childhood" stage. Shakespeare has said it in his famous lines in *As You Like It*. The passage refers not only to regression and second childhood, but also portrays varying identities in the growth, development, and maturation of man:

All the world's a stage,
And all the men and women merely players.

[78]

They have their exits and their entrances;
And one man in his time plays many parts,
His acts being seven ages. At first the infant,
Mewling and puking in the nurse's arms.
And then the whining school-boy, with his satchel
And shining face, creeping like snail
Unwillingly to school. And then the lover,
Sighing like a furnace, with a woeful ballad
Made to his mistress' eyebrow. Then a soldier,
Full of strange oaths, and bearded like the pard;
Jealous in honour, sudden and quick in quarrel,
Seeking the bubble reputation
Even in the cannon's mouth. And then the justice,
In fair round belly with good capon lined,
With eyes severe and beard of formal cut,
Full of wise saws and modern instances;
And so he plays his part. The sixth age shifts
Into the lean and slipper'd pantaloon,
With spectacles on nose and pouch on side;
His youthful hose, well saved, a world too wide
For his shrunk shank; And his big manly voice,
Turning again toward childish treble, pipes
And whittles in his sound. Last scene of all,
That ends this strange eventful history,
Is second childishness, and mere oblivion,
Sans teeth, sans eyes, sans taste, sans everything.

Some attempt at clarification of the concept of regression is
in order. It is a defensive operation of the ego. In conditions of
stress and conflict, wishes may be partly or wholly given up and
the person may, to avoid anxiety, return to earlier aims and
desires. Thus, for example, a person faced with a genital or
phallic desire which is accompanied by severe conflict over a
form of wish or behavior felt as taboo, forbidden, incapable of
fulfillment, dirty, or dangerous, will regress to anal or oral
aims and wishes. The purpose is thereby to achieve some

degree of satisfaction, gratification, pleasure, or equilibrium within the psychic structure. The maneuver may succeed to varying degrees or may fail, but the effort and striving occurs. We are familiar with the pathological meaning of regression, which is not usually characterized as a healthy defense. The unhealthy and pathological significance of regression is especially obvious in such severe disturbances as the schizophrenias where regression and fixation are the most prominent features of the disorder. It is also clear that we must think of regression as representing varying degrees of health or illness. In this connection, Kris (1952) has pointed out that regression may be used normally, without carrying the stigma of illness, as when it is used "in the service of the ego." That is, in normal conditions, such as joking and wit, one may regress momentarily into primary-process thinking which enables one to appreciate the joke while still maintaining ego mastery of the regressive aspect of the primary-process consideration. Artists too may use regression and dip into their own unconscious, into their own primary processes, which are then utilized in artistic expression and creativity. Such uses of regression are not considered to be pathological, although parenthetically we must add that sometimes the artist who has such close communion with his primary processes may be in difficulty when he tries to find his way back to the more adaptive secondary processes necessary for a sane and civilized existence — a fact which is poignantly attested to by the frequency of psychic disorders in creative, artistic people.

We have pointed up two extremes in the spectrum of what is called regression. Where in this range shall we place the phenomenon of regression in the aged? Before an answer to this question can be attempted, a closer scrutiny of the determinants of regression in the aged would be helpful. The criteria which establish whether a given regression is to be considered pathological or not would be the determinants which bring it into being.

It is already observable that one feature of the difference between pathological regression and regression in the service of the ego is what brings about the regression. In the pathological case, regression may come about as a consequence of trauma, while the not so pathological regression may be stimulated by creative needs. In the aged person, the need for regression arises out of the inexorable fact that genital primacy, which was the maturational goal arrived at, now diminishes to varying degrees, sometimes disappearing altogether. There is no choice left for the aged person except to retreat to previous libidinal positions. Under the impact of the "normal crisis" of aging, regression manifests itself. Since the whole crisis of aging is a slow-motion condition, regression may likewise occur in slow motion, that is, it develops gradually—a *marche à petits pas*. What may be observed is a recapitulation in reverse of previous maturational ontogeny.

The differences in degree of regression may be determined by previously achieved states of maturity, early object relations, or what was achieved in the narcissistic object-relations balance. An analogy here is Freud's theoretical consideration of depression and suicide. The question arises why suicide is hardly considered to be a problem with compulsive obsessives, who, like the depressed, are full of self-reproaches and self-hatred. The answer is contained in the theoretical assumption that the depressed suicidal patient regresses to the oral or narcissistic level, while the compulsive does not—the assumption being that some early object relation now sustains him and suicide is not sought as a way out of a hopeless dilemma. So it is with the aged person: the degree of regression, and what is more significant, his acceptance of regression as a way of life, is determined by earlier conditions. Of course, this raises the serious question of what is "successful aging."

The clinically observable conditions we refer to as regressed are those in which the anal and oral drives are manifested, for

[81]

along what other route is retreat or substitution possible? The preoccupation of the aged with food and bowel conditions, so common and so well recognized, are obvious manifestations of the regression that has occurred. That this may be accompanied by diminished genital primacy is indicated in familiar colloquial references and jokes in which an old man asserts that the act of defecation now gives him far greater pleasure than that experienced in sexual relations. Or the fact of diminished genital primacy and sexual desires, as well as memory defect, are contained in the simple joke about the old, old man who chases a pretty girl around a table, but can't remember why.

What must not be lost sight of in regressive phenomena is not only that actual physical sexual life as a manifestation of genital primacy may decline, but the more significant fact that concomitant character changes arise which are consistent with the various libidinal levels of organization. To consider genital primacy only in its overtly sexual function is an injustice to the whole theoretical framework of which we speak, as well as a constriction of and injustice to the understanding of the aged.

While Freud did not have much to say about aging, and wrote no paper devoted to this subject, some pertinent comments about aging are nevertheless interspersed in various of his papers. I would like to quote one which is related to the subject at hand.

It is a well-known fact, and one that has given much ground for complaint, that after women have lost their genital function their character often undergoes a peculiar alteration. They become quarrelsome, vexatious and overbearing, petty and stingy; that is to say, they exhibit typically sadistic and anal-erotic traits which they did not possess earlier, during their period of womanliness. Writers of comedy and satirists have in all ages directed their invectives against the "old dragon" into which the charming

[82]

girl, the loving wife and the tender mother have been transformed. We can see that this alteration of character corresponds to a regression of sexual life to the pregenital sadistic and anal-erotic stage, in which we have discovered the disposition to obsessional neurosis. It seems, then, to be not only the precursor of the genital phase but often enough its successor as well, its termination after the genitals have fulfilled their function [Freud, 1913, pp. 323-324].

The concept of characterology as related to different levels of libidinal organization would require classification of a variety of character traits as we know and see them clinically, a classification I shall not undertake at this time. The existence of regressive character changes in the aged is well known: what Shakespeare called the "second childishness" implies a whole range of character and symptom formation.

There is, however, one other characteristic of regression in the aged which should be mentioned. The young adult may regress when he encounters conflict on being confronted with a test situation, for example, when called upon to function and behave as a mature sexual adult. At such times regression may occur to oral and anal levels of behavior. The aged person, however, is in a different position. When regression occurs, because of his diminished genitality, the retreat to oral and anal positions has a different color. The aged person may have functioned successfully at genital levels, and so from memory and experience knows what it has been and what it has meant to him to operate successfully. He must now adapt himself to a lesser position forced upon him. (It is possible that recent memory defects may be related to this situation — to remove the painful aspect of giving up a cherished level of biological maturation.) Many aged people refuse to give up genital primacy and seek to prove they are what they once were. In consequence, we sometimes see aging people trying to behave both sexually and occupationally as if they had not changed — hence

[83]

the colloquial comment, "there's no fool like an old fool." Sometimes the effort to recapture a lost position, especially in sexual matters, leads to tragic legal consequences. There is frequently a hollowness in this striving; some old people seem to live in a kind of afterimage. Conversely, those who can accept regressive changes, both physically and psychically, may be considered to possess an active ingredient necessary for so-called successful aging. It is quite likely that the superego and ego ideal significantly determine the course of successful and unsuccessful aging.

TIMELESSNESS OF THE UNCONSCIOUS
(PERSISTENCE AND RETURN OF THE REPRESSED)

This psychological phenomenon should be discussed in conjunction with regression, for they are essentially coupled — which does not mean they are the same thing, for they are not. When regression occurs, previously repressed material may now become conscious. On the other hand, much drive material was never repressed and has remained conscious throughout life, but at a period of life when it should normally become repressed, it does not. This is especially obvious in regard to sexual drives. At a period of life when the sexual drive is not physiologically active, there nevertheless remains an active fantasy life which bears little or no relation to external reality. Thus a woman who, since puberty, had been phobic about being attacked and raped if she walked on the street, verbalized the same phobic fear (and wish) in her seventies. Recently, there was a newspaper item about a 78-year-old man who killed another man in a quarrel over the attentions of a mutual girlfriend.

Some of the paranoid breakdowns among the aged reveal the same timelessness of sexual fantasy life, sometimes to a point of absurdity — as in the case of the 80-year-old man who was preoccupied with delusional fear that his 80-year-old wife was attractive to other men and that she was being actively unfaithful to him!

We are indebted to a report by Linden (1953), which graphically and interestingly illustrates this fact:

Nellie: "Why, Susie, you know you flirt with all the boys."

Susie: "I do not. How can you say that? I'm respectable. You're the one who always says you're getting married." (General laughter)

Bertha: "That may be true about Nellie, but I saw you out there on the bench with that painter. You were making eyes at him and kidding him. You're with him every day at lunch. I don't blame you. He's sort of nice."

Susie: "Oh, you couldn't have seen me, because I didn't do it. Doctor, I hope you don't believe them. They're making it up. They're just trying to tease me."

Nellie: "Aw go on, don't try to look like an angel in front of the Doctor. Lately you've been dressing up fit to kill —had your hair done twice in the beauty parlor, putting on all your jewelry. You're not fooling anybody."

Susie: "You're making it all up. How could I get serious about that painter—if he's the one you mean, why he's too old for me. Why don't you just forget about me and pay attention to yourself? You've got plenty of explaining to do. Go on, tell the Doctor what you told me yesterday." (General laughter)

Nellie: (Reddening, but smiling) "Okay, I will if you tell him what you told me." (Both titter)

Mary: "Oh, you're both being childish—after all what's wrong if you do like a man. Is that abnormal? I should think that by this time of our lives we could face such things and talk about them without trying to pretend that we don't have such feelings."

[85]

Mayfield: "That's the way I feel about it. I'm not ashamed
to tell everybody that I'd like to get married. Maybe
that sounds silly to you, Doctor, but that's really the
way I feel. I guess it'll never happen, but I dream
about it."

One could easily believe that this conversation took place
among a group of adolescent girls, but here are the facts:
Nellie is 70, Susie is 77, Bertha is 65, Mary is 68, and Mayfield
is 76.

The unconscious is indeed timeless, and so are instinctual
drives and wishes. A parody of a famous quotation seems to fit
the facts just presented, namely, "Old wishes never die, they
don't even fade away."

There is something forlorn and empty about older people
clinging to their pursuits of earlier days; their behavior is more
an afterimage than it is the genuine article. Shakespeare no
doubt had this in mind when he remarked, "Is it not strange
that desire should so many years outlive performance?" (*King
Henry IV,* Part II).

The image of the old person striving unrealistically for performance based on past experience should be clarified in at
least one area, by linking it to what was previously discussed
under regression. Two points are pertinent here: (1) behavior
not realistically realizable may occur after regression takes
place, and (2) this behavior may occur when the necessity for
regressive change is denied and consequently overcompensated
for. I am reminded here of a 55-year-old woman whom I saw
in consultation some years ago. Her appearance in the interview was quite bizarre. Her clothing was quite flashy and out
of keeping with her age. Her face was made up heavily with
lipstick, eye shadow, and various paints, and her manner was
coy and flirtatious. The understanding of her appearance and
behavior came from the knowledge that at the age of 18 she
had indeed been a beautiful girl, and had in fact won a beauty

[86]

contest. The narcissistic gratification derived from this victory had never left her, and she had tried in all the intervening years to maintain the image of herself as a beautiful, admired adolescent girl — a position incompatible with reality and consequently full of pain and despair.

Not only are unconscious wishes and drives timeless, but so are the various defensive and adaptive mechanisms the psyche uses in order to achieve and maintain a state of equilibrium. It is in this area of ego functions that we see what we call character and character traits which persist for a lifetime, whether the characterological formations are healthy ones or unhealthy ones. In this connection, I recall seeing an elderly man when he was 79. I had known his early history from personal sources. He had been involved in litigation year after year. In his earlier years he had been diagnosed as paranoid. At 79 he had been declared mentally incompetent by several psychiatrists and still bore the diagnosis of paranoia. In his interview with me, he continued to be preoccupied with many paranoid ideas but had become much more quiet about them and had more or less resigned himself to the knowledge that there was little he could do to make the world around him believe in his ideas, ideas which involved his daughter, her lawyer, and some community plans. He had in a certain way mellowed and muted his paranoia, but it was still there. Some years later I received a call from him, and he came to see me. He was now 90. He was much thinner, much older-looking, infirm, stooped over, and walked quite slowly. His voice, strong, resonant, and robust at 79, was now weak and barely audible — but the content of his thinking had not changed. He was still paranoid, and still wanted to prove his accusations against his daughter and her lawyer.

Timelessness then involves the unconscious, that which is repressed in the unconscious; it involves drives and wishes which are correlated with drives; and it involves defensive and adaptive mechanisms of the ego.

[87]

INDEPENDENCE

Another phenomenon, the wish to be independent, occurs among aged people with startling regularity in an intense form, and sometimes under the most unrealistic conditions. I first became acquainted with this phenomenon during a research study of community aging problems among cases being managed by a social service agency. While I was surprised to see the striving for independence when I first met it, I have since learned that it has been well known among lay observers.

Time and again, in the most adverse physical circumstances, economic deprivation, isolation from others, these aged people would insist upon being what they called *independent!* They would refuse care and dependent relationships. Thus, a man in his seventies with a severe cardiac disorder, frequent decompensation, and difficulty in breathing, who was so disabled that he could at times hardly even walk, lived in a fourth-floor walk-up apartment. It was pointed out to him that walking up and down four flights of stairs was dangerous, and he was asked to accept financial help from his children, which would enable him to rent a ground-floor apartment. He refused, stating he wanted to be independent. He insisted that, if he were to accept any help at all, the only thing he wanted was to install a telephone so that he might call his doctor in an emergency. This is only one illustration of many similar situations. In each instance these people preferred living under hardships and deprivations in order to maintain what was for them an image of themselves as independent.

Such a repetitive clinical observation deserves closer study. From the examination of a number of cases, it is apparent that a number of determinants cause what seems clinically to be a wish for independence. "Independence" is the term used by the patients. It is not necessarily an accurate term, for, as we shall see, independence may shade into rebellion and domination, etc.

The following classification is not unique to the aging; it applies at various developmental levels. However, it seems particularly useful when applied to the aging.

1. *Independence as a normal maturation process.*

It ought not be overlooked that the expressed wish for independence may be reality-oriented, and may be based on a lifelong maturity pattern in the aged person. Such independence is real and object-related. It is accompanied by a sense of well-being as well as an absence or minimum of anxiety.

2. *Various meanings of the concept of independence.*

a. The notion of independence may by equated with the concept of strength. The corollary is that dependence represents a weakness. To assert independence is to assert strength and deny weakness and helplessness.

b. Related to this is the equation of independence and youthfulness. To assert independence is an effort to deny being old.

c. In this same grouping is the equation of independence — representing activity or motility as a quality of life — with being alive, with contact with ego boundaries, while passivity shades off into ego dissolution and the threat of extinction. To assert independence, therefore, is to assert that one is alive. (This particular category deserves much more theoretical discussion than can be given here.)

d. Asserting independence may be a compensatory device, used to combat feelings of inferiority and inadequacy, which may always have been present but are now exaggerated by actual physical and psychological decline. Such people tend to become overassertive, rebellious, and domineering. This category is closely related to the concept of strength noted in (a) above.

3. *Ways in which independence may be used—and its secondary gains.*

[89]

a. To assert independence and thereby deny others in their efforts to help, and consequently to live in a state of deprivation, may arouse concern, guilt, and anxiety in others, mainly in the person's children. It is therefore an unconscious act of hostility and punishment.

b. This capacity to arouse anxiety and guilt in others by asserting independence serves another need. Many people have never been able to express or feel closeness with or tenderness for others, even their own children, in any really mature way. It is not at all infrequent for such people to establish and maintain a relationship, but one in which closeness and tenderness are warded off. The children, who are the usual targets of this maneuver, are kept in a state of constant uneasiness and suspense, and the old person therefore cannot be forgotten or deprived of attention.

c. The wish for independence may enable the old person to avoid exploitation by others, especially by his own children — exploitation of either his services or his material goods. As one old woman put it, her daughter had always come to her with problems, demanding help, and now she felt it was time she was free of this demanding one. As she said it, "I just don't want to be her slave any more." Another woman likewise expressed her wish not to live near her children for fear of being exploited as a baby-sitter. This maneuver may represent a projection as well as a wish for dependency.

d. A state of independence may be claimed by the obsessive-compulsive person who needs to isolate affects and ties with others.

e. Some old people assert a position of independence through the fear that they may, if dependent, impose on others. In this way an old person may try to live up to certain conventional standards in order to ensure approval of and acceptance by others.

f. Independence may be really antidependence.

SOME PROBLEMS OF DRIVE AND ENERGY CONCEPTS

It is a tacit assumption and generally accepted that the energy quanta and drive energy diminish in the aged. This assumption should be critically reviewed in order that we may be satisfied that it is true or, if necessary, modify or correct our concepts in this significant area. There is room for doubt and reservations about the validity of the assumption that drives decrease as one gets older, but the question remains open. Let us briefly review some of the aspects involved.

In the first place, to go back to a different chronological era of growth, we are accustomed to speak of the adolescent as manifesting increased instinctual drives. Thus, Anna Freud (1936) stated that after childhood "the latency period sets in, with a physiologically conditioned decline in the strength of the instincts. . ."; after latency come puberty and adolescence, at which point "no qualitative change has taken place in the instinctual life, but the quantity of instinctual energy has increased. This increase is not confined to the sexual life. There is more libido at the id's disposal and it cathects indiscriminately any id impulses which are at hand."

One question which arises in attempting to determine any relative increase of quantity of instinctual energy is that of methodology. We have no way of accurately measuring such quantities. Estimates of increased drive or decreased drive are based primarily on behavior and clinical phenomena.

In the case of the adolescent, who is usually in some kind of psychic turmoil, behavior in motor terms connotes something which we interpret as increase in drive. Thus the adolescent can be observed to have a marked increase of interest in sexual matters; there is a shift from pregenital organizations to genital primacy, with overt genital sex play, increased interest in the opposite sex, and a marked increase in intellectual and philosophical concerns, as well as an increaed interest in world

[91]

affairs. Conflicts around independence and dependence, rebellion and submission, are prominent and are acted out in many ways, sometimes dangerously. But do these behaviors signify an increased quantity of drive? If so, then the infant who screams when he is hungry also manifests a high quantity of drive. If, furthermore, the infant has high drive intensity, why is it believed that there is, in adolescence, an *increase* in drive? Is it possible that drive intensity remains the same, but in the adolescent, because of a shift of emphasis, we see manifestations not of increased drive, but rather of *new conflict situations*? The clinical manifestations may not be the result of increased drive, but rather of a disturbance in a previous equilibrium, a disturbance that demands a resolution which in turn is accompanied by considerable turmoil. This point is not neglected by Anna Freud in her superb discussion of adolescence.

Looked at in another way, what may be going on is that the ego, with all its defenses and adaptations, manages drives in a fashion that prevents and defies measurements, e.g., in the latency period defenses are strong and drives are held in check. In the case of the obsessive-compulsive personality, a similar process is at work in which the defenses of isolation and reaction formation give the appearance of quietness and equanimity. We know, however, how incorrect such an evaluation of drive quantity is, for the compulsive achieves an equilibrium based largely on inhibition of drive. The degree of inhibition is a measure of the degree of drive in a loose one-to-one ratio — i.e., the degree to which inhibition is used is roughly equivalent to the degree of instinctual drive being inhibited. One sees the compulsive personality as the "caricature of equanimity," as Brenner (1955) aptly describes it. The opposite is true of the impulse-ridden character or the agitated existence of certain hysterical personalities.

In what way is this discussion relevant to the problem of drive quantity in the aged? As already mentioned, it is taken

[92]

for granted that drive and energy decrease in the aged. It is tacitly assumed that drives decrease gradually to a final point where death occurs as the inevitable and inexorable result. Certainly it is a clinical fact that sexual interests decline with age, but those regressive oral and anal phenomena which seem to replace sexual interests carry a not inconsiderable quantity of drive, a fact also clinically demonstrable in the intensity of interest in oral and anal functions. Is there really, therefore, a diminishing of drives, or is there a shift of interest, the quantity of drive remaining the same?

The issue is complicated by the fact that energy is required to maintain adaptive or defensive equilibrium. Gitelson (1948) remarks that "the failure of adaptive strengths which goes with age is associated with a weakening of the defenses against the instinctual drives." As a result one may see a number of gross psychiatric disturbances. But if so, then what seems to be occurring is that the defenses are weakened while the drive intensity remains the same. Or can drive and defense diminish together? If so, there must be relative imbalance between the two, otherwise symptoms would not be likely. A further question relates to the problem of energy sources of the defenses themselves. If defenses weaken, the drives too must have diminished. I do not know the answers to the questions I have raised. I raise them only that they may not be neglected, and that hopefully we may with further study arrive at some answers.

THE CONSULTATIVE POSITION

It is disquieting to think of regression as representing only morbidity—for this means essentially that all senility is morbidity. There may be room for discussion on this point, for if this were true, both biologically and psychologically the aged would correctly be regarded as undesirable pathological elements in society. But such is not the case, although attitudes toward aging vary in different cultures. An answer to certain aspects of the question of whether senility is morbidity was attempted under the topic of regression. I should like now to suggest something further in terms of identity of self in the aged, which presents a more positive condition than the acceptance of one's own regressive changes with a certain equanimity.

What follows is based on Erikson's (1959) concept as stated in *Identity and the Life Cycle*. Briefly, he has offered a classification of different age periods from infancy through adolescence, young adulthood, adulthood, and mature age. Erikson suggests a specific identity for each age period. For example: "A child in the multiplicity of successive and tentative identifications, thus begins early to build up expectations of what it will be like to be older, and what it will feel like to have been younger—expectations which become part of an identity as they are, step by step, verified in decisive experiences of psychosocial 'fittedness' " (p. 114).

Leaving aside for the moment that part of his classification which deals with earlier maturation, we begin with adulthood, that stage which involves the libidinal genital organization, and includes the capacity for developing a sex relationship with a loved partner of the opposite sex, and capacity for love, kindness, tenderness, in other words, a mature object relation. Erikson calls this stage "intimacy and distantiation versus self-absorption"—which offers a spectrum from health to morbidity.

The subsequent stage is "generativity versus stagnation." Generativity is concerned with parenthood, with the production and care of offspring. Actually, the wellsprings of generativity include many sublimated facets designed not only for the care of one's own children but in general for the future generation as well. Thus artists and poets work not only for contemporary society but for the next generation, i.e., for posterity as well.

For mature age, Erikson suggests the concepts of "integrity versus despair and disgust." This he defines as "the acceptance of one's own and only life cycle and of the people who have become significant to it as something that had to be and that, by necessity, permitted of no substitutions" (p. 98).

I would like to suggest a concept which is either a corollary or an extrapolation of Erikson's classification as it applies to old age. I am not certain what age group Erikson refers to in his grouping of "mature age." In any event, whatever it may refer to, there is a concept significant for the image and identity of integrity in old age. I shall call it "the consultative position," denoting, specifically, a role, an identity the elderly assume in relation to those around them, those who are younger, and who are statistically bound to be in the majority.

The consultative position implies that the aged person, by reason of having lived and survived a full life, has profited in experience, training, discrimination, judgment, wisdom, and the like. By virtue of such achievement, he is available now to help others as an objective philosopher, as it were. These implications are not necessarily objective facts about any one aged person. The assumption that it is so is usually explicitly or implicitly made, both by the oldster and those around him. Lest we get involved in the problem of a value judgment about the "consultant," let us specify that this is not the main point. For our purpose, it makes no difference whether the consultant is a good or a bad one. The question of ability is not the issue.

A simple and well-recognized illustration of the assumed identity of the consultative position is an old person's being asked to what he attributes his longevity. Invariably an anwer will be given, an answer usually intended as consultative for others; that is, he will indicate a way of life which, in his opinion, and through his years of experience, explains how he has managed to live so long, with the expectation that others may now go and do likewise and so be guided to a ripe old age. In terms of the value of such replies, we sometimes hear

[95]

opposing absurdities, such as the advice never to drink whiskey, or to drink as much as one wishes. The point is not that a good or bad answer is given, but that an answer is asked for and an answer is given which fulfills the old person's role of consultant.

Another illustration of the consultative position is to be seen in the conduct of Bernard Baruch, the famous financier and advisor to Presidents. In his eighties, he sat on his park bench in New York while the great and near-great went to see him as an oracle and consulted him about the affairs of the world. In a broader sense, the consultative position is accredited and discernible among certain classes of people whom society generally honors in this category, such as judges, physicians. educators, scientists, and "Chairmen of the Board."

In a sense, the consultative stage is a continuation of the generative stage, but without the accompanying responsibility. Caring for, and being interested in, other people's children without the accompanying responsibility is frequently observable in the relationship of grandparents to their grandchildren. It is not dissimilar either from the actual role of the medical consultant who evaluates a medical condition, but leaves responsibility for the care of the patient with the referring physician.

The motive force for this consultative position is still unclear. However, whether it is biologically determined, or is a psychological outgrowth and further development of previous psychological states, or represents a culturally determined position, or is a combination of these things, is a subject which bears further study.

Precursors of the consultative position seem to be within the structure of the generative organization. They may be observed in children who actually play out this role, as when an older brother takes a younger brother in tow and gives him advice and guidance. It seems that children are inclined to play not only at games of procreation, as in various forms of

[96]

sex play, but also at games representing generativity and consultative roles, such as family games.

I was quite delighted to find confirmation of my thesis about this consultative position in Cicero's *De Senectute:* "Old age, especially when honoured, has influence so great that it is of more value than all the pleasures of early manhood."

When the consultative role can be filled reasonably, it is a significant ingredient of successful aging. When this role cannot be lived up to, then one may see a "collapse of the self-esteem," as Edward Bibring (1953) has phrased it, and various depressive reactions may follow. In other words, when the consultative position is available, then the satisfaction and gratification derived contribute one quality, among others, which enables the aged person to manage the physiological involutions and psychological regressions which inevitably occur. It may, in a special way, be a replacement for the lost genital primacy.

Psychodynamic Considerations in Normal Aging

IRVING KAUFMAN, M.D.

I T IS INDEED APPROPRIATE for a child analyst also to be interested in the aging. Children and adults at an advanced age often require similar help. This includes help in the management of such external realities as food, shelter, and activities. Sometimes a protective service is required. As indicated by the phrase "second childhood," the regressive patterns observed in the older age group have many similarities to children's behavior.

In this paper I will discuss some of the psychodynamic phenomena associated with the normal process of aging. The data are drawn primarily from my clinical experience as director of consultation service for the Family Service Association of Greater Boston, and particularly the Services to Older Persons division, and from cases seen in private practice. Included in the discussion are observations on the timelessness of the unconscious, regressive phenomena, a consideration of the ego-adaptive processes associated with the physiological and psychological aspects of aging, countertransference reactions, and the implications these have for management and treatment of older people. These five areas are very closely interrelated, and require consideration in all cases. The following case illustrates some of these phenomena.

An 83-year-old woman referred herself to an agency with a request for financial help. She was an extraordinarily independent woman, who presented the picture of a vivacious, alert, and competent person. When the relationship began, she started to read textbooks on casework procedure and offered advice to her therapist. She also read many novels and recommended what was, in her opinion, the best current literature. During the previous five years, she had weathered a series of medical difficulties including arteriosclerotic heart disease with myocardial infarction, gall bladder surgery, and neurological changes secondary to arteriosclerosis. She was very secretive about her marriage and her family, and only discussed very carefully selected current realities which primarily related to finances. Throughout her therapy sessions, which were conducted in the worker's office, she maintained this competent exterior. Therefore it was particularly striking to learn from other sources how she had compartmentalized the various parts of her life and functioned at widely disparate levels in different situations. Her range of adaptation was particularly highlighted when, because of her advancing age and the need to supervise her medical care, it was recommended that she leave her rooming house, where she lived alone, and move into a group facility. When she moved into this group setting, which included several other elderly women, she became upset and reacted negatively. She became irritable and hostile to the other women, and began to lose control over her bowels, particularly at meal times. This loss of sphincter control caused considerable distress and counterhostility from the other women. During this time, it was observed that she was exposing herself to the other women.

Outside of this house, she was able to attend the interviews, maintain her relationship with her church and minister, and carry on such business activities as making hooked rugs and pet-sitting for people who wished to have their pets cared for while they were away. In the course of treatment, it became evident that the patient was experiencing a homosexual panic leading to this regressive behavior. The panic was stimulated and intensified by the presence of the other women in the home. Before another placement plan could be worked out, the patient took matters in her own hands. She went to a local hotel and told them she had decided to move in. When they told her that they had no available room for her, she informed them that she was certain they had a room, and after some encouragement from her, they finally found one. In this setting, where she could be alone, she was able to regain much of her previous, more effective functioning and continue with many of her activities.

This case illustrates the five areas listed for consideration. The patient, demonstrating the timelessness of the unconscious, behaved much like an adolescent girl, reacted to the group setting, and experienced homosexual panic. The underlying unconscious drives and conflicts were seeking expression in spite of her age. However, the tendency to regress as a part of all ego reactions to stress is particularly characteristic of the older patient. The capacity to compartmentalize enabled this patient to confine her more severe pathological behavior to the relatively limited setting of the group placement. The secretiveness, the loss of sphincter control, the struggle for control of and competition with the therapist, were all expressions of the anal level at which this woman was now functioning. The reactions to her were varied. Her therapist and her minister had a very positive relationship with her. The woman directing the group home was distressed and angry at her hostile and provocative behavior. She posed a particularly complicated management problem.

Ordinarily, it would be desirable to help a patient of this age, with her physical and emotional needs, work out a group placement. However, because of the homosexual panic which the group placement stimulated, it was necessary to help her work out her life situation within the more isolated and less protected setting of the hotel.

The following vignette also demonstrates the timelessness of the unconscious expression of id derivatives, and the similarity of conflicts seen in patients of all ages.

A woman in her mid-seventies described an upsetting situation to her caseworker. She said this occurred when she went to her hairdresser. While she sat in a chair, she saw him pour himself a glass of ginger ale. Thereupon she loudly announced to him that she knew "what he was up to" and ran out of the beauty parlor in a panic.

Such hysterialike behavior is generally thought to be associated with younger patients. However, fear of rape and other sexual and aggressive fears and wishes can occur at all ages, and must be dealt with within the context of the implications their expressions have for the ego strengths of the patient. What may appear clinically as an intensification of instinctual forces, during this phase of personality functioning may primarily reflect a diminution of ego and superego control as a result of the ego changes secondary to both physical and emotional alterations of functioning which are associated with the aging process. In this sense, the gross manifestations of instinctual energy may also have a regressive component in the fixations characteristic of the person.

Not all the regressive phenomena are associated with pathology. In some persons the aging process produces a diminution of the constricting and inhibiting forces which have kept creativity at a minimum. One man seen in treatment for the past year is now an author. He was a rather dull and unimaginitive person until he reached an advanced age, at which point he wrote several books which are now being seriously considered for publication. Perhaps Grandma Moses is another example of the flowering of creativity in the older person. The ego-adaptive patterns of this stage of life are similar to those of adolescence. Some adolescents for a time develop a capacity for creative expression in music, art, or poetry. Many of these same adolescents lose their creative capacity as they mature, only to regain it at an advanced age. The vicissitudes of the creative process at various points in the person's life are worthy of further study.

In some persons the regression which occurs comes under the service of the ego and leads to a late flowering of creativity. In others, the regression may lead to crude expression of libidinal and aggressive impulses, such as irritable and angry outbursts or the sexual molestation of little children.

The person brings to his aging years those strengths and weaknesses he possessed at various stages of his development. Therefore, one of the best guides for an evaluation of potential capacity to master the stresses associated with aging could be a careful appraisal of how the person handled stress earlier in his life.

Although it is not possible to create new strengths which are not inherent in the personality, it is possible to maximize the ego's capacity by helping the person in his planning, and by gaining some understanding of the meaning of his wishes. For example, planning which gives the older person an opportunity to maintain himself in his familiar life pattern and feel self-worth in his activity is a most important psychological support. Support of the ego processes, which seem to take over with advancing age, can in many ways further help the patient to manage the stresses and environmental strains confronting him. For example, the increasing utilization of denial and isolation in the severe illnesses which often accompany aging may be a last-ditch stand to hold together some ego integrity, and usually should not be challenged.

Another interesting phenomenon often noted in the aging patient is a disparity in memory patterns — memory for recent events is often diminished and memory for the more remote

[103]

past seems to take over. This memory defect may have an ego-adaptive function. In elderly patients who become depressed over the stresses of current living, it seems to protect them against an overwhelming depression. In treatment, respect for this adaptive pattern seems to be useful. Pressure to make patients face and concentrate on their stresses and worries may either drive them out of treatment or produce an overwhelming depression. This technique is different from the treatment techniques utilized with the younger patient.

An ever-present problem for those who work with the older patient is the countertransference reaction to the patient, to the aging process, and to the whole issue of hope. Some therapists find aging and its implications threatening. This is particularly true when the associated physical illnesses of cancer and heart disease are present, as they are in so many cases. However, for therapists who take the time to see what can be done in many of these cases, and particularly with the utilization of realistic objectives, the patients begin to emerge as people with problems whom the therapist wishes to help, many of whom he finds he can help.

In summary, then, we find in the older patient many conflicts and patterns of stress also seen in younger patients. The force of the instinctual drives is ever-present and potent. It is necessary to remember the timelessness of the unconscious, with its libidinal and aggressive energies and the associated conflicts, which are manifest at this stage of development too. Therefore, one should be prepared to deal with conflicts about heterosexuality and homosexuality, and with aggressive and hostile phenomena, particularly jealousy and revenge. Mental conflicts and struggles for dependence and independence in the readjustment of the marital relationship sometimes take on the intensity of the independence-dependence struggles of adolescence.

The loosening of some of the synthesizing functions of the ego and some diminution of superego controls can lead to a variety of phenomena, including expression of underlying pathological tendencies or, in some persons, a flowering of latent creative capacities. Help, protection, guidance, and management from treatment personnel who utilize a dynamic diagnostic framework in their evaluation and management of these cases can make a major difference for these patients during their later years of life.

Regression and Recession in the Psychoses of the Aging

MAURICE E. LINDEN, M.D.

RECENT COMMUNICATIONS in the field of gerontology reveal the increasing emergence of two fundamental attitudes that exist side by side among the students and workers in this field. On the one hand, there is a contagious element of optimism about the potentialities of older persons to respond to rationally structured therapeutic programs. On the other hand, there is an equally insistent note of caution, prudence, and subdued optimism about what may be the responses to all of the rehabilitative and reconstructive treatment systems designed for older persons. Reflective examination and evaluation of these divergent attitudes lead invariably to the conclusion that both points of view are correct, but that they relate to different groups of older persons and different stages in the life in given people.

Gerontology, in addition to being an objective science, possesses a human element of devotion to the relief of human suffering. Such devotion requires a fundamentally optimistic view of the elasticity and flexibility of people. This is desirable and lies at the foundation of every conceivable therapeutic approach. Still, the true scientist is capable of accepting certain realities that are at variance with his best intentions.

[107]

It is necessary to recognize in treating the aging and aged that three modes of therapeutic response may be expected.
1. The complete reversal of abnormal, socially undesirable, and problematical psychological conditions. This occurs in a minority of the gerontological and geriatric group of patients.
2. Partial reversal of abnormal intrapsychic systems of accommodation and the achievement of limited therapeutic goals. Responses to therapy that fit this category are by far the most frequent.
3. Complete and absolute failure to respond to all efforts.

THE REVERSIBILITY OF PSYCHIATRIC CONDITIONS
IN THE SENIUM

A certain degree of reversibility is intrinsic in all psychological functions in the human mind because:
1. The emotional relationships within the psychic structure, as well as those that relate to the external milieu of people, are based on interpersonal communications, or as we say in psychiatry, object relations, which are by their nature variable, fluctuating, and inconstant. The capacity for every form of object relation within the human mental apparatus is found to be operative at roughly two levels: (a) the level of automatic and unconscious thinking (primary process); and (b) the level of voluntary, intentional, and logical thinking (secondary process).
The natural laws relating to organization, operation, and function are different modes of approach to be modified.
2. Emotional energy is in a constant state of flux, but may be contained in closed and open systems of operation. The closed systems constitute self-limiting channels of expression which comprise the rigidities of human nature. The open systems possess a certain nascent malleability that may be regarded as the adaptational equipment of the human psyche derived originally from its instinctual endowment.

3. The psychic energy systems follow patterns of expression not unlike the laws of physics that relate to energies. In essence, this means that psychological energy orbits always seek modes of relieving tension deriving from any kind of restraint. In the closed systems, the relief of tension is obtained through relatively unvarying systems of behavior. In the open systems, changing adaptations become the order of operations.

4. There appears to exist in the psychological structure of living things a deep-seated compulsion to repeat past and learned modes of performance. In the aging, this principle is manifested in efforts to re-establish familiar patterns of behavior from which the organism has departed or from which a departure by the organism is threatened or forced.

5. The mere process of living at any age from birth to exitus involves inexorable and continuous psychic accommodations to changing internal and external realities. This is related to what may be regarded as purely psychological adaptation as well as to changes in the material substance of the organism of which the psychological apparatus is a function.

Clearly the capacity for automatic reversal of behavior in the human organism is minimal largely because of the prevalence of closed systems and profoundly rooted compulsions. Before these factors can be considered in somewhat greater detail, we are obliged to examine, at least briefly and in a general way, the problem of psychological accommodation to the various realities.

ADAPTATION IN DEPTH

The student, worker, researcher, therapist and, for that matter, all persons interested in the welfare of the people included in gerontological considerations, should have a realistic concept of systems of human adjustment. This is admittedly a vast field of study. However, some general principles are worthy of attention at this juncture.

Many investigators are convinced that the concept of "faulty adaptation," or "abnormal adjustment," of the human being is erroneous. Such objections are based on the conclusions of observers of human behavior that every mode of accommodation is appropriate to need and possesses a greater or lesser degree of effectiveness. In this sense, of course, there is no such thing as abnormality; there are only factors of necessity and efficiency.

An understanding of this requires the recognition of at least the two levels of operation of the human psychic structure mentioned before. The level with which we are the most familiar, because it lends itself most readily to direct conscious observation, may be termed the level of volition. While the existence of even this self-determinative level of thought is somewhat theoretical and subject to debate, those who are convinced of its existence speak of it as the conscious ego possessing an agglomeration of functions. It is presumed to be the psychic area possessing an autonomous capacity for logic, reasoning, conscious awareness, readily recallable memory, and voluntary control as well as certain other functions. This is the level of self-awareness.

According to this concept, the ego possesses a variety of layers and mixtures of mental activity. Topographically, the ego component of the mental apparatus has several facets. It must, in addition to being aware of itself, develop an interphase of definition between itself and the outside world. At its deeper levels it faces and commingles with the very profound, primitive, inherent psychological endowment from which it originated. In addition, it possesses what may be regarded as an internalized structure, the essential functions of which are the rendering of critical judgments, evaluation of motives for behavior, and the exercise of prohibitory authority over other ego functions. Thus the operation of the higher levels of consciousness must mediate and compromise among a large assortment of demands and interests that impinge on the ego.

[110]

The ego itself possesses various levels of consciousness. For the sake of our descriptive considerations we may regard the group of functions enumerated above as residing in the conscious and relatively conscious ego.

There is reason to believe that among the most profound depths of the human mind there exists a vast repository of affects, memories, impulses, and strivings which are essentially outside of the control of the relatively conscious and conscious ego. For the sake of delineation we may call this the unconscious ego. An enormous system of adaptations, memory complexes, and roots of behavior in all probability reside in the unconscious reservoir. The two levels of the ego, the more superficial and the more profound, possess their own intrinsic rational systems.

The deeper level of operations manifests a logic that is related to primitive orientations and the ancient experiences of childhood and infancy. The more superficial and conscious levels of ego operation manifest the more familiar and customary logical systems related to social living.

Our division of the mind into two gross structures is quite artificial, since in effect the mental apparatus appears to be a continuum in depth, with various layers of organization not unlike the geological layers of the earth's crust. This purely descriptive device for comprehending the levels of the mind is, of course, not necessarily actual, but is of value in communication. Nevertheless, it suggests that the different layers exist in the mental apparatus in association with chronological factors in the development of the person. In this sense, then, as layers are peeled off by some process, the subsequent levels that are uncovered are found to be progressively more primitive.

It is possible to conceive of the psychological necessity for the establishment of some demarcation between the essentially nonsocial primitive organization deep within the mind and the essentially social and less primitive organization at the upper levels. If we indulge our conceptual scheme a little further, we

[111]

can think of the layers of the mind as forces and the boundary between unconscious and conscious as an interphase of forces — in a sense a dynamic wall invested with energy to some extent capable of preventing the fields of psychical activity on both of its faces from becoming aware of one another.

As we know, intercommunication does take place between consciousness and unconsciousness, in a variety of forms of breakthrough and failure of integrity of the barrier, as well as in the conditions of dreamful sleep.

For the sake of practical consideration it is probably not too great an error to regard the barrier between the two fields as the level at which psychological defenses operate. The material behind or beneath the barrier is composed of the developmental experiences of infancy and childhood up to the set of events that terminated infantile thinking and permitted the beginning of adult and responsible psychological organization. In most people the more or less complete establishment of this intrapsychic barrier starts around the age of six, continuing into early adolescence. As a consequence, there is experienced in the conscious mind an amnesia for most of the experiences that took place before this age. Were it not for this amnesia, the reasoning and logical adult mind would constantly be harassed by intrusions of infantile thinking and feeling which would disturb the rational continuity of thought and the striving after mature social goals.

Psychiatric investigations have uncovered that the forgotten mental material of infancy consists in itself of developmental layers of organization. Much of this material concerns problems of early childhood that have been only partially solved, unresolved, or resolved with difficulty. The elemental problems of infancy and young childhood, coupled with the pleasures, discomforts, and disturbances of the early periods of life, follow a fairly uniform pattern among people in a given culture. In their forward course they constitute progressive physiological and behavioral growth in the direction of adult orientation. They progress, as it were, from relatively complete dependency toward autonomy and mature organization.

The neurotic systems of adaptation that are so common in a given culture gain their first footholds in the early stages of psychic organization. Special problems that are invested with a high degree of mental energy are thought of in psychiatry as fixations or psychological arrests. In most people such fixations constitute only a partial involvement or binding of mental energies. Despite the entrapment of these forces, much of the mental apparatus continues in its forward developmental course. In a pictorial sense, the problem events of childhood are in effect scars layered in depth and their memories are never lost, merely buried. This means that they exist as psychic records to which the mental apparatus may return should such return become necessary.

Threats to Adaptation

The developing individual maintains his goals of social adaptation so long as there are rewards for doing so. The main rewards for social adaptation are acceptance, membership, and recognition. From one point of view, such rewards are obtained through conformity so that a certain degree of universality of behavior patterns is seen in each social group. The reward for conformity is the conferring upon the individual, partly from within himself but largely from outside of himself, of a vast assortment of psychological supplies such as love, material gratification, participation, and compliments for achievement. The internal sense of self-esteem and self-valuation requires a fair degree of continuous emotional nourishment and replenishment from the environment. In addition, the integrity and wholesome functioning of the physiological apparatus lend support to the mental attitudes that summate in self-esteem. In colloquial terms, this means that if a person feels healthy and is accepted, he likes himself.

Through the earlier phases of life, both of these conditions

[113]

(health and emotional supplies from the environment) are usually present in fair measure. In the later stages of life, the human organism is beset by four main sets of factors that contribute to psychic stress: (1) the resurgence of lifelong neurotic components of the personality; (2) social attitudes toward the process of aging; (3) physiological involution and recession; and (4) the progressive reduction in the circle of friendly contacts from which psychological support can be expected.

It is not my purpose to consider the details of these factors, but to pinpoint the group of events that follows their introduction into the aging process. By far the most important factors in the aging process are the emotional deprivations that are experienced as a result of cultural attitudes of rejection toward the aged and the loss of external sources of supply, as well as internal involution and alteration of organic structure and function. These are blows to a person's sense of self-esteem. The integrity of the mental apparatus of the older person cannot long endure such impoverishment with its lack of emotional gratifications. It would appear that as the external milieu seems to grow increasingly remote from the aging ego, the rational, conscious aspect of the personality finds less and less in the outside world to which to relate itself. The outcome is an increase in dominance of the deeper areas of the mind because the balance is shifted in their favor. On this account the ego suffers the threat of being overwhelmed by the very forces against which all of its life it has erected barriers.

The choice of pathways of behavior available to the person depends now to a considerable extent on the intensity of the unconscious compelling forces, and the integrity and effectiveness of the defensive barriers long erected against primitive drives. The purpose of the defensive barriers has been to prevent the anxiety and discomfort that primitive strivings would produce if they were to reach conscious perception.

In addition to the anxiety occasioned by primitive strivings that are contrary to civilized principle is the intense unconscious anxiety that exists at the roots of neuroses. In general, the neuroses have been formed in the personality as a fairly efficient method of disguising and compromising with untenable wishes in the child's mind that are directed toward parents and parent substitutes and which, if expressed, would bring real or imagined punishment and mutilation to the child. There are thus at least two sources of anxiety and fear in the human organism.

REGRESSION

In older persons whose unconscious mainstream of psychological activity has been dominated by incompletely resolved, serious problems stemming from childhood, the loss of ego effectiveness leads to so great a summation of unconscious forces that these forces tend to overcome the defensive barrier, enter the ego, and neutralize its activities. Such entry into consciousness of the profound forces can be viewed in two ways. Both amount essentially to the same thing. The upsurge of unconscious drives may be thought of as a return into consciousness of what was long held out of consciousness (return of the repressed). Or the sequence may be viewed as the awareness function of the ego becoming focused on reactivated archaic events from out of the remote past (return to the repressed). In both instances the process constitutes regression, which in the aged may be regarded as the catastrophic event in a series leading ultimately to the development of psychosis.

Regression contains a certain element of suddenness, and reveals itself first in a withdrawal of interest from other human objects. This is accompanied by retrogressive steps of psychological behavior back to some point or points of early fixation among the deeper layers of the psyche. Customarily we look upon this as a disease, but in actuality it is the attempt at cure. The disease that threatens consists of the enormous feelings of anxiety, fright, terror, and panic that would be sensed by the

[115]

aging person as the effectiveness of his defenses is reduced. In older persons the regression to an earlier level of psychological orientation is a restitutive process that permits the ego to reorient itself more appropriately to familiar demands in accordance with the most efficient methods that were devised when such demands were first introduced into their lives. The psychosis is both psychologically realistic and self-deceptive. It consists in the main of a return into awareness of the fantasies, magical thinking, and wishes that were once in the consciousness of the infant. Such fantasies support self-esteem, and in some persons they may become entirely organized into an intrapsychically rational, delusional set through which much of reality is misperceived. The last stage of psychotic regression consists of such unrealistic or dereistic preoccupations.

The sequence of psychological events in the case of regression is somewhat as follows:

1. Social rejection of the older person occurs.

2. Social rejection is incorporated in the self-concept and, coupled with neurotic forces, develops into self-rejection.

3. Loss of self-esteem mitigates the effectiveness of defenses.

4. Conscious anxiety and an intrapsychic state of panic and terror develop.

5. Frenzied efforts to reconstruct crumbling defenses lead to psychophysiological exhaustion and enfeeblement.

6. The unconscious mainstream overrides the ego, and what is clinically seen as psychological regression develops.

7. Ego consciousness becomes dominated by the intrapsychic events and withdraws its interest from external reality and people who comprise it. This may be termed the withdrawal of object interest.

8. Efforts to overcome anxiety and fear involve the use of primitive and infantile defense mechanisms which are clinically seen as pathological. This process consists of restitu-

tive phenomena with the enhancement of pathological mechanisms.

9. The fantasy systems that dominate consciousness are misinterpreted as real and develop into dereistic preoccupations. This is the last stage in the development of a psychosis. If the psychotic system of adaptation is untreated, it will then proceed into a more or less gradual decline of the organism that is sometimes called deterioration, but which is actually another phenomenon which we are about to consider, more appropriately designated as recession.

It is well to remember that regression often does not follow or parallel the steps of physiological disintegration and degeneration in the aged person, but may occur as a sudden or somewhat gradual event in the course of late senescence.

In regression the backward steps that the mental apparatus takes reach points of psychological fixation that may well identify the stages in the child's early development at which serious disturbances of interpersonal relationships, mainly with the parents, took place. Thus the configuration of the psychosis seen in the aging mind, whether based on more or less purely psychological needs or triggered by certain somatic events (arteriosclerotic phenomena, etc.), is closely patterned on events in early childhood, may thus be understood, and may be treated according to the needs implied in those stages of life, provided that the vestiges of adult psychological organization are honored.

RECESSION

Psychological recession may be thought of as a fairly systematic retrogressive process that parallels the degenerative course into very late maturity. It may be thought of as de-education. It is analogous to the early stages of childhood during which the educative process moved in a forward direction, but in late age this process moves backward. In recession the aged

[117]

person appears to proceed through a series of retrogressive steps through level after level of the infantile developmental stages all the way back to psychological infancy. The last stage of recession is thus the last stage of dementia before death and corresponds in many ways to fetal and neonatal organization.

Recession, like regression, follows a fairly universal sequence of events and also contains some elements of emotional deprivation for the same reasons observed in regression. These sequential stages are seen clinically as follows:

1. Disillusionment following the loss of psychological supplies and ego bolsters.

2. Partial neurotic surrender as some defenses are lost or weakened. This leads to an increase in the need to replenish the defenses. Without adequate refurbishment, such neurotic surrender seriously threatens self-esteem and leads to the next stage.

3. Senescent melancholy. A mild, moderate, or severe depression is practically universal among the aged at this stage.

4. The relatively secure ego at this level makes attempts at internal reorganization in order to achieve some comfort. Clinically this is seen as general improvement. It is followed by further aging with its attendant emotional reorganization leading to the next stage.

5. Secondary neurotic surrender.

6. Senescent decline. This physiological recession is accompanied by the next stage.

7. Systematic emotional recession.

Regression and recession often occur simultaneously in the same person. This is a complicating factor which frequently makes the clinical picture more intricate.

THE EMOTIONAL DISTURBANCES OF SENESCENCE

The clinical picture of the regressive phenomena in senescence in the majority of instances appears to have the following architecture.

[118]

As the late senescent is beset by a variety of events that constitute rejections and emotional impoverishments, he is seen to show a loss of self-confidence, a reduction in his feeling of usefulness, a greatly reduced sense of self-esteem, and a growing feeling of insecurity. Such feelings are usually hidden from the older person's circle of contacts and are in fact also hidden from his own awareness, if he can succeed in isolating them from consciousness. Nonetheless, there follows an intense sense of loneliness.

As his psychological mechanisms of defense begin to crumble and shatter, the senescent experiences feelings of anxiety, terror, and panic. Such feelings are often masked by an outer shell of pride, but the older person covertly searches for emotional support and reinforcement from his external environment. Very often this need goes ungratified and his panic-ridden attempts at internal repair progress to exhaustion.

The problem is then largely internalized and the individual is made the lonelier by the remoteness of his external milieu and his own withdrawal, so that he is now forced to redirect his interest and attention away from extrapsychic realities. He thereupon discovers in the deeper recesses of his own mind a multitude of memories with corresponding object images that derive from his own past. Ancient pleasure strivings are reactivated as the aged person invests his interest in such archaic memory objects.

In many aged people, fantasy preoccupation possesses an attendant euphoria so long as the pleasant aspects of the memories are dominant. Nevertheless, a complication occurs as time goes on. The revitalized old memory objects have attached to themselves the childish misperceptions, errors, and misconceptions and an assortment of associated appropriate mixed emotions which were part and parcel of infantile experience and which have hitherto been repressed. As these memory complexes with their mixed emotions proceed toward awareness, the aged mind becomes irritable and goes through

[119]

mercurial and almost kaleidoscopic changes in mood. Such mood changes are frequently incomprehensible to the observer but are in all probability logically associated with the memories and thoughts that pervade consciousness at a particular time. Simultaneously, external reality makes insistent demands on the older person's attention so that his mental interest is drawn to and fro, as it were, by the competing intrapsychic and extrapsychic objects that demand attention.

At this stage the mental apparatus of the aged is struggling in a conflict between what amounts to attention to daydreams and attention to reality. This state of affairs results in confusion and perplexity. Since the rewards from external reality are the least satisfactory, the aged ego increasingly turns its interest inward. Clinically this is seen as waning alertness. Whatever ego resources are not involved in the process of internal preoccupation with reactivated memories become concentrated on efforts to repair psychological defenses and to bring some order out of the chaos that threatens. Further fatigue and enfeeblement ensue.

For the sake of economy, in order to conserve mental energy and achieve some pleasure, the aged mind progressively yields to the pressures from the unconscious. Outmoded and hackneyed defensive systems are re-established against a flood of primitive ideational and emotional memory systems. The ego is now relatively impotent and it surrenders to the superior force of the recently activated unconscious memories. The more completely the ego is absorbed in re-experiencing its own memories, the more gratification the patient enjoys. Owing to the ego's tendency to organize ideas, to systematize thoughts, and to elaborate disjointed mental events into a coherent totality, the fantasies that rise into consciousness become progressively bound together through secondary elaboration into what now constitutes a new psychic structure—the dereistic sphere of fantasy.

The dereistic mental construction usually consists of three

main areas: a mental re-experiencing of old events, delusional misinterpretation of external realities, and the denial of death accompanied by fantastic concepts of immortality. The more the fantasy systems and the external realities become interwoven in the aged mind, the more the thought structure becomes dominated by delusion formations.

In true senile recession, the stages of infantile psychosexual development are traversed backward, one after the other, until a return to infantilism is realized.

Psychophysiological interrelations are so intimate that in the emotionally disturbed aged, whose problems are partly the result of physiological recession, the ailing ego appears to have a destructive effect on somatic integrity and further degeneration is introduced and accelerated. The unimpeded cycle thus established can only result in total decline and death.

The Rationale of Therapy with the Aged

The choice of a therapy in all conditions must be determined by diagnostic accuracy. Knowledge of the origin of symptoms and a conceptual scheme of causation lie at the foundation of treatment systems. This applies as well to the emotional disorders of the aging. Most of the symptoms that are seen in the regressive and recessive disorders of the aged mind can be related to special needs. I shall not enumerate here the many manifestations of emotional problems. In general, however, it is important to remember that although the regressive behavior of the aged resembles childishness, the total personality of the older person still possesses important vestiges of its own socially responsible adult psychological structure. Therapeutic systems in the aged are designed to keep such social rudiments alive and replenished. With a very large number of older persons suffering indispositions caused by regression and recession, it is possible to reach by appropriate methods those elements of the ego that remain unaffected by the psychotic process. It is to the more "normal" areas of the ego, the unaltered areas, that external reality (therapy) may be directed. A rule of thumb may be of some help here: the greater the regression or recession, the greater the involvement of the ego in the psychotic organization, and the lesser the probability of response to a system of therapy.

In general, the products of recession are less likely to respond to therapeutic efforts than are the products of unadorned regression. That is, the psychoses of the senium may respond much more readily to therapy than the alterations of function that are due to senile dementia. Such psychoses and dereistic fantasy systems are virtually dream states occurring in partially conscious persons. The goals of therapy with the aged must perforce be less ambitious than with younger patients. In most instances the therapist must be content not to try to reconstruct a whole personality along less neurotic lines, but rather to diminish the appeal of the psychotic dream state by increasing the attractiveness of reality.

The Relation of Regressive
Phenomena to the Aging Process

NORMAN E. ZINBERG, M.D.

IT IS BY NOW A TRUISM that today the wards of a general hospital are in essence geriatric wards. My experience on such wards bears out Dr. Goldfarb's contention that aged men have fewer somatic complaints in institutions than in their own homes while, in contrast, there is no change in the volume of complaints from women. To state this point in general social terms, the women at an earlier time in their lives are much less secure about their value. From the time that their children are in school and require less attention, they frequently feel almost useless. Often they do not know what to do with themselves and feel at loose ends. At this same period the husband may be at the height of his productivity, obtaining much sustenance from his work. It is at this period that the women usually turn to clubs, organizations, and equivalent activities in order to obtain group support for their morale by "joining" with others in a similar situation. But when the husband, if he lives (and now certainly there has been a shift in the longevity of men and women), retires, the woman's role in the family again becomes a more important one. She continues to have her housekeeping duties while the man loses his vigor and masculinity in the sense of his capacity to work and produce. Our society has no place for him. The lack of social reinforcement for his function makes it difficult for him to retain self-esteem, and he may take refuge in groups in a way that he did not when he was more active. The women, on the other hand, by now have often become less committed to their organizations. This is often stated directly in a comment such as, "I worked for the WCTU for years and now I've had enough. Let the younger women do it—and anyway my husband is home more now." It is also probably true that, from childhood, women make less of a commitment to groups than do men. The wards of a hospital offer a companionship to the men that they obviously do not to the women. The men really enjoy sitting around with each other and talking, getting support from each other for being retired, and feeling that they have permission for this kind of leisure. It may also revive an important latency or adolescent form of activity that was very supportive at that time of life. The women on the wards who have husbands often cannot wait to get back home and do whatever little it is they can do. It is a fairly consistent phenomenon.

The term "regression," when applied to the aged, poses the problem of defining the difference between a developmental phase and a psychopathological defense. "Regression" is a word and a concept that has been used in a number of different ways. It seems to be important to distinguish between a return to first objects that have been libidinally invested, and a return of the whole sexual organization to earlier stages of psychosexual development. We also have to realize that temporal regression, the return of the entire sexual organization, is essentially a genetic concept, and some of the earlier psychoanalysts tended to regard it very schematically as a reinstatement of earlier stages, including the gratifications appropriate to those stages. Although there is a theory of fixation, a theory of development, regression implies that the regressed state is in an important way similar to the earlier developmental state.

This is to a certain extent true. But there are important differences resulting from the development subsequent to the state to which there is regression. When an old man is soiling, one can speculate about the possibilities of there being a certain kind of gratification. However, the development subsequent to that state, on which he bases his self-esteem and dignity, makes it impossible to view the loss of sphincter control primarily in terms of the more primitive gratifications.

Hartmann's (1951) definition of secondary autonomy of the ego, as "relative functional independence despite genetic continuity which invites marking off more clearly the functional aspect from the genetic one," applies here. The patient's relation to the world, based on his capacity to control his sphincters, has become so autonomatized or "reified" that a view of his soiling as gratifying is inadequate and misleading.

Dr. Kaufman, in discussing lapses of memory, emphasizes that these acts of repression do not serve primarily a defensive or gratifying function for the patient, but rather an adaptive one. Dr. Goldfarb makes a similar point in his criticism of the phrase "healthy dependency," by which I understand him to mean that we have to be sharper in both our definitions and our understanding of behavior. Dependency in an adult usually represents a problem. But for an adult to permit himself to be cared for in the special conditions of illness or debilitation due to age may be adaptive.

It is my contention, as I have stated elsewhere, that for any person, young or old, to utilize most effectively the hospital environment (whether the environment of a modern hospital is essentially therapeutic is another problem which does not belong here), it is necessary for the patient partially to surrender many secondary autonomous age functions. This surrender is usually regarded both consciously and unconsciously as temporary. Certain personality mechanisms characteristic of the patient when in a physically and emotionally more compensated state are accentuated. The result is that ways of thinking, perceptual distortions and preoccupations, specific actions that one would expect in an earlier stage of development—i.e., during childhood—become pre-eminent. It is necessary to regard this loss in the aged not as pathological, but as part of a developmental phase of the human animal. In a sense, we are trying to define certain aspects of what is an adaptive state in an aged person. In discussing this, especially in regard to hospitalization and illness, I shall sttempt to differentiate between regression as a pathological defense, which involves the whole ego, and regression in the service of the ego, which is primarily intrasystemic and transient (Gill and Brenman, 1959). We know that in certain conditions the latter may turn into the former. One might say that transient regression results from both the environment (in this case the hospital) and the internal condition of the organism, compounded of the illness and the intrapsychic state. To keep this differentiation sharp, we must also specify what initiates the process of a regression and separate this clearly from the dynamic situation once such a regressive process is established. To clarify the issue of regression in relation to the aging process it is most helpful to paraphrase the work of Gill and Brenman on hypnosis (1959).

In regression, as a pathological entity, the ego is overwhelmed. The psychic boundaries between the abstractions id, ego, and superego are loosened and often seem to have been dissolved. Superego and id may invade ego, and the ego withdraws to earlier positions. Savage self-destructive urges may coexist with frank instinctual urges. The move is away from abstract thinking and verbalization and toward concrete thinking and action.

In regression in the service of the ego, the attempt is to synthesize.[1] The ego lends itself to and uses primitive regressive

---

[1] It is understood that in one sense all regression, even in schizophrenia, is adaptive, but that is not the sense in which we wish to be understood.

mental activity for its own purpose. This should be considered an intrasystemic process in which part of the ego has allowed a usually unconscious and unacceptable mode of functioning to become syntonic. Such changes are specific and transient by definition. Intrapsychic boundaries in general remain. However, the superego, which seems always to require nutriment from the external world, may be much affected.

If the organism was functioning previously in a relatively satisfactory equilibrium according to its stage of development, an alteration is necessary to initiate a regression. The force of fixation operates to facilitate regression. This temporal regression to earlier developmental stages is a genetic concept. We might use the same three essential shifts that Edward Bibring (1953) viewed as initiating depression in describing the initiation of regression: (1) Increase in strength of instinctual impulses; (2) change in the apparatus available to the ego from disease, bodily injury, intoxication, etc.; and (3) alteration, real or fancied, in the external situation. The geriatric patient fits all three of these criteria for the initiation of a regression. There is a threat from without in the altered social situation. There is a threat from within, that is, a shift in the ability to deal with impulses. Finally, there is a weakening of capacity due to the morbid process and its sequelae.

The dynamics of the regressed state itself can be discussed only in relative terms. The tendency must be toward earlier developmental concerns and away from later ones, toward primary-process, and away from secondary-process thinking, toward pleasure-principle and away from reality-principle functioning. Therefore, the adaptive or synthetic functions of the ego will be impaired. In this sense, then, some morbidity must accompany regressive changes in the aged.

Some of the shifts that were discussed as the dynamics of a regressed state have already occurred in old age as a result of these regressive pressures. The weakening of the synthetic function of the ego and the reinstatement in part of primary-

[127]

process and pleasure-principle functioning are exemplified best in preoccupations with bodily needs. With all of these changes, which are a retreat to earlier developmental states as well as to libidinally invested objects from the past, the state of the aged person shows elements of both pathological regression and regression in the service of the ego.

In a younger person who is physically ill, we can see a fairly sharp differentiation between his psychological state during illness and after recovery. One advantage for the physician of the pre-eminence of more primitive and rigid defense mechanisms during illness is the ease with which a salient personality conflict can be recognized. The person who, when in a compensated state, has certain conflicts around masochism which are well controlled and not obvious, may, when ill, see each move of a doctor or a nurse as a personal attack. I have often had the experience of talking with a patient on rounds in the general hospital and, by asking just a few questions, bringing out clearly the anxieties on his mind. The frankness of the patient's language is consistently surprising. A few weeks later, the same patient, now relatively well, may come to see me in my office. After an hour's intensive interview I may feel quite uncertain about a clear-cut formulation of his difficulties. When the patient is more compensated, many character traits and defenses, as one might expect, obscure and protect against the anxieties that were obvious when he was ill.

The anxieties of old age, likewise, are often transparent. This makes it possible for the skilled geriatrician to make quickly an educated guess about how to approach the patient in a tactful way—a way that goes along with the patient's already strained defenses and does not cause even greater defensive activity. For instance, with a hysterical patient who has great trouble remembering what the doctor says, it is not helpful to go into long intellectual explanations. The patient's anxieties are already requiring much repression—why add more material to be repressed?

[128]

Let us now turn to some ideas about psychotherapy with the aged and try to connect them with ideas about regression. The case of a 70-year-old man, whom I saw in psychotherapy for some time, serves as a clinical illustration of the special nature of geriatric psychiatry.

Mr. A. came with complaints of insomnia, restlessness, acute anxiety, a sense of incompetence and self-degradation, and, especially, poor judgment. He had recently been dislodged from the top position in a business by a nephew whom he had taken into the business. Mr. A. suffered terribly from guilt and self-recriminations for having permitted this betrayal. When Mr. A. was 40, his father had died and he had inherited the business, which was at that time quite small. Eight years later his mother had also died suddenly. He reported his concern in conventional terms, but my feeling was that he had experienced more grief on the death of his mother. The business began to grow enormously when Mr. A. assumed complete control.

At the beginning of treatment his wife came in with him, and he was loath to see me at all without her. Except in child psychotherapy, where it is common for the mother to come in with the patient for the first one or two sessions, this procedure is unusual. It went on, however, for several weeks, and it is my impression that the man could not have been treated if he had not initially had this support. The procedure during our meetings was for him to tell me a few things and then turn to his wife for confirmation. Another thing that was immediately clear was that he could not be bound by a 50-minute hour. It was obvious that I could not give him endless time on the occasions when he wanted to stay, but I tried to schedule him when I had some leeway. On the other side, I quickly learned to use the degree of his restlessness as an index to when it was time to terminate the session. It was clear that often at the end of 20 or 25 minutes he had had enough. It was also difficult to decide how often to schedule appointments because it became obvious that for him to ask for more appointments was to admit weakness. I took the hint, and would suggest that I would like to see him the next day or in two days, depending on my "feel" of the current situation. This fitted into an important wish of his — to see me as the usual medical doctor. Mr. A. used this view of me as a way to control me and the session. Perhaps even more importantly, not seeing me as a psychiatrist was used to protect himself from the unpleasant feelings associated with having an emotional upset and with the reason for the disturbance. He would tell me each time about his symptoms, and outline his entire day in a repetitious, compulsive, narcissistic fashion. There were details about how he had slept, what he had eaten, and the condition of his gastrointestinal tract, presented in a form that one usually thinks of as being reserved for a nonpsychiatric physician. As he became less anxious, this ritual lessened, but never disappeared.

Before the development of the business situation which precipitated Mr. A.'s disturbance, he had been as vigorous and active as a man many years younger. This fact, plus the acute onset of his difficulties, made his prognosis from the beginning a favorable one. When I first saw him, he moved slowly, spoke slowly, and even his response to usual conversational gambits was characterized by deliberateness. This sluggishness gave a perceptible rhythm to the therapy, a rhythm which is especially marked with the geriatric patient whether in psychotherapy or on the general hospital wards. I felt a necessity to acclimate myself to the rhythm — things had to go a certain way. It was not helpful to ask unexpected questions or make offhand remarks that represented a change of pace. In fact, I found that any new questions, comments, or clarifications that I had to make had to come within the framework set up by the patient. When he said certain things in a certain way, then I might ask the question, but not with any variation.

Sometimes I would speak to him in terms of a third person, a book, or a movie, in order to make a point pertinent to him.

He often "reported" to me that he had gone to the movies the night before, or that he had been able to read a book. Then he would very politely tell me what the movie or book was about. I would then express an interest in what had interested him in the entertainment. Many times the things of interest to him were pertinent to thoughts about himself which he could not reveal directly. Some of our most animated discussions occurred in this third person fashion. We examined carefully and critically *By Love Possessed*, by James Gould Cozzens. Only occasionally would the direct personal relevance of the comments about the characters in the book be made explicit.

This is very reminiscent of child therapy as I recall it. My recollection of child psychiatry, especially with latency boys, is that we played checkers. The first game would be played with hardly a word exchanged; in the second game there would be a casual interchange, and suddenly, in the middle of the third game the child would look up and say, "I kicked my mother in the teeth yesterday." We would then return to playing the game, and although nothing more might be said for the remainder of the session, we both knew that a form of communication had taken place from which a degree of understanding was possible. It was really almost like this with Mr. A. Much could be said to him and there were many things that he would tell me, but all communication had to occur at properly measured intervals.

In much of the psychiatric literature dealing with geriatric problems, the emphasis is on what is lost in the process of aging that is used by young people to make therapy feasible. Mr. A. certainly had lost, as is usually described, much flexibility and spontaneity of affect connected to other people. He had quite good contact with affect that concerned himself. One of the things less frequently emphasized about the aged patient is the gain of distance, which is a therapeutic advantage. By distance is meant a vantage point from which to take a long view of himself and others. Mr. A.'s knowledge and acceptance of

[131]

the frailties and vanities of the human animal as facts of life made easy the introduction of many things which would stir up a great deal of resistance in younger people. When we talked about a book, he would, in a disillusioned, somewhat cynical way, describe how the world is, and use this knowledge to make telling points that related to him personally. I find this fairly consistent among my geriatric patients. One can speak readily with them of corrosive anger and the cutting, biting nature of envy in human affairs (including the patient's) and meet with understanding. Mr. A. was able in one of the early sessions to quote a statement of Samuel Johnson's: ". . . envy is mere and unmixed genuine evil; it pursues a hateful end by despicable means, and desires not so much its own happiness as another's misery" (*Rambler* # 183). He could talk about this as personally relevant in a way that would be rare in a reasonably well integrated younger patient.

The intellect, as a way of dealing with others and with one's feelings about others, is much more heavily relied on by the aged patient. This follows an awareness that one's emotions are more likely to concern oneself and less likely to concern others. Therefore, in order to maintain satisfactory object relations, the older person begins to distrust spontaneous affect and to rely more heavily on cognition. But at the same time he is, in fact, losing his intellectual facility, so that he begins to doubt whether he can control the growing regressive, narcissistic trend of his libido.[2]

For the therapist it becomes a technical problem of some magnitude to reconcile the dichotomy between the patient's loss of faith in his intellectual power and his justified growing

---

[2] While I do not believe there is necessarily a diminution of instinctual energy, there are qualitative shifts in its use over the life span which may be based on a degree of instinctual diffusion. With children there is the problem of fusion with neutralization of psychic energy in childhood and there may be a reverse in aging during the developmental process I discussed earlier as regression.

reliance on intellectual control. Again, an analogy with children exists. Almost from the beginning we try to teach the child to use his mind, his intellectual awareness of how to live with people, to master the rampant, narcissistically invested instinctual forces. As we reach adulthood, often our effort is to try to get back to better terms with our feelings; but, following the riddle of the Sphinx, in old age we return to our beginning task.

In order to resolve this therapeutic dilemma, it is necessary to understand another important way in which geriatric patients differ, by necessity, from younger people; that is, in the use of the past. For this group of patients, the past is both closer in psychic reality and further away in objective reality. The tricks of memory that keep the past alive make the shopworn psychotherapeutic comment, "past thoughts, feelings, ways of dealing with conflicts and people are still active and effective in the present," a cliché of which the patient is far more keenly aware than is the younger therapist. Often this greater acceptance of the past can become a major resistance, because the patient can use the realistic concept of greater distance in time to express an attitude of helplessness and hopelessness. The clarity and persistence of the past in current ideation may be experienced by the patient as part of the loss of intellectual agility. A quote from Mr. A. may express this feeling better: "Yes, the dead past influences my present behavior. So what? My father has been dead for over thirty years. Of course I envied him and more than anything I wanted to surpass him. How many times did I sit in my office and gloat over my success and think how much I wanted him to see the business now? Now it is ashes, he is dead, and I will be soon. What effect did this have on my taking my nephew into the business? I don't know. Was this family feeling? Was this obligation or guilt? It is done and I have not time to undo it." Here is understanding without insight. The past, and even the understanding of it, is used as resistance.

[133]

Now I will try to tie together the three areas I have mentioned as potentially therapeutically useful with older patients: the ability, because of the patient's regression, to assess quickly the salient personality conflict, the use of the intellect, and the use of the past. My efforts have taken the form of never proposing anything new to this group of patients. I ask them to use their intellectual clarity and distance about the past to search for solutions or ways of looking at things that worked for them earlier in their lives. These questions are always phrased in terms that seem to me to fit their leading characterological traits. For instance, those struggling with dependency and deprivation may be approached with the phrase, "It would be helpful to you if you could think of . . ."; to someone who is angry, one might say, "We are trying to work out a solution. We know that this is a laborious and inefficient method but it is the best we have. If you can stand it for a little while, we will see if it bears fruit, but if it doesn't, we will not trouble you further in this fashion."

In studying the ward situation, I am impressed by the truth of the comment that our culture is future-oriented. The physicians frequently and inadvertently ask the patient to consider something new — to learn something fresh. It may be a new approach to an old condition, a new drug, or even something as simple as the name of a new doctor. I always ask the older patients if I remind them of anyone. Even though psychiatrists' training in the use of the patients' ways of phrasing and thinking is helpful, they tend, on the basis of their experience with younger patients, to introduce concepts without adequate searching for the previously acceptable structure that permitted the emergence of a particular idea or feeling. The fact of being part of a future-oriented culture indicates that the older person is psychologically out of step. Therefore, the past automatically assumes a more basic importance. More energy is needed for getting through the day, both physically and psychologically, when the older person is called upon to face fresh problems. To learn something new, it is necessary to detach libido assigned to the past for this fresh duty. To say the same thing in a more succinct way, it is necessary, as much as possible, not to de-automatize existing automatic responses. Rarely propose a fresh solution to the older patient. Whenever possible, find a past solution that has already been "learned," and present even this idea so that it does not clash with the patient's needs or defenses. The physician's recognition of the patient's salient personality conflict and the defense against it were discussed earlier.

With Mr. A., it was important to take into account his ambivalent attitudes toward strength and weakness. When his symptoms were discussed it was important not to promise him too much quick reassurance that he would get well. That would stir up his guilt and his dependency wishes. It was possible to tell him that he had always been a strong man and that even if he did not improve one hundred percent, it was clear that he could take it. This formulation allowed him recognition for past and current "strength," but permitted him the degree of symptomatology that was necessary for discharge and secondary gain. It was soon obvious that, within the confines of our relationship, he preferred to gain my respect by exhibiting how well he could do even with his symptoms. This approach to the patient, and to the understanding of the patient, is illustrated in the works of Grete Bibring (1956) and Edward Bibring (1953, 1954).

The emphasis on the gerontologic patient's regressive concerns with orality and anality often obscures very specific later vicissitudes of the oedipal triangle. There is also a need to reconsider the importance of the oedipal conflict in the aged person. The obvious nature of the pregenital interests and the frequent fact of organic sexual incapacity have seemingly obscured, as they one did in childhood, the extent of the libidinal interests still extant. Berezin (cf. pp. 75-97) liberally illustrates the importance of sexual interests in this older group.

[135]

The hours with Mr. A. provided me with material, especially those comments connected with the feelings about the death of his father and how that even influenced his present decompensation, to buttress conjectures about a later vicissitude of the oedipal conflict concerned with the fantasy that one has outdone one's father. Sophocles was 89 when he wrote *Oedipus at Colonnus*, in which he stresses that Oedipus, previously overwhelmed by his tragic experience, is now preoccupied with the meaning of his survival. He begins to wonder if he has not in a way triumphed, and then wonders about his becoming an Olympian. It is only the gods who triumph over their fathers and can, with impunity, forego the incest taboo. Oedipus becomes convinced of his own omnipotence, and foretells that he can choose the place of his death, and that the chosen city, Athens, will be a hallowed place.

Mr. A., along with many of the older patients whom I have seen, felt that he had outlived and outdone his father in the world by attainments, and also by longer contact with his father's wife and, in fantasy, continuing that relationship by replacing his mother with his wife. The preoccupation with omnipotent fantasies, if unchecked by careful re-establishment and reinforcement of the reality principle, can lead to the loss of ego boundaries and the re-emergence of archaic superego primacy. The reliance on the superego permits an alliance with the id which may show itself clinically in grandiose fantasies, extended and hollow claims in relation to others seen as unfriendly or rivals, and attempts at physical or psychological feats clearly beyond the person's powers.

In conclusion, it is stressed that in discussing regression in the service of the ego, an attempt is made to explain the relationship of regression to external reality by way of the intrapsychic representation of the outside world which makes possible experimental action on the environment. The incorporation of the external environment is conceived of as taking place by a series of steps which results in a hierarchy of organizations. It is noteworthy that each successive level of the hierarchy is a derivative of the preceding one, plus a new piece of the external environment. Therefore, the successive levels of the hierarchy are increasingly determined by the nature of the real world. For the older person, it is a changed world in which he is a changed person who must shift his mode of functioning. The new mode is determined more by internal drives and less by external reality, and the question is whether we, in our relationship with older people or in our thinking about their relationship with themselves, can help them to accept this new mode and adapt to inevitable change.

Libido Equilibrium

SIDNEY LEVIN, M.D.

At all ages the maintenance of a satisfactory libido equilibrium[1] is essential to mental health, and when disturbances in this equilibrium persist they are typically accompanied by depressive reactions. In the aging population, many new factors capable of creating such disturbances enter the picture, and as a consequence depressive reactions are frequently encountered.

In a paper entitled "Old Age and Aging: The Psychoanalytic Point of View," M. Ralph Kaufman (1940) notes some of the differences between aging in the female and in the male. He points out that menopause comes as a narcissistic injury, and that there are two climacteric phases. In the first phase there is an attempt at compensation in which the libido is strongly directed toward objects with a strong narcissistic longing to be loved. In the second phase there is a turning away from reality and reversed oedipal fantasies. As a consequence, the son now takes the place of the father, and the daughter the place of the mother. In comparing the reactions of the female

---

[1] The use of this concept implies the assumptions of Rapaport that "drive-needs of the organism are disequilibria in energy-distribution" and that "such disequilibria tend toward reestablishment of equilibrium" (1951, p. 689).

[139]

with those of the male, Kaufman states: "The function of reproduction and the loss of direct object relationships are the center of conflict in the aging woman. During the corresponding age period in the male, the focus of conflict also centers about the sexual problem. We find that failure of potency, inaugurated as in the woman with a loss of object relationships and regressions, is typical of the psychic illnesses of this period. The principal difference, however, between males and females in old age, is in the field of sublimations" (p. 76). Kaufman also notes that with the waning of sexuality there may come increased anxiety. He attributes the lack of elasticity in old age primarily to deeper repression of this anxiety, with increasing fixity of reaction formations originally laid down as character traits. As a consequence, the individual is more vulnerable to regression and, in the face of conflicts which cannot be solved, will have recourse less to the psychoneurotic type of reaction and more to the psychotic type of reaction.

The restrictions in activity which occur with aging may contribute significantly to disturbances in libido equilibrium, since such restrictions can lead to a loss of important satisfactions which have helped to maintain this equilibrium. Older people may become restricted by fears of "overdoing it" and harming themselves physically. For example, the fear of having a heart attack or a cerebral hemorrhage can lead to considerable inhibition of activity. Furthermore, precautionary attitudes of relatives can reinforce those inhibitions. The effects of restriction of activity in the aged are often experienced rather suddenly as a consequence of some illness which forces a person to give up some activities that have yielded important satisfactions, such as playing golf.

Since most activities in our society are geared to the young and middle-aged population, the older person often finds it hard to keep up with the pace. I am reminded of an aged woman who commented that she rarely went downtown to do her shopping because she had to wait for long periods of time for the streetcar. She stated that since there was no place for her to sit down while waiting, she would often become tired and her feet would hurt. In a facetious way she expressed an interest in creating what she called "A Society for the Promotion of Seating Facilities for the Aged."

The physical discomforts of old age are also significant factors in disturbing the libido equilibrium. These discomforts mobilize or accentuate fears of serious illness or death, especially in those with hypochondriacal tendencies. Therefore, the type of medical care which is directed not only toward maintaining health but also toward *adequate relief of discomfort* is essential to the libido equilibrium of the aged person.

The major object relations of the aged may be even more important than those of younger people. It is not uncommon for an older person to begin to slip both mentally and physically after the death of the spouse. There is also reason to believe that the aged die more rapidly after such a loss. The reactions of older people to loss may therefore be similar to those observed in children. Spitz (1946) described the development of "anaclitic depression" in a group of children who were institutionalized and separated from their mothers. These children showed all the manifestations of "hospitalism," including marasmus and a high mortality rate. In these children the sustaining object was the mother; in the aging person the sustaining object may be the spouse, and a comparable type of anaclitic depression may result from loss of this object. The breakdown of an older person's relationships with his children can have a similar effect, especially if the children have been the sustaining objects. Unfortunately, as people age, their increasing irritability may contribute to such a breakdown. Furthermore, older people often feel unwanted, especially if they are people who tended to feel rejected in earlier life. Such people may withdraw from their children without being rejected by them, and as a consequence a vicious circle of depression and further withdrawal may be created.

[141]

Aging is typically accompanied by interference with two major functions involved in narcissistic equilibrium, namely the functions of the genitals and of the brain. As a consequence of such interference, feelings may develop not only of sexual impotence, but also of mental enfeeblement. The latter may be aroused not only by impairment of intellectual ability, but also by impairment of important sensory functions, such as sight and hearing. In many instances the loss of mental ability is more apparent than real, and may be based on emotional problems. For example, symptoms such as difficulty in concentration, a sense of memory impairment, and slips of memory can all develop on a dynamic basis in older people, just as they can in younger ones.

When there is a weakening of ego functions in the aged, there may be a decrease in efficiency of the ego which makes mastery more difficult. As a consequence, readjustments to new situations may be limited, and the unfamiliar may evoke increased anxiety and suspicion. It is therefore characteristic for older persons to cling to their habitual patterns of behavior. Atkin (1940) has pointed out that conservatism in the aged is often an ego defense against anxiety. However, he hastens to add, "The concept of the psychology of conservatism as an ego defense against anxiety does not contradict that of conservatism as a synthetic and socially constructive attribute of late maturity attributable, perhaps, to wisdom and judgment, enhanced by experience" (p. 82). Atkin calls attention to the fact that although genital primacy may break down and lead to regression of pleasure striving to more primitive pleasure zones, in the majority of the aging population the ego is sufficiently strong for them to make an adjustment to the failings of old age without any gross regressive manifestations. He notes that since men appear to have more available social sublimations than women, their adaptation to sexual aging is likely to be a more gradual and less eventful transition. Furthermore, since women identify their meaning as individuals in society and in the erotic sphere with their reproductive function, they are more subject to emotional disturbances when this function is lost.

The maintenance of narcissistic equilibrium in the aged can be thought of in terms of the person's attitudes toward the past, the present, and the future. Many an older person maintains his self-esteem on the basis of past performance. I noted this especially in one old man who was confined to his home, but who was able to reminisce with great satisfaction about the days when he was a prominent figure in politics. He was still admired in the community and was considered to be somewhat of an elder statesman whom the younger generation listened to with respect, even though they did not take his advice.

The importance of attitudes toward the present includes not only the person's confidence in maintaining object relations, but also his confidence in performing certain tasks adequately, with resulting narcissistic satisfaction. Such satisfaction can also be obtained from the successful performance of offspring and grandchildren, who become built into the individual's concept of "self."

The significance of attitudes toward the future in the maintenance of narcissistic equilibrium has to do mainly with the person's anticipations of what the future will bring to himself and to his love objects. The notion that the aged person usually has little to look forward to is far from correct, as indicated by the fact that he often anticipates with considerable enthusiasm events such as weddings, births, graduations from school, and so forth.

The disturbances in libido equilibrium which occur in the aged are also significantly influenced by cultural forces. The current attitude in our society is one which is not as accepting of sexual activity in the aged as it is in younger individuals. Just as a person can be thought of as "too young" to participate in sexual activity, one can also be considered "too old." As a consequence of these attitudes, the older person may be more fearful of making moves in the direction of obtaining sexual gratification than he was in his earlier years. For the same reasons, an older person may be more reluctant to seek privacy, or to do a variety of things which might facilitate his sexual gratification. Cultural attitudes may also play a role in inhibiting the widow or widower from seeking a second mate. Such persons often feel that to remarry would be considered disrespectful to the dead spouse, and to go out on a "date" would be frowned upon. The persons involved may therefore feel humiliated if they are seen by their children or their friends in a "dating" situation, and may therefore avoid it. Older people may also be inhibited in making themselves attractive, by clothes or other means, owing to the fear of being ridiculed for "trying to appear young." Some of these attitudes are seen in a more pronounced form when an older man marries a younger woman and has to face the critical attitudes of a community. Many older people overreact to these cultural forces and manifest excessive inhibitions. Such overreactions can often be resolved by psychotherapy.

The relationships of older people with their children are also culturally restricted. For example, there is considerable feeling in our society that parents should not live with their married children, because of the possibility of increased tension.

Psychotherapy is also restricted by cultural attitudes. There is a general feeling that people can be too old to undertake treatment and that there is something shameful about an older person going to a "young doctor" to get help for emotional problems. These attitudes can reinforce the person's embarrassment about seeking therapy. The older person is likely to feel that he must continue to be a parent and be in the "giving" role, and that to enter therapy would imply that he is accepting the dependent and "receiving" role of the child.

The importance of cultural attitudes toward the aged has been pointed out by many authors. Lawton (1940) maintains: "Senescence in the United States is even more a cultural artifact than it is a biological reality" (p. 86). Grotjahn (1951) states: "The aging people of this country feel more apologetic than proud of their age and try to keep up with the younger ones. . . . Until recently, the older generation constituted the tragic group of 'the hidden relatives,' They are, in the eyes of the younger generation, the representatives of the dark past and the old country" (p. 302).

It is common to find that therapists, as well as others, have an emotional reluctance to work with the aged. Part of this reluctance comes from a realistic anticipation of greater resistance on the part of older patients, and of reduced opportunity for therapeutic success. However, some of it comes from countertransference problems, which may be rationalized in terms of a poor prognosis. These problems may involve the therapist's unresolved conflicts concerning his parents and grandparents, as well as his own conflicts about the process of aging. For example, the therapist may prefer to deny the realities of aging, and may find himself avoiding the aged patient because he does not want to see his own fears played out in the life of another person.

In recent years the attitudes of psychiatrists toward the elderly members of our society have been changing. The therapeutic nihilism of the past is giving way to increasing efforts to apply our psychological insights to this segment of the population. These efforts are accompanied by greater optimism and a more general acceptance of the proposition that the aged have many untapped potentialities for further psychological development. I would like to conclude by quoting some poetry written by Longfellow which is dedicated to this proposition:

It is too late! Ah, nothing is too late
Till the tired heart shall cease to palpitate.
Cato learned Greek at eighty; Sophocles
Wrote his grand Oedipus, and Simonides

SIDNEY LEVIN

Bore off the prize of verse from his compeers,
When each had numbered more than four-score years, —
Chaucer, at Woodstock with the nightingales,
At sixty wrote the Canterbury Tales;
Goethe at Weimar, toiling to the last,
Completed Faust when eighty years were past.
These are indeed exceptions; but they show
How far the gulf-stream of our youth may flow
Into the arctic regions of our lives.
For age is opportunity no less
Than youth itself, tho' in another dress
And as the evening twilight fades away
The sky is filled with stars invisible by day.
                              —*Morituri Salutamus*

Discussion

ALVIN I. GOLDFARB, M.D.

Even if we should cover all the ground that we would like to, there would still be one very important reason left for the existence of the Gerontologic Society. The Society should continue to exist so as to discuss some of the friendly disagreements that arise when we approach psychiatric concepts about the aged. For example, weak analogies are often made between gerontologic psychiatry and work with children. I look forward to seeing what Dr. Berezin has said about independence on the printed page so that I will be better able to grasp it; but I would like to make one remark now.

In my developing theoretic scheme, dependency has come to mean one thing — an interrelationship of at least two people in which the weaker exploits the stronger. Of course it is not necessarily active; it can be passive. But when seemingly passive exploitation is examined microscopically, the passivity is recognized as being very active indeed. "Healthy dependency" is a term which comes up very frequently, but I do not think that any such term should be utilized in psychiatric literature. I believe that people have capacities for cooperative behavior. But the term "healthy dependency" should be abandoned and we should talk about parasitism, mutual or otherwise, where it exists. We could talk about symbiosis as a relatively healthy state, but I think that we can talk about mutual cooperation, as did the Russian Kropotkin, as the healthy state of social interaction.

With respect to the term "senile," I think that it should be given the deference which it is due. It means infirm, it means weak — and there is no use in sugar-coating it. But it should not be used as a euphemism. It means, as we in our society see it, morbidity, but unfortunately it is now too often used to hide or deny morbidity. True pathology is acknowledged with reluctance, and is undesirable, but the person in whom it occurs is not necessarily undesirable. The person may be regarded with affection, even though he is behaving morbidly. I think it is Flügel who said in his book on the family that a society can be measured by the kind of care it accords its aged population. We are stirred more by humanitarian aims and a desire to preserve and perpetuate our culture than we are by love, or not-love, of the healthy, and we can certainly continue to have affection and regard for a person after the advent of illness.

As Dr. Linden knows, the term "regression" is one which often troubles me. Although I have considered respect for it, I find that sometimes it intrudes itself upon my logical processes. Before saying something very briefly about that, I would like to call attention to a description of life's trajectory which preceded Shakespeare's "seven ages of man." It is a notation in the *Pirke Avoth* in which the stages of development are described — as they usually are in our culture — in terms of performance rather than in terms of desires or wishes. It goes something like this: at five the person is ready to learn; at ten, to examine; at 18 he's ready for marriage; at 20 he's ready to earn a living; at 30 he reaches full strength; and at 40, wisdom; at 50 a man is ready to give counsel; but at 60 he attains green old age; at 70, ripe old age; at 80, white old age. In his nineties, he bends with the weight of years over the grave; and at 100, is as good as dead.

Now, what is successful aging? There can be successful ag-

[148]

ing. Successful aging is—not to age, but to live a long time. Obvious!

Now I would like to say something about the matter of "regression." I have no great quarrel with Dr. Berezin, but still, it is difficult for me to visualize or understand the incontinent, failing, aging patient as one who has actually returned to a previous point of pleasure or gratification, and who may be deriving true libidinal gratification, in this primitive sense, from his behavior. In my own psychotherapeutic attempts and in my attempts to initiate people into how to bring about pleasurable relationships on a psychiatric basis with the aged, I have come to ask them to look at the person's development of a painful invalid state as the means by which he hopes to achieve, or by being ill achieves, the illusion that he will gain some form of gratification. This would be a pain-dependent pleasure mechanism, sometimes called a masochistic mechanism. It is an adept, adroit, adult, adaptive maneuver, and not, as I see it, a return to a previously effective infantile method, complete in itself, of achieving pleasure, although it certainly has, as its core, patterns of human relationships which were learned early in life, which may not now have direct reference to the particular orifice or area involved. I can, for example, mention that in certain cultural groups a woman changes from tenderness and coy sexual delight to a scolding nag, not so much as a metamorphosis but as a revelation. As her value in the sexual respect is decreased, pursuit yields to indifference, gratitude for her favors becomes more a recollection than a present event; then, what was given to her on demand, or could be coaxed in trade, she must now ask for or force by use of "invalid" techniques. One sees this in the "beautiful woman" whose marriage was good till she and her mate began to age. Her coercing techniques are then accompanied or followed by a need for self-punishment, which joins her desire to punish her husband. This grows, and is manifested in complaints. Her husband suffers, and she suffers so that he will

[149]

suffer. She also suffers so that she will be forgiven and need not suffer. Many of these patterns of personal behavior can therefore be regarded as patterns similar to the hysterical neurosis but which have less flexibility because they are rather basic, elemental and unelaborated.

Discussion: Psychobiologic Aspects of Aging

JOSEPH J. MICHAELS, M.D.

AGING MAY BE REGARDED as a normal psychobiological phenomenon inherent in the very nature of life itself. One of the difficulties in studying the process of aging from a psychoanalytic point of view is the fact that persons over fifty years of age cannot easily be analyzed unless they have undergone an earlier period of analysis. There have been occasional reports of persons who have been analyzed at a late age, but these have been very few.

As a result of this handicap, we have to do the best we can, and find ourselves applying psychoanalytic principles. In addition, some psychoanalysts have had significant experience in dealing with the aged. The contributors to this symposium have discussed their different observations and approaches. In order to add to our knowledge of the process of aging, they called on the humanities. Freud himself stated that it was the poets who discovered the unconscious and that he went on to study the unconscious scientifically.

Dr. Berezin, in his paper, concentrated on the intrapsychic aspects of aging with special attention to the factors of regression, timelessness of the unconscious, independence, some

[151]

problems about drive and energy concepts, and, finally, the consultative position. In considering first the problem of regression, Dr. Zinberg, in his presentation, has made my task easier. I would like to emphasize the need to clarify the various ways in which the concept of regression is used. When psychoanalysts speak of "regression," they mean a specific psychological mechanism. The term has been applied loosely to certain changes that occur in aging. There is a need to define and specify the natural decline of the individual in all his psychobiological functions and structures. A return to earlier modes of funcitoning in aging need not necessarily be regarded as pathological. When there is an exaggerated return to a lower level of functioning, beyond what may be appropriate for aging, that is pathological. The degree of pathological regression is probably dependent on the ratio of immature to mature levels of attainment in the person. To the extent that there is a high degree of maturity, the degree of regression will be less pathological; the greater the degree of immaturity, the more pathological the regression. The concepts of evolution and dissolution, integration and disintegration, which apply to the central nervous system, might have a parallel application in the psychobiology of aging.

There is a general decline of the life force which occurs in the process of aging and terminates in death which we have to accept. Persons vary in their attitudes toward such a natural decline depending on their training and philosophy. Freud's concept of the death instinct met with a variety of feelings, questions, and controversy, which revealed significant differences in scientific and personal philosophies. There is considerable difference of opinion among psychoanalysts about whether there is an instinct of aggressiveness — the neo-Freudian (culturalist) psychoanalyst explains aggressiveness as primarily a reactive phenomenon. In a parallel manner, such psychoanalysts tend to explain aging and death as due to external factors. Szasz, in discussing the psychoanalytic theory of instincts, stated that "aging and death appear to develop only in response to environmental interferences with the life instinct" (1952, p. 44). This conception precludes belief in an innate instinct of aggression, implies that life need never end, and expresses the hope that man will conquer death.

Dr. Berezin elaborated on libidinal and ego regression. He also emphasized characterological changes. We are beginning to study character structure and the total personality, so as to inquire what happens to the total organism in the aging process. In classical psychiatry we learned that one of the significant features of organic disease of the brain was a caricature of the previous character of the person. To what extent does such a caricature of the character and personality occur in the normal process of aging?

In regard to the "timelessness of the unconscious," I have some reservations about describing it in this way. I would suggest using the term "persistence of unconscious wishes and drives." Dr. Berezin raises the interesting question of a decrease in quantity of drive in aging. If one adheres to a biological frame of reference in regard to life in general, then one believes in a beginning, a middle, and an end. During the various phases of human development—infancy, latency, puberty, adulthood, and the climacterium—there is a constant shifting of forces and change in equilibrium. If we use adolescence as an example, we find an upsurge of instinctual forces with the maturation of the sexual functions and organs, and hormonal changes. In aging there is a reverse process, with the involution of the sexual functions and their respective hormonal changes.

It is an interesting biological fact that in infancy there is the fastest rate of growth, the highest rate of metabolism, and the greatest amount of time spent in sleep. In aging a reversal occurs, in that there is probably the lowest rate of growth and metabolism and the least amount of sleep. Edward Bibring (1941), in his lectures on instinct theory, spoke of the life po-

[153]

tential which was highest at birth and declined to zero at death. One would expect anabolism to be greater than catabolism in infancy and the reverse in aging.

It is of some interest to consider how the person, in the process of aging, comes to terms with the inevitability of his death. I have the impression that those persons who meet this problem with the most equanimity are those who have resolved their castration anxieties. These persons come to regard death as a natural physiological phenomenon, free of symbolic meanings, and thus face it realistically.

In assessing the factors of independence versus dependence in aging. I believe that, to the extent that the person has resolved his preoedipal problems, the conflicts over dependence and independence will also be mastered.

Dr. Berezin concluded his presentation by emphasizing some of the positive aspects of becoming old. It is apparent that the process of aging has biological, physiological, and sociological aspects, all of which should be considered. It was comforting to those persons, who are now in the process of aging, to realize that they may be in a consultative position. I am not sure whether this is the most apt term to describe this respected and venerable period of mellowness. At present I cannot suggest a more appropriate term, but I was reminded of Robert Bowning's *Rabbi Ben Ezra*. It would be in keeping with the taste for literary quotations which the panel members have shown to conclude with the first stanza of that memorable poem:

> Grow old along with me!
> The best is yet to be,
> The last of life, for which the first was made:
> Our times are in His hand
> Who saith, "A whole I planned,
> Youth shows but half; trust God: see all, nor be afraid!"

PART TWO

Normal Psychology
of the Aging Process
Revisited — I

Introduction

MARTIN A. BEREZIN, M.D.

THIS SYMPOSIUM CELEBRATES the fifteenth anniversary of the Boston Society for Gerontologic Psychiatry. Age "15" puts the Society in the beginning of its adolescence and on its way through the maturational and developmental phases toward the geriatric position.

The proceedings of the Society's first symposium are published in Part One of this volume. While we believed we were able to cover the field of normal psychology in our first symposium, since then so much has been published, both in professional and popular journals, that it would be impossible to deal adequately with this topic in just one symposium. As a consequence, we are re-examining this topic and will present it in several symposia. You will note that the present symposium is numbered I; it is our plan to have "revisits" II, III, and IV for future symposia to cover various conditions subsumed under the heading of "normal psychology."

It is felicitous that three participants in the Society's first symposium are also participating in this one: Dr. Norman E. Zinberg, Dr. Irving Kaufman, and myself. The presentations scheduled for this symposium have titles which might suggest a disparity of content. It will be observed, however, that without prior planning the material in each of the papers touches upon issues related to each other. There is a thread and even at times an overlap in the presentations.

Social Learning and
Self-Image in Aging

NORMAN E. ZINBERG, M.D.

Despite increased interest in and research related to the aging process over the last two decades, some misconceptions still exist about problems associated with aging. For example, our culture has accepted almost unquestioningly the notion that sexual activity slows down in the middle years and is minimal or nonexistent by the time people are in their sixties (Bowman, 1954; Zinberg and Kaufman, 1963; D. Kent, 1968; Alvarez, 1969; Berezin, 1969, 1972; Verwoerdt, Pfeiffer, and Wang, 1969b).

Although careful studies in this area have made it clear that such convictions are based not on physiology but on a legacy of Western puritanism, the prophecy of a decline in sexual activity in the aged is often self-fulfilling. Many older people accept the cultural stereotype and unconsciously inhibit their sexual activities and, more basically, their desires. Many of the aged who are not inhibited are embarrassed, so completely have they accepted the social norm. Workers in general hospitals where patients do *not* go because of psychological difficulty have reported that both seriously disturbed and well-functioning older patients appear to accept culturally induced inhibitions around sexuality as well as around other activities (Shock, 1960; Zinberg and Kaufman, 1963; Berezin, 1969; Nadelson, 1969; Davies, 1972; P. Cameron and Biber, 1973; Pfeiffer, 1975). They tend to have a negative self-image that reflects the stereotype of the social norm rather than an objective and realistic view of their physiological and psychological capacities (Newman and Nichols, 1960; Cumming and Henry, 1961; Tuckman, Lorge, and Zeman, 1961; Zinberg, 1964; D. Kent, 1968; Berezin and Stotsky, 1970).

Psychiatrists working with older patients have found that in many cases previously accepted stereotypical inhibitions can be reduced markedly by psychotherapy (Goldfarb, 1955; Meerloo, 1961; Zinberg and Kaufman, 1963; Berezin, 1972). The idea that therapy is most effective with the young is one more indication of the same distorted stereotype of aging (Cumming and Henry, 1961; Berezin, 1969; Berezin and Stotsky, 1970).

At times, links can be made between a patient's presenting condition and his or her past life. However, some psychiatrists working with older patients hypothesize that aging persons' inhibitions result more from their acceptance and internalization of the culture's taboos into their self-image than from any overwhelming, long-standing, unresolved conflicts (Zinberg and Kaufman, 1963; D. Kent, 1968; Ahrens, 1972; Schaie, 1973; Anastasi, 1974; Bier, 1974; Lowy, 1974; Davis, 1975). There is some indication as well that successful psychotherapy earlier in life, while generally resulting in a more comfortable, less emotionally restricted person, does little to interfere with the influence of negative cultural dicta later in life (Zinberg, 1964, 1970).

Through neither clinical nor metapsychological theory has psychoanalysis made many systematic attempts to study the impact of social learning on the continuing, lifelong development of the individual. This is particularly surprising because the necessary theoretical constructs exist in the work of Hartmann (1939) and Rapaport (1958) on ego autonomy, and these constructs are in general use. These theorists contend that ego autonomy is dependent on the input of the social environment. But they are not explicit about how particular, culturally accepted ideas are integrated into ego functioning and affect ego development. (In part, the reluctance to follow through with these concepts may have been an overreaction to the struggle with the work of Sullivan, Horney, and other "environmentalists.") It is as if the input from the social environment had the same timeless, unchanging quality as the input from other maintainers of ego autonomy, that is, instincts (Zinberg, 1975).

Now many of the earlier cultural stereotypes are changing, causing an upsurge of interest in older patients accompanied by an increase in conflict not only in society as it views aging, but also within the aging person as he or she becomes more aware of these socially imposed limitations. In order to understand and treat such patients effectively, knowledge of the clinical and theoretical relation between cultural input and ego response is useful (Berezin and Cath, 1965; Riese, 1971; Sanders, 1972; Howell, 1973). In this essay I shall use the formulations of Rapaport (1958) in relation to two cases to show how social learning affects ego functioning.

CASE 1

A 64-year-old man consulted a psychiatrist because of a growing depression over a two-year period, loss of interest in a highly successful business, general apathy, and an absence of any fulfilling or committing interests in his life.

Mr. A. was the oldest of three children, with a brother two years younger and a sister four years younger. His father had been an aggressive, moderately successful, hard-working businessman who died 25 years earlier. The patient felt that he was his father's favorite and that his own success had been a source of great satisfaction to his father.

[161]

His mother was described as aggressive like his father, involved in the business, working side by side with his father, at times for as long as 16 to 18 hours a day. She was demanding of her children and took little pleasure in their success, always expecting more. Her dissatisfaction continued after her husband's death and during her subsequent, brief remarriage, so that she was an active, bitter, complaining woman until her own death five years before Mr. A. decided to visit a psychiatrist. The patient felt she favored his siblings. He and his mother simply never got along well.

While in college, Mr. A married a girl his own age when she was three-months pregnant. She came from a solid, middle-class, professional family, no wealthier than his, but better educated and more socially aware. He did not feel he loved her, but they had been unsure of her pregnancy, had missed the opportunity for an early abortion, and had sought no recourse but marriage. They had four children during their marriage, who were ages 44, 42, 38, and 34 at the time the patient consulted the psychiatrist, but the couple had never had a mutually pleasant relationship. Intense competition and bitter struggles for control characterized each year, until their divorce ten years earlier. During much of the marriage, the patient had had brief affairs with "high-class" prostitutes, usually at conventions, but he was chiefly preoccupied with running his business and making money—two activities at which he excelled.

Despite his bitterness about the marriage, it was his wife who actually sought the divorce. He knew he never got on as well with women as with men, and he was actually conscious of feelings that his wife was very much like his mother—a bitter, dissatisfied woman who would allow him no peace. In one sense he was sorry about the divorce: he felt it made life awkward in many respects for him and for his children, but he had no real personal sense of missing his wife. He was upset, but experienced little overt depression. He plunged into his business with ever-increasing activity. Finally, he negotiated a business venture that was much more profitable than he had expected and made him an extremely wealthy man.

During this period he had numerous brief affairs. The woman whom he found most attractive and with whom he had the most satisfying sexual relationship of his life eventually rejected him because he was much older than she was. He still had many kind thoughts about her, but at no time did he feel her decision was other than proper. He felt no anger toward her and, even during the period of rejection, contrasted her kindliness with his wife's and mother's bitter acceptance of him and their constant complaints about him through all the years past.

He continued to seek out women, but with reduced vigor. Occasionally he was impotent and suffered more and more consistently from *ejaculatio retardata*. He believed his symptoms were a result of his age and accepted them with little struggle. At the time he saw the psychiatrist, the patient's initial complaints of loss of interest and apathy did not include his sexual decline. He so clearly accepted the cultural attitude that his sexual activity labeled him a "dirty old man" and believed it right and proper that he cease such activity, that he felt it unnecessary to even comment on this. It was only after he had seen the psychiatrist several times that he mentioned his impotence which, at that time, was of almost three years' duration, the last two years coinciding with his depression, and that he had made no effort at sexual relations.

His problems seemed to him to have begun with the highly successful business venture. He felt there were no further goals to strive for after that, and he bitterly regretted having carried it out. He felt he had been happier before, and once he had accomplished what, from a financial point of view, was the pinnacle of his life, there was nothing left to aim for.

Mr. A.'s enormous wish to be taken care of emerged early

[163]

in treatment. He had always believed that both his wife and his mother would never care for him in any way because they were too preoccupied with themselves. The girl he had cared for, he felt, looked up to him as a father and wanted many things from him in terms of advice, support, and succor, but she had little interest in caring for him. In fact, he felt that her rejection of him as too old was based in part on her fear that she *would* have to take care of him.

After some time in treatment he began to see his aggressiveness and vigor in business as stemming directly from his fear of rejection and his wish to be cared for. He talked at great length about the long-term background of his current dissatisfaction and depression. He felt he always expended a great deal of energy not only in acting against the outside world, but also in the struggle against his own passive-dependent wishes.

His mood soon began to improve and, although he felt chronically depressed, he decided he would like to leave treatment for a while and embark on a period of travel, an old ambition he had abandoned during his severely depressed state. Although there had been much discussion about the ease with which he had accepted his sexual decline, and this had been considered as part of his rejection of his previously active and vigorous state, he had shown no particular interest in resuming sexual activity. In short, he left treatment feeling somewhat improved, but with his chronic depression a potent factor.

Six months later he returned to the psychiatrist looking quite a different man. He was tanned and had put on a few pounds, but the greatest change was in his expression. He seemed far more confident, had lost his previously characteristic hangdog look, and was obviously more cheerful. He told of his stay with his oldest son and his family immediately after leaving treatment.

Mr. A. had long been fascinated by young people, but had kept his distance from them in his usual isolated way. However, he had gotten to know his 20-year-old granddaughter and met a number of her friends at his son's summer home. During the few weeks he was there, he was involved in long discussions with the young people about changing social mores and changing concepts of life style. He was impressed by their ideas and attitudes, and he contrasted these with his own traditionalism and rigidity. He was particularly impressed by their ideas about sex which he quickly began to idealize. It was his feeling that they saw beyond what he and his generation could envision; that is, sex could be a friendly, pleasant experience, characterized by neither the bitterness that had gone on between him and his wife nor the subterfuge and clandestine, shameful quality that had characterized his other sexual experiences. For the first time in years he had a renewed interest in sexual activity. He specifically described having been "educated" by these young people and denied any direct sexual interest in them.

Following this visit he did indeed travel, but stayed away from many familiar places. In particular, he completely avoided one winter resort where he had spent eight to ten weeks every winter for the previous 20 years, a place filled with people who thought as he did and followed the same traditional patterns he had espoused. He traveled instead to places he had previously thought of as somewhat racy, although respectable.

At one resort he met a woman in her late forties, once divorced and more recently widowed, who belonged to a different social circle from his. They became friendly in a situation which did not lead to any direct pairing off. He found that this woman and some of her friends shared attitudes more like those of his granddaughter and her friends than his. Again he described himself as having been "educated."

It was very difficult, however, for him to believe that the freedom these people expressed was genuine. He constantly tested them, searching for the guilt and other attitudes he had

[165]

clung to. He explored at great length the "double standard."
Through most of his life he had thought that what was right
for men was not right for women, and he was particularly impressed by these women's relative freedom. Eventually he and
his new-found female friend did begin to date, and he felt
great trepidation about potential sexual activity. He confided
his fears to her, a considerable breakthrough for him. She
laughed at him, insisting that he was not too old, and she indicated that if he had any real trouble she would be more than
pleased to help him out and care for him.This frank and
rather generous reaction to what he regarded as a shameful
admission stimulated him enormously. He did attempt sexual
activity with her and found himself quite successful, with none
of his previous symptoms.

By the time he returned to the psychiatrist he had been
seeing this woman for several months, was planning to marry
her, and felt there was no physiologic basis for his previous sexual difficulties.

CASE 2

Mr. B. was a 71-year-old man, retired for two years. During
the last year he had developed headaches, a growing sense of
isolation, and a strong death wish. Careful medical examination revealed no discernible organic pathology. His wife, age
63, was in good health, as were his three children, two
daughters aged 44 and 39, and a son aged 41. Mr. B. went to
see a psychiatrist at the insistence of his son who thought his
father was depressed. Indeed, when asked about his problems,
the patient stated that as far as he was concerned he was dead.

Questioning revealed that the patient had chosen to retire
from a business he had founded and run successfully. His son
did not want him to leave and stated plainly that there was
more than enough for both of them to do. Mr. B. decided,
however, that it was time to leave and remarked that he had

"earned a rest" and it was "time to see the world." He thought that he "should" get out and give others a chance. But he began to develop considerable guilt about his wish to stay.

A short time after retirement, Mr. B. realized he was miserable. Travel without a specific goal, that is, some business-related venture, bored him, and he simply could not keep himself occupied.

Mr. B. believed there was something wrong with him. He realized that he had left the business only because he believed he should, and he had tried to convince himself that he wanted to. He was full of anecdotes about people who had stayed on too long and had aroused bitterness and hatred. Years before, Mr. B. had vowed never to allow that to happen to him. At some point, however, he felt caught between his continued drive to work and function and his belief that this was wrong and selfish.

During the course of a relatively brief therapy (eight months) it became clear that Mr. B. had always had serious difficulties in dealing with aggressive wishes. He was a perfectionist, had wanted people to like him, and had been willing to sacrifice certain advantages to himself for this goal. He had been tenacious and competent, with an aptitude for organizing affairs well. He described situations where he had brought people together and had generally made arrangements so that things could move along smoothly without his having to take over. In certain respects he had never liked being the head of the business, and for many years part of him longed for his son to take over.

Whatever secret resentments he may have had were thoroughly buried and were of little concern to him. For over 50 years he had managed quite successfully to deal with conflicts of that nature. However, retirement posed a different problem. When younger, he had worked for a man who became testy and aggressive at the time he was about to retire. Mr. B.'s own father had continued working long past his peak and, in fact, had lost much of the fortune he had accumulated during those years because he was no longer competent. Throughout his life, Mr. B. had been very responsive to what he imagined people expected of him, and the one thing of which he was clearly convinced was that for someone to be a decent human being, to behave gracefully, the person should get out when the going was good and not outstay his welcome. Although it was clear in this particular case that Mr. B. had not outstayed his welcome, it was hard for him to deal with this idea.

In the course of a very few discussions it became obvious that in this case the insistence on retirement was irrational. Although the standard age for retirement in our society is 65 and he had stayed on longer, retirement was inappropriate in his situation. The idea of returning to head the business — which his son quite freely offered him — was unacceptable to him. He felt he did not belong and was embarrassed, shy, self-conscious, and otherwise ill-at-ease whenever he went into the front offices of the plant.

After just a few weeks of therapy, however, Mr. B. began to devote himself to the question of what he could really do. From the moment he undertook the project of finding a place in the business for himself, when he decided he could neither return to head the business nor do anything else, his mood began to change perceptibly. After only three weeks he learned that a portion of the plant was not functioning well. Thus, in effect, he returned to the same role of minor efficiency expert he had held in his earliest years in his business. He went back to the job of getting people together and trying to get things worked out right — of being, as he himself described it, a "facilitator." This position required only a moderate commitment of time and energy, but it was enough. When he was not specifically on the job, he could think and plan about how he could do things better. By the time he stopped therapy, not only was he on his way to having completed the initial task he had set for himself, but he had found three other areas where he could work in the same capacity. He felt he was set for years to come and he no longer felt depressed.

DISCUSSION

These two cases are of middle-class men with resources of wealth and family. But I have interviewed low-skilled, working-class people who demonstrated identical problems, although I did not get to know them in sufficient depth to include their cases in this discussion. Class structure undoubtedly makes a difference, but in any social class some of the same principles operate.

In order to function as an independent entity, a person must maintain relative ego autonomy. Those factors were delineated by David Rapaport in 1958. He observed that non-living matter cannot escape the impact of the environment, and thus the results of the interaction are invariant and statistically predictable. This is not true of living matter, however. At times psychoanalytic theory has tried to pretend that inner forces are strong enough to develop some sort of predictability despite the uncounted variables acting through the social and physical environment. This has not worked out. Using the Berkeleyian and Cartesian positions to develop a dialectic, Rapaport pointed out that in the Berkeleyian view man is totally independent of the environment and totally dependent on inner forces and drives. He need have little concern for the external world since it is "created" by inherent forces. The cartoon psychiatrist who is shown asking someone who has been hit by a car—"How did you cause this to happen to you?"—is an exaggerated clinical version of this position.

Descartes, on the other hand, saw man as a clean slate upon which experience writes. He is totally dependent upon, and thus in harmony with, the outside world, and totally independent of, that is, autonomous from, internal desires. In essence,

[169]

Cartesians, like behaviorists, view such drives and the unconscious supposedly containing them as nonexistent.

Rapaport (1958) reasoned that neither of these totally divergent positions speaks to man's experience: that to understand how the ego, whose functions determine and delineate a sense of self, remained relatively autonomous and coped with both the demands of the external environment and of the basic, inborn forces Freud termed "instinctual drives" required consideration of both and their interactions. The autonomy Rapaport postulated was always relative, and the inside drives and the outside environment carefully balanced each other. Drives prevented man from becoming a stimulus-response slave,[1] while the constant stress of stimulus nutriment from the environment mediated and moderated the primitive drives[2] by sustaining primary ego apparatuses such as motor capacity, thinking, memory, perceptual and discharge thresholds, and the capacity for logical communication. In addition, external reality nurtured those secondary ego apparatuses such as competence, cognitive organization, values, ideals, and a mature conscience, determined by each particular culture as adaptive, and allowed these traits to become successfully estranged from the original drive functions.

Thus the relation between the ego's relative autonomy from the id and the ego's relative autonomy from the environment is one of interdependence. When drives are at peak tension, as in puberty, the ego's autonomy from the id is in jeopardy. Adolescents try to combat their tendency to subjectivity, seclusive-

[1] Rapaport (1958) tells the story of a man who did not march in step to an enthralling military band because he was pondering, and points out how falling in love saved the protagonist of *1984* (Orwell, 1949), at least temporarily, from the press of that overwhelming environment.

[2] Here, Rapaport (1958) uses the story of Moses and the great king who had been told by his seers and phrenologists that Moses was cruel, vain, and greedy. Upon finding Moses gentle, wise, and compassionate, the king planned to put his wise men to death. Moses demurred, saying, "They saw truly what I am. What they could not see was what I have made of it."

[170]

ness, and rebellion by the external reality-related converse of these — intellectualization, efforts at total companionship, and distance from primary objects. But it is an unequal and often painful struggle.

The ego's autonomy from the id can also be disrupted by minimizing the balancing input from external reality. Experiments with stimulus deprivation (Bexton, Heron, and Scott, 1954; Heron, Bexton, and Hebb, 1953; Heron, Doone, and Scott, 1956; Lilly, 1956) showed how susceptible individuals became autistic and suffered from magical fantasies, disordered thought sequences, disturbed reality testing, primitive defenses, and poor memory under such conditions.

Similarly, conditions which permit only restricted and frightening forms of stimulus nutriment impair the ego's relative autonomy from the external environment. When, as in a concentration camp, external conditions maximize the individual's sense of danger and arouse fears and neediness, the drives no longer act as guarantors of autonomy from the environment, but prompt surrender. The deprivation of varied stimulus nutriment and its replacement by insistent streams of instructions in the stimulus-deprivation experiments (Heron, Bexton, and Hebb, 1953; Heron, Doone, and Scott, 1956; Lilly, 1956) give those instructions power and engender belief. In order to maintain a sense of separate identity, values, ideologies, and orderly thought structures, people require support for existing verbal and memory structures. Not surprisingly, Rapaport used George Orwell's *1984* as a text — one which described in exact, clinical detail how this interdependence functioned under environmental conditions intended to turn the individual into a stimulus-response slave.

Throughout his discussion Rapaport insisted that the superego in particular was dependent on consistent stimulus nutriment. The convention, or American Legionnaire, syndrome, when moderate, respectable men and women remove themselves from their usual routines and social relations and

[171]

behave in an impulsive and uncontrolled manner, makes it very clear how heavily the strictures of conscience depend on social structure (Zinberg, 1975).

The aging have lost various sorts of stimulus nutriment. Sometimes families have been alienated and previous social relations severed. Important connections such as the ability to see themselves and be seen by others as functional have been interfered with. If contact with certain social relations has remained, it has changed in character and is seen either by others or by the older people themselves as being of a different order. Sources of stimulus and support begin to have a different meaning: Mr. A. no longer saw himself as an aggressive and vigorous man; Mr. B. felt that in order to remain a likable and reasonable person he would have to leave a job he treasured.

Our older people believe, and are often supported in their belief, that were they to continue, in Mr. A.'s case as a sexually potent person, in Mr. B's case as a functioning businessman, they would be declared deviant by the larger society and would no longer maintain their sense of worth and dignity. The social input available to them was changed to a negative view of themselves, and they had rational support for this view from any sampling of the reigning cultural outlook. Any input from the inside, any interest in gratification and pleasure by way of continued status or by way of direct sexual gratification, was increasingly seen by them as wrong. As a result they became further estranged from internal inputs and at the same time from reasonable and consistent stimulus nutriment that would support their feelings about themselves as worthwhile people. Obviously some accept this transition of concepts and find different areas from which to gain self-esteem and a coherent self-image. But, and this is where I quarrel with theorists like Erikson (1950, 1959), no one person's defenses are all-purpose, to be used for every phase of life in a particular society.

[172]

According to Rapaport's (1958) formulation a regressive state should develop when the ego is unable to maintain autonomy from either the id or the external environment. In such a state the barriers differentiating ego and id processes become fluid. Images, ideas, and fantasies rise to consciousness and a reliance develops on more and more primitive defenses. The sense of voluntariness and of having inner control over one's actions in relation to oneself and to the external environment is interfered with. Is that not exactly what I have described as the general clinical picture in these two cases?

Both of these elderly men continued to desire interactions with the environment which they saw at the time as tinged with primitive drive factors. Their desires increased their dependence on the environment at a time when they felt these desires were improper, based on their life experiences in our particular culture. Thus the ego's autonomy from the id was impaired. At the same time decreased contact with usual environmental supports impaired the ego's autonomy from the id. Both of these men's efforts to continue some coherent relations with whatever objects and social institutions were left to them made them extremely dependent on external cues. They sought, and were able to find, cultural dicta against sex, in one case, and for retirement, in the other.

However, the external cues could no longer be seen in a rational and objective way and tended to be distorted. Both men suffered constantly from doubts about their ability to maintain relations with the outside, and they tended to cling to culturally stereotyped views of themselves. Clinging to what remained of the external environment maximized the ego's autonomy from the id, but at the cost of minimizing the conscious input of and trust in affective and ideational signals that usually regulate judgment and decision, that is, at the cost of impairing the ego's autonomy from the environment.

Thus in this society older people's relative autonomy from both id and external environment can become impaired. They

[173]

are isolated from their own useful emotions and from those views of the world that permit a coherent and integrated sense of self. The need to block any primitive impulses leaves them at the mercy of an overwhelming sense of longing that invades or nearly blocks out a capacity to perceive and integrate "objective" reality. They become filled with doubts, and as a result of this impaired autonomy, the ego attempts to make do with insufficient or distorted input from both id and external environment. The ego attempts to modify its structure to conform to this new, more restricted, and primitive pattern. It is my clinical impression that the ego fights to retain whatever level of ego functioning can be saved, but in these older people it can be seen that this is a reduced capacity to function and a marked impairment of the sense of self.

Within the average expectable environment, adaptation demands that their attention awareness mechanisms assign priority to the items that are culturally acceptable. Perceptual thresholds develop which allow the individual to notice most easily what he needs to notice in order to function successfully. A form of self-programming results, leading to the availability of those percepts which contribute to organized thinking. This, in turn, leads to a rigidity of thinking that makes it difficult to conceive of any other way to look at familiar internal experiences. It would, of course, be a mistake to think that this inflexibility is total. The average expectable environment changes, though slowly, and an experience considered alarming in one historical era becomes commonplace in another.

In my own experience I found that a study of representative high school students over the period 1967 to 1973 showed the development of an entirely new response to marijuana and alcohol. At the beginning of the period a highly ideological position was evident. Marijuana smokers desired insight, were secretly terrified of hidden dangers (even the rebels half believed the propaganda), practiced elaborate group rituals

[174]

around getting "high," were recognized by themselves and others as a delineated group, and eschewed alcohol. By the end of that short time span the students had abandoned any ideological connection with the drug, were no longer a delineated group, had dropped or attenuated most rituals surrounding getting high, had lost any awe of the drug, wanted only brief pleasure from it, and used marijuana and alcohol either together or separately in order to get high. Further, during this same time span, teachers who had been violent and persistent critics of drugs and drug use became almost unaware of its much more current and widespread use (Zinberg, Boris, and Boris, 1976).

Input into the social setting from the experiences of individuals continues to change it, and the social setting, in turn, changes these experiences. Layers of attitudes exist in the social setting which can be rearranged so that layers chosen by individuals to reach awareness, that is, what is considered the range of reality-related ideas and what is available and acceptable to perceive and describe, become part of a dynamic equilibrium. Social rituals are developed to legitimize new perceptions and attitudes. For example, the rituals of the early marijuana smokers made this deviant behavior a social activity and acted as both a method of controlled drug use and a form of legitimation.

In a social age when cultural dictates tend to limit sexual activity to certain and few approved situations, anyone, for example, an older person, who no longer accepts these dictates and the rituals (often joked about) that go with the acceptance, needs a new social group with different rituals and different educational patterns. He must, if you will, find a group with which to establish those rituals that make his "deviance" acceptable. Such social rituals can act as both a patterning and disruptive force, patterning for the new and disruptive for the old.

Thus, although the social setting cannot be considered a

[175]

part of any controlled, experimental design, it can be affected even by investigations that may stimulate greater interest in what old people themselves learn about aging in this culture. The reverberations of new ideas through the social setting can be treated as one more subjective, changing element when this whole notion is being studied.

This theory of the importance of social learning in the development of individuals and social attitudes becomes of particular interest when one looks at cases such as those of Mr. A. and Mr. B. These men accepted the stereotyped social views of themselves even though such views were clearly maladaptive. The views, however, were presented in such a consistent and repetitious way that they had the force to dominate the intake of stimulus nutriment. The consistency of such stimulus nutriment interfered with the capacity of these individuals' egos to function. These men's responses were not to a fantasy but to a real social occasion.

Psychotherapy could and did offer something. It helped to reduce the pressure of the superego and to restore ego stability by pointing out the extent to which the patients were responding to social views that were not consistent with all of their own attitudes toward the same events. Nevertheless, the most effective form of therapy with these men, and with others whose symptoms may be more or less mild, would be a changed social view of the aged. This does not mean that all men and women need to be overwhelmingly sexually active in the very late stages of their lives, nor does it mean tht they should not be sexually active in the late stages of their lives. This view does not imply that people need to retire and find nothing to do, nor does it mean to say that retirement should be avoided at all costs. What it does mean to say is that recognition of individual differences and variations must be acknowledged so that genuine choices are available to people who have a variety of views.

[176]

Discussion

W. W. MEISSNER, s.j., m.d.

IT IS ALWAYS CHALLENGING to be asked to comment on a paper by Dr. Zinberg, since his approach to problems usually tends to be interesting, expansive, and even provocative. In the present paper, from one perspective, Dr. Zinberg is approaching a form of social disengagement theory. Such a theory would hold that the mutual withdrawal of the aging individual from his society and the correlative withdrawal of the society from the individual create the circumstances within which so many of the psychological problems of aging arise. Such a mutual disengagement would presumably be correlative to the hypothesis of diminishing stimulus nutriment to which his argument appeals.

Yet the argument has its opposite side as well. He writes: "Older people accept cultural stereotypes and unconsciously inhibit their activities, and more basically their desires." And again, ". . . the aging person's inhibitions result more from his or her acceptance and internalization of the culture's taboos than from any overwhelming, long-standing, unresolved conflicts." In terms of the approach through stimulus nutriment, then, there seems to be some ambiguity as to whether the individual is engaged or not engaged, and consequently whether the social stimulus is being maintained or not being maintained. In terms of the stimulus nutriment model, the aging

[177]

person is being deprived of stimulus nutriment, yet at the same time is subject to social and cultural influences which strongly influence and pattern his response.

The object of my remarks here will have to do with the inadequacies and limitations of the Rapaport model of autonomy and the correlative concept of stimulus nutriment. I shall argue that a critical variable between the level of social learning theory and the organization and integration of autonomy has to do with the vicissitudes of narcissism. From that point of view, the basic problem for the aging person is that of narcissistic loss. Such a position places the problems of aging in continuity with the problems of human life in general, insofar as human life is a process of continual loss. What makes it possible to sustain such losses and to carry on the course of our lives, and even to grow and mature through them, is our capacity to gain restitution for what is lost. It may be that the capacity for restitution is what spells the difference between the psychology of the aged and that of younger age groups.

It should be clear that there can be little argument with Dr. Zinberg's appeal for an effective social learning theory and for its integration with psychoanalytic variables. He seems to feel, though, that the theoretical apparatus is ready to hand for such an endeavor. My own point of view differs somewhat. I feel the reason such a theoretical advance has been slow to develop is that the theoretical substructures are not by any means available as yet. Some of the work of Erikson in his attempts to expand ego psychology to include social and cultural variables may be pointing the way, but what seems to be required in this context, particularly in terms of the integration and internalization of social value systems, which are the core elements of any culture, is a theory of superego and ego integration. The fact is that we do not have such a theory. The psychoanalytic structural theory is derived from the notion of conflict between superego and ego rather than from their integration.

[178]

Ultimately what is required is a notion of the way in which superego and ego structures can be integrated gradually through the life cycle in relation to critical narcissistic transformations. Here Erikson's psychosocial crises can be envisioned in terms of the critical resolution of narcissistic issues at various stages of the life cycle and their integration with progressive structural modifications and integrations of superego and ego. Another critical theoretical issue that must be joined in order to articulate a theory of this sort is that of internalization, especially those critical internalizations having to do with higher-order, culturally derived components, particularly value systems. It is at this juncture that the interface between cultural influences, learning phenomena, and the organization and integration of inner psychic structure become crucial. Historically, no one was more sensitive to this problem of the difficulty between the integration of inner structure and the inputs provided from learning than Rapaport. The problem of integrating learning parameters with structural formation and modification was a central focus of his lifework, and one which he himself had to declare unsatisfactory. The problem remains a current one in our theoretical approach to such issues.

Let me turn my attention to the Rapaport (1958) model of autonomy. In his schema, the basic notion of autonomy concerns independence of drives and reality determinants. Thus the guarantee of relative autonomy from the drives comes from the side of reality or the environment, while the guarantee of the independence from reality determinants comes through the operation of drives and drive derivatives. In this sense, Rapaport's notion of ego autonomy is a negative notion connoting independence of specific determinants, and ends up being trapped between the instinctual forces, on one side, and the environment, on the other. Autonomy is an autonomy *from* instincts and *from* environment.

The problem with such a negative model of autonomy can be seen clearly in the notion of the obsessional patient, who

[179]

preserves his autonomy by an immersion in the details of reality, thus presumably defending himself against the influence of drive derivatives. However, if we consider the obsessional state, it seems ludicrous to think of the obsessional patient as possessing autonomy from the drives, since he is hardly independent of his drives; indeed, he is plagued by them, despite his immersion in reality. In such a case, the model seems to break down. Rather than considering autonomy as caught between these dichotomous polarities, it may be more useful to think of it as an internalized attribute. This would allow us to think of autonomy as being simultaneously independent both of the instincts and of the environment. Alternatively, we may be able to think of it as involving the simultaneous congruence with both drives and reality. In this sense, the ego can be strengthened by drive components, rather than weakened.

These difficulties lead us in the direction of a somewhat different notion of autonomy than that articulated by Hartmann and Rapaport. To begin with, in the Hartmann-Rapaport model autonomy is strictly speaking a functional autonomy, that is, it is an autonomy that has to do with the relative independence of specific ego functions. This functional view, which is related to the ego-psychological notion of the ego as an organization of functional systems, is relatively impersonal and concerns itself with the maintenance of structural integrity in the separate functions of the ego. Such autonomy is then a matter of conflict-free functioning within an average expectable environment (Hartmann, 1939). Consequently ego autonomy must be reduced to a consideration of the autonomy of separate functions, an argument that has been articulated by Beres (1971).

This limitation of the functional view of autonomy sets it appart from the notion of autonomy that has to do with the cohesiveness, integration, and independence of the self, that is, an inherent quality or possession of the self. It is this view of autonomy that Erikson has tried to describe in his epigenetic schema as a critical developmental achievement for the growing child.

With these limitations of the Rapaport model in mind, we can turn back again to Zinberg's stress on the role of stimulus nutriment and social learning. The problem with such an approach is that it tends to ignore or underplay the role of the narcissistic factors involved in the integration of self-autonomy and the maintenance of self-coherence. Rather, such an approach tends to settle for a form of "social compliance" along the lines described by Hartmann (1964). He understood such compliance as referring to the relation of congruence between the person's mental structure and his social environment:

> This gives us the right to speak of *social compliance*, by which we understand the fact that social factors must also be described psychologically in such a way as to demonstrate their selective effects; they operate in the direction of the selection and effectuation of certain tendencies and their expression, and of certain developmental trends, among those which, at any given moment, are potentially demonstrable in the structure of the individual [p. 27].

If, however, we rely too exclusively on extrinsic factors, we run a definite risk in our conceptualization, namely of substituting a form of "false-self" conformity for real autonomy. The false-self organization, as Winnicott (1960) has pointed out, which is based on conformity to social and extrinsic expectations and norms, results in a splitting of the inner organization of the personality with potentially serious pathological results.

The whole point of this criticism of the Rapaport model of autonomy and its correlative notion of stimulus nutriment is that these concepts are indeed quite difficult and problematical, and they do not yield to any simple analysis. We are confronted with the complex relations among the notions of adaptation, autonomy, and social conformity, on the one hand, and with their relation to problems in false-self organization, on the other. Thus the problem for old age is not to settle for some condition of external conformity or compliance, but to achieve that form of internal autonomous and adaptive growth which enables older people to sustain the trials and tribulations of old age. But this, in fact, is the therapeutic problem and the challenge at all levels of human existence. The social learning approach runs the risk of thinking that changing social attitudes toward the old aged and having them accept such changes will solve the problems. The argument I am making here seriously challenges that presumption.

I have suggested that a critical variable left out by the approach through social learning is that having to do with the narcissistic vicissitudes of old age. As I see it, the basic problem of aging is that of narcissistic loss. The losses associated with advancing age form a type of narcissistic assault. As Rochlin (1965) writes:

> The greatest test of narcissism is aging or old age. All that has come to represent value and with which narcissism has long been associated is jeopardized by growing old. The skills, mastery, and powers, all painfully acquired, which provided gratification as they functioned to effect adaptation wane in the last phase of life. One's resources, energies, adaptability, and functions, the intimacies of relationship upon which one depended, family and friends, are continually being depleted and lost. The longer one lives (as the longer one gambles), the more regularly one loses. Aging is an assault upon narcissism. Just as in early life the precariousness of existence is made clear to the child, so the friability of what is valued is made plain to the aging. Narcissism, therefore, has no lesser role in aging than it had in the years before [pp. 377-378].

There are certain specifiable results of narcissistic trauma and loss. The first of these is regression, which is accompanied by a reactivation of infantile needs and conflicts. It is interest-

[182]

ing in this regard to reflect on Dr. Zinberg's cases, since the effects of narcissism can be traced in both of them. In the first case, it seems clear that the depression is related to narcissistic loss, and that the improvement followed on a degree of narcissistic restitution which took the form of sexual acceptance and involvement with the divorced woman. Similarly, in the second case, the severe narcissistic loss and deprivation led to the mobilization of dependent and aggressive conflicts, which only turned the therapeutic corner when self-esteem was restored by the mobilization of meaningful work projects which allowed this man to regain some sense of effectiveness and self-worth. In the two cases the locus of narcissistic trauma was different, but in each case it was the capacity to restore and make up the loss and redeem the narcissistic equilibrium that made the difference.

Such narcissistic traumata are accompanied by an increase in the titre of unresolved narcissistic needs. Along with this there is also an increase in the level of aggression and agggressive conflicts. This includes what Kohut (1972) has described as "narcissistic rage." In addition, narcissistic traumata can produce depression, along with heightened anxiety, increased propensity for guilt, loss of hope, and diminution of the capacity for restitution. Such narcissistic depletion may also result in the development of paranoid trends as a defense against narcissistic loss, eventuating in forms of criticism, blaming, increasing disengagement, and even paranoid projection (Meissner, 1977). It is in these terms that we can think of the problems of the "generation gap" as an expression of these trends.

Perhaps the greatest loss of all is the encroaching deprivation and the ultimate narcissistic trauma of death. This raises the specter of loss without the concomitant elements of restitution. Here Rochlin's (1965) words are again to the point:

Aging is the only phase of human development which is characteristically, generally, and regularly resisted. The re-

[183]

sistance to aging reveals an awareness that impoverishment well understood in advance leads to the end of life. Among persons whose characters are more primitively organized, it is not chiefly impoverishment, however, so much as deprivation that is feared. It is a fear that is always responded to with regression. Although recognized as having its own characteristics, aging has been neglected as a developmental phase. It has been regarded instead as a static terminal period in which psychological functions fail or shut down, as does the sclerotic arterial system. Even more frequently overlooked is the dynamic importance of aging as an experience in which limitations will not be transcended nor losses restored. Life is made more precarious, when it nears its end, by the replacement of a promise of restitution with the disquiet of impoverishment, to which, in some cases, the danger of deprivation is added [pp. 365-366].

In terms of the relation of social factors to such inner deprivations, one might speculate about the ways in which society deprives older people of the promise of restitution. This is certainly operative in terms of the means society makes available for such restitution, even in the basic material terms of financial security and a reasonably secure, comfortable life. Another form of deprivation stems from our society's value systems which tend to deprive people of the restitutive resources of religious belief systems. Such systems, particularly those having to do with life after death and the promised rewards for religious fidelity in the next life, serve as a powerful restitutive resource for restoring and recovering the potential trauma of narcissistic loss which is to be faced in death. Insofar as society undermines and deprives people of that resource without effectively replacing it, it compounds and multiplies the damage.

Consequently I cannot help but feel that the theory of narcissism and the related theory of object relations lie considerably closer to the core conflicts in the aged. It should be clear from the tenor of these remarks that, in advancing the notion of narcissism here, I am not proposing it as an exclusive alternative to the social learning dimension stressed by Dr. Zinberg. My emphasis here rather is that there is some difficult theoretical work ahead which is required to bring the pertinent dimensions of a social learning schema into conjunction with more psychoanalytically based notions. I conceive of the operation of narcissism as a critical linking phase between the cultural context and the problems of stimulus nutriment—even though I have indicated some reservations about the use of this concept in the context of the problems of aging—and the maintenance of the internal autonomy and effective adaptive functioning of the individual.

The point of my remarks is that a theory of social learning and cultural influences cannot stand on its own, it cannot afford to bypass the linking variables concerned with narcissism and object relations. It would be totally incorrect to assume that in addressing a theory of narcissism in this context we would be opting for a form of totally internalized and self-involuted understanding. We need to remind ourselves that narcissism has to do with the integration and cohesion of the self, and that the self can only be defined and maintained in its relation to, as well as its distinction from, others. A theory of narcissistic loss in old age must explain how social influences both impinge on and undermine the capacity for adaptive reaction in the aged, as well as the ways in which social functions and structures can influence the restitutive aspects of narcissistic equilibrium. It is hoped discussions such as these can advance these concepts along this difficult path.

Marital Adaptation in the Aging

IRVING KAUFMAN, M.D.

I SHALL DISCUSS THE RELATION between the social institution of marriage and the biologic fact of aging, and the psychoanalytic implications of their interrelation. There are many definitions of the term "aging," and there is an enormous difference from person to person as to the rapidity of the aging and the forms it takes. Rather arbitrarily, I shall define the aging as the group of people who are over 55. There will be many exceptions to the generalizations presented here. No attempt has been made to cover the literature. Instead, there are selected references to illustrate certain concepts emphasized in this presentation.

There are developmental tasks, cultural pressures, and adaptive or maladaptive ways of integrating all of these factors at all ages. In addition, continuous changes in the culture put enormous pressure on the individual's ego capacity to adapt. In the face of these tasks and stresses, what happens to people who remain married over a long period of time? Some of the studies of marital satisfaction over time have produced contradictory findings. For example, Blood and Wolfe (1960) found the trend of marital satisfaction to be a general decline, while Rollins and Feldman (1970) found the trend to be a U-shaped

[187]

curve, a decline in the earlier stages followed by an increase in satisfaction in later stages. The studies of Rollins and Cannon (1974) confirm the Rollins and Feldman findings that marital satisfaction over the years tended to follow a U-shaped curve.

Those of us in the mental health field primarily deal with the problems that confront people adapting to a variety of life circumstances. There will be a discussion of the problems associated with marital adaptation in the aging. However, it is refreshing to find studies that indicate there are also successes in managing one's life. I am therefore presenting one such study in some detail.

Stinnett, Carter, and Montgomery (1972) report that in studies by Fried and Stern (1948), Bossard and Boll (1955), and Lipman (1961) many older persons find their marriages to be satisfactory or better than satisfactory in later years. Although Stinnett et al. did a study of their own to determine people's attitudes toward their marriages, because studies by Townsend (1957), Blood and Wolfe (1960), and Saphilios-Rothschild (1967) reported that people found less satisfaction during their later years, especially in lower socioeconomic groups, in general, the literature reveals that marriages perceived as satisfactory in the early years continued to be so in the later years. The reverse is also true. Those marriages perceived as unsatisfactory from the beginning tended to be perceived as unsatisfactory over the course of time.

In a previous study, Stinnett, Collins, and Montgomery (1970) found that love was the greatest area of marital need satisfaction for both husbands and wives. "Respect" was the area of least satisfaction for husbands and "communication" was the area of least satisfaction for the wives.

Although it is obvious that both men and women need narcissistic supplies, self-esteem and self-respect, closeness and object interaction, there apears to be some difference between men and women in the relative emphasis on the way these needs are met. How much of this is cultural, biologic, or

[188]

reflects some inherent difference in the personalities of men and women is extremely difficult to determine. There are, however, repeated findings that point to both the needs and the differences in achieving them. For example, an article in the *Boston Globe* (October 25, 1975) reports:

Mrs. X was a perfect wife: Her children were outstanding students, her tasteful home was spotless, she was a gourmet cook and charming hostess on the many occasions when her husband's job required they entertain.

Nor did she neglect herself. She kept her body in trim with regular exercise, her mind honed through challenging community projects and continuing graduate level courses.

Now, with both children away at college, she looked forward to having more time with her husband.

That's when he announced he was going mountain climbing in the Himalayas at Christmas.

He returned — to pursue the adventurous life, driving a Maserati and living in a singles apartment at the marina. Baffled and stunned, final divorce papers in hand, Mrs. X retreated with the family dog to Milwaukee, where she had been a popular and carefree career girl before her marriage.

What happened? Dr. Edmund C. Hallberg, professor of guidance at California State University, Los Angeles, states Mr. and Mrs. X were victims of what he calls the male metapause syndrome. He defines the word literally, meta, meaning change, and pause, a time to stop and think — in this context about one's identity and direction. It occurs in the middle age, which Hallberg brackets as between 35 and 55.

"A man hits 40, he finds a few gray hairs, he realizes all of a sudden his kids don't need him much any more and that he is not going to move up to be president of his company," Hallberg said.

[189]

IRVING KAUFMAN

Suddenly he's asking, "Who am I and where am I going?"

"Symptoms of male metapause run the gamut from unhappiness at work to fear of losing sexuality," said Hallberg, who is writing a book on the syndrome.

"The American male ties so much of himself into his
work," he said. "He pins his hopes on going far in a company, then in mid-life he begins thinking, 'I'm in a rut.' He
knows in his heart that, while he probably can remain in
the company until retirement — and there's another depres-
sing thought, he won't advance much."

Sexual changes cause a certain amount of fear; the feeling that it's all over really bothers a great many men. They
are confused by two things: their Victorian conditioning,
which contrasts with today's swinger philosophy, and the
mythologies of the numbers game — the "how many times"
and "how long it is" tales we grew up with in the locker
room.

"The emancipation of woman to personhood changes
the dominoes in the family," he said. "She returns to school
or gets a job, and the division of her time changes. She finds
excitement at a time when her husband is bored."

Through it all, Hallberg said, the man continues to ask,
"Who am I?" — and to seek answers through change.

"Some things are subtle. A man grows his hair longer,
the checks in his jacket get larger, he buys a sports car," he
said.

"Males going through metapause need excitement.
After his divorce — the second largest divorce rate occurs
when the husband is between 35 and 55 — he moves to the
marina or Newport or Aspen. He takes up sky diving or
hang gliding or climbs mountains — to prove he can do it.
He goes out of town on business and picks up an 18 year old
girl."

"He has drinking problems. Look at the advertising.

[190]

'Gusto — you only go around once. Kamchatka — come catch me.' A man's fears also may be exaggerated because he thinks he is the only male who has them," Hallberg said.

Some of the answers, Hallberg thinks, may lie in getting rid of two erroneous concepts.

"The first is that, once we're graduated from college, we are educated," he said. "The second is, that as we leave college or begin a career, we are 'adjusted.' The truth is that all of us go through predictable crises."

"Men play roles, as women do, and as the years pass they find that some are not as important as they used to be. But retirement is a process that can be terribly devastating.

We must recognize that education is definitely becoming a lifelong process. We must consider alternative careers and avocational interests.

We all have a need to be a personage, and dropping out isn't the answer."

There are other ways to view the problem presented by Hallberg. The difference in emphasis of needs, "respect" for men, which involves their narcissism, "self-respect, self-esteem, and communication" for women, which involves object interaction, closeness, and intimacy, will be discussed from the psychoanalytic point of view as two of the major issues around which the marriage will succeed or fail.

Some of the common problems facing all married people who are aging are reduced income, unavailability of suitable housing, lack of social opportunity and participation, and failing mental and physical health (Barron, 1961). These are again stresses on the marriage which may or may not be able to tolerate these pressures.

In the study by Stinnett, Carter, and Montgomery (1972) of the attitude of married couples to their marriages, they chose an age range of 60 to 89 years. These were 408 couples in senior citizens centers. The sample was 96 percent white. The largest

[191]

of occupations was clerical-sales (40 percent), and farming constituted the smallest percentage (13 percent). Their findings are as follows: (1) The greatest proportion of the couples rated their marriages as very happy (45.4 percent), or happy (49.5 percent). (2) The majority (53.3 percent) of older husbands and wives reported that their marriages had become better over time. (3) The present time was reported to be the happiest period of the marriage by most of the couples (54.9 percent). (4) Approximately 50 percent of the sample felt that most marriages become better over time. (5) The two most rewarding aspects of the present marriage relationship were most often reported by older husbands and wives as "companionship" (18.4 percent) and "being able to express true feelings to each other" (17.8 percent). (6) The two aspects of the present marriage relationship most often reported as being troublesome were "having different values and philosophies of life" (13.8 percent) and "lack of mutual interest" (12.5 percent). (7) The two most important characteristics of a successful marriage were most often reported as "respect" (38.2 percent) and sharing common interests (26.5 percent). This again goes back to the issues of self-respect, narcissistic supplies, closeness, and object interaction, which are necessary for both men and women. The greatest marital success occurred when these needs were most completely met. (8) The most important factor in achieving marital success was most often reported as being in love (48 percent). (9) The most frequently mentioned major problems of the present period in the sample were housing (27.5 percent), poor health (21.2 percent) and money (20 percent). (10) The present time was reported to be the happiest period of life by the greatest proportion of the couples in this study (50.3 percent).

The principal factor, "love," is one that most of us in the field, with the exception of Freud, have not dared to define. However, from Freud's (1914) research on the subject, we know it includes an intense object interaction with an over-

[192]

idealization of the object and a heightening of self-esteem. In simpler words, nothing makes a person feel so good about himself as being in love.

This obviously includes narcissistic supplies and close object interaction. If they can be obtained in the marriage, these are major factors to success. If for some reason the marriage does not supply these needs, then the individual either suffers it out or searches for these needs to be met in some way outside the marriage.

As Stinnett, Collins, and Montgomery (1970) have pointed out, there is a continued need and desire in aging couples to be in love. One wonders about the impact of the cultural attitudes about romantic love and youth and whether for many people there is a diminished expectation that this will be part of their lives. Feldman (1964), in an earlier study, found that older couples valued being in love less than did younger couples. Perhaps more successful marriages include a retention of this ideal, and perhaps there is even some current liberation of older people from all the cultural constraints.

Sexual satisfaction was the fourth (5.4 percent) most important characteristic of a successful marriage. Since sexual closeness and satisfaction are usually found together in a love relationship, one wonders why it was placed as fourth. There are several possible explanations. In part, this may be culturally determined where it is not considered as "seemly" to seek or admit to the desire for sexual satisfaction beyond a certain undefined age. This is despite the fact that many studies show that people do desire and gain sexual satisfaction during the later years of their lives.

In addition, however, there may be some real difference in the ego's managing of libidinal desires. Freud (1913) has pointed out that there can be a regression from the genital to the anal stage with advancing age. This could lead not necessarily to an absence of genital desire, but to a different way of perceiving the desire. As in the anal stage, need satisfaction

[193]

may be perceived in more diffuse ways. Or, to express it the other way, the progression of libidinal patterns through oral, anal, to genital, is from the most diffuse to the most specific. The anal stage is midway. Erotic desires at this stage are perceived in a more polymorphous form or in the form of role playing, which becomes so evident in adult patients fixated at this stage. Therefore, rating "respect," "sharing common interests," and "effective expression of true feelings" before sexual satisfaction is compatible with the concept that warmth, closeness and sexuality are viewed in these more diffuse rather than genital terms, even though there may well be considerable genital sexual interaction. Apparently marriage does work for some people. Certain basic needs have to be met for it to succeed, and there are many external and internal factors which both support and threaten marriage.

Recently there has been increasing question about the institution of marriage. Various alternative procedures have been attempted, primarily by younger couples. There is an increasing awareness of a kind of role reversal where new patterns of behavior initiated by youth are first tolerated, then accepted, and sometimes adopted by older persons (Somerville, 1971).

In these shifting times with the greater stress on individual expression and need satisfaction, the institution of marriage is not only questioned, but more frequently interrupted.

As a consequence of both the demand for self-fulfillment and the reduction in the community's condemnation of divorce, interruption of marriage is more frequent and more acceptable, but it is still traumatic. For some people the interruption represents an awareness of a new identity and a need for different ways to fulfill it. In some instances this can lead to growth. For others it can be a part of ego dissolution and represent a vain hope to save oneself. Between these two extremes lies a wide range of possibilities which are beyond the scope of this paper.

Needs for companionship, sex, and economic security can

[194]

be satisfied in ways other than marriage. With women becoming both economically and personally independent, marriage as we know it, as a basis for security, may change.

Many of these questions have been raised by women especially in terms of their wish for a career. A recent study by Epstein and Bronzaft (1972) showed that in a sample of 1063 women entering a tuition-free public university, a plurality of 48 percent saw their role in 15 years as that of a married career woman with children. These students came from predominantly lower-middle-class and working-class backgrounds. In this rather large sample "marriage and children" was one of their major goals. Along with this, we observe that the greatest amount of experimentation occurs among younger age groups. But in some ways this may serve to prepare the older person for the kind of life he will have to face. In the older couple's lives the focus on children and work shifts. The children move out at an increasingly earlier age, and the age of retirement continues to be reduced. Coupled with this are the reduced patterns of family interaction. So with children and job focus diminished, the couple have to turn to each other and to other couples for emotional satisfaction. While this may or may not lead to communal living, the group homes for the elderly are a type of group living. To what extent this would include the emotional and sexual sharing that we find in some of the youth group living patterns remains to be seen.

Somerville (1971) refers to the term "command generation," applied to persons in their forties and fifties who are at the height of their power, influence, and economic capacity. This term refers to a small group of people and definitely does not apply to the lower socioeconomic groups who are faced with decreasing returns from their habitual life patterns. So, for some people, external gratification adds to their sense of well-being, and the marriage may be supported. For others, the problems of aging, economic security, ill-health, loss of children and friends may put too much stress on the marriage, and the couple may turn against each other because they hurt and the marriage is not solving the problem.

Earlier (Zinberg and Kaufman, 1963), we pointed out the dynamic shift between id, ego, and superego. As the id's drive power becomes less intense, there is some regression in the service of the ego, and the ego defenses take on a different pattern to handle the changes confronting the aging. Marriage, too, is a dynamic process, and its success depends partly on the individual's personality structure, but equally on whether the personality patterns mesh satisfactorily with the patterns of the partner.

For example, one couple, now in their late fifties, who married and had several children, had been very happy with each other, shared many interests, had an excellent sex life, and found their children to be mostly a source of joy. They came in for therapy because this blissful pattern had seriously deteriorated. As their interrelation was examined, it became clear that the husband had been extremely dependent on his wife. She had been very able while he was struggling to find himself. Although he had developed a successful career in the manufacturing business, his achievement fell short of his goal. There was a shift in the couple's relationship at the point when their last child left home for college. At that time the wife became depressed, and became less of a companion to her husband. As a result, he turned his energies away from her, and the business began to flourish. He also began to travel more to conferences and to indulge in incidental romantic encounters. Apparently, for many years, he had been chronically depressed and dependent. He had unconsciously made a trade-off, gaining supplies through his dependence on his wife, and foregoing narcissistic supplies for lesser achievement in his career. His wife, who was very nurturant, and needed her children and her husband to be dependent on her, gained her self-worth and self-esteem in this fashion. When she lost the youngest child, who went off to college, the entire equilibrium collapsed, and a new, maladaptive pattern emerged. She became depressed and needy. The husband resented having a wife who was no longer "any fun or support" and turned to his business, which prospered and made him feel good, and to other women, who also gave him nurturance and boosted his self-esteem. So the marriage changed from a state of balance which had been relatively satisfactory, and the inherent problems now began to surface. In terms of their pain, there were his many years of chronic dissatisfaction and unhappiness now matched by her acute pain and unhappiness. So at this point their defense systems no longer meshed, and the under-lying problems also became manifest in the marital disruption.

This case also illustrates the complexity of the balance of narcissistic and object supplies. The husband was unconscious-ly willing to forego a fuller quota of narcissistic supplies as long as his wife was nurturant and a playmate. She achieved the gratification of feeling useful and needed, and thus gained her narcissistic and object supplies from the same source. When the relative quota of object supplies was taken away from her with the departure of her last child for college, she regressed and turned into herself toward the introjected objects she mourned. She felt empty and could not give. She felt worthless and devalued, and her self-esteem was shattered.

Therapy for both partners had to be directed at the under-lying personality issues, helping them resolve the chronic per-sonality problems. The many years of dependency and its loss had created a resentment in the husband which made him feel entitled to live and become a meaningful person in his own right. He did not feel grateful for what his wife had done for him, but unconsciously felt he had been victimized, partly by her and mostly by himself. His need to balance good with bad and make trade-offs was another manifestation of a maladaptive ego pattern. Now he was trading "success" for his marriage. She needed help both to resolve her current depression and to develop more effective ways of gaining

[197]

emotional and narcissistic supplies other than by the dependency of those around her.

The literature describes the patterns of interaction between husbands and wives in a variety of ways. For example, Levinger (1968) discusses the repeatedly reported finding that husbands and wives differ in the kinds of family tasks they perform. On the other hand, in the social-emotional realm, with one exception, there tended to be little difference in the husband's and wife's activity. The area that seemed different was the wife's greater willingness to "talk about one's feelings with the spouse when one is bothered or upset." (This may be partly a cultural phenomenon where admitting to or talking about feelings may seem less masculine to some men and hence less acceptable.)

In contrast to this study, Bott (1955) describes families in which, at one extreme, the husband and wife carried out all tasks separately and independently of each other; she had her tasks and he had his. In their leisure time he went to football games and she visited her family. The felt their behavior was normal, and typical of their social circle. Bott then describes another couple who did everything jointly, sharing as many activities as possible. This included interchanging household tasks whether they were cooking, repairing, or gardening. They shared their interest in politics, music, and literature in their leisure time. They too felt that their behavior was typical of their social circle. There were many degrees of variation between these extremes of a joint conjugal role relationship versus a segregated conjugal role relationship.

Bott's research reveals that the degree of segregation of conjugal roles is related to the network of family connectedness. Those families with a high degree of segregation in the role relationship of husband and wife had a highly connected network; many of their friends, neighbors, and relatives knew one another. Families that had a relatively joint role relationship between husband and wife had a dispersed network. Few of their relatives, neighbors, or friends knew one another. There were many degrees of variation between these two extremes. Bott further describes the sociologic factors affecting the development of joint versus segregated conjugal role relationships.

The studies of Levinger and Bott are significant because they introduce several important issues. Traditionally, there had been a division of tasks inside and outside the house. With women becoming more involved in careers and in their own development there is a tendency for less task differentiation. However, over 20 years ago, before this movement had gained its current momentum, some people had developed joint conjugal role relationships. The effects of these patterns can yield mixed blessings. In societies where there is clear role definition and training for the tasks, there tends to be more stability. In our culture there is little preparation for the major events of life such as marriage, parenting, aging, illness, and death. As a result, it is as though each generation has to rediscover the wheel and fire. This is an extreme statement, but it has some validity. The problem posed by a rigid structure includes stripping of individuality and interference with mutual fulfillment within marriage. So we are confronted with the issues of stability and security versus autonomy and greater self-expression. Perhaps a way can be found to capture the best of each.

For the aging couple these problems remain and may be intensified. For example, one couple had a relatively stable marriage. They thought they had been happy and fulfilled throughout their marriage. They were a middle-class family. The husband had steady employment, and there were no economic problems. Their children had grown up, completed their education, and were married and launched in their careers. The couple had looked forward to the husband's retirement when they could do some of the things they had always wanted to do but never had the time for. The wife had always

[199]

stayed at home, cared for the children and the home, and had never worked.

When the husband retired, problems emerged. He missed his work both in terms of giving a purpose to his life and the companionship of his fellow employees. The hobbies and other activities in which he engaged seemed trivial, dull, and boring to him. He sat around the house complaining and criticizing his wife. She, on the other hand, became increasingly irritated with him. He did not want to move when she had to vacuum. He was irritable and unpleasant, and she had managed without his executive assistance all their married life. They fought over innumerable issues and tried to draw the children into the conflict. Finally the couple sought therapy. The role pattern for the wife had remained the same, but with the disruption of the husband's sources of emotional and narcissistic supplies from his work, he had become depressed, and in a complaining way was saying he was hurting. They had never shared a great deal and were not prepared to cope with the void in the husband's life. He needed help in resolving his depression, feelings of loss of self-esteem, and some meaningful way to gain supplies both with and away from his wife. She also needed help in understanding what was happening to her and to him, and perhaps to develop ways to share more activities with him.

In summary, I have discussed some of the general issues involved in marriage, some of the social, cultural, and psychological factors affecting the marriage as the partners go through their aging process. Whether or not the process is adaptive or maladaptive will depend on the balance of the ego patterns in the partners and whether they mesh or conflict. There is always a need for object and narcissistic supplies for both partners. Shifts in this area are most crucial to marital functioning. These supplies are needed by both men and women, though there appears to be some difference in the emphasis of men on narcissistic and women on object supplies. Whether this will change as women become more involved in developing their autonomy, including careers, remains to be seen. However, whatever the balance, it is necessary to direct one's attention to these areas, both to consider ways to strengthen marriages if that is what the couple wants, and to deal with those situations where there has been a problem and the marital partners are in a state of crisis.

Discussion

DAVID BLAU, M.D.

SINCE THE FIRST SYMPOSIUM on the "Normal Psychology of the Aging Process" took place, there have been some changes in our thinking. Zinberg and Kaufman (1963) placed particular emphasis on the adaptive-ego functions. Standing closer in time to the work of Hartmann, Anna Freud, and others, the emphasis is quite understandable and significant. Since 1960 other areas of psychoanalytic thought and focus have received increasing attention.

Dr. Kaufman, for example, in his paper "Marital Adaptation in the Aging" (1976), highlights the importance of object relations as well as the significance of narcissism. This, too, is reflective of current psychoanalytic focus in which we have reappraised some old concepts and viewed them in a new light. I cannot refrain from observing that Dr. Kaufman's paper, like the marriages in the Stinnett study, improves as it goes along. The last half of the paper is much more satisfying than the beginning.

Although it has not been said in the particular paper, I am sure that Dr. Kaufman agrees that when we discuss a subject as complex as marital adaptation, we become involved in some of the most intriguing and intricate forms of balance and interlocking needs which transcend individual psychopathology.

For example, we have all seen people who were relatively happy in their marriages and yet were quite disturbed intrapsychically. We have also seen people with much less pathology who were unhappy in their marriages and relatively comfortable intrapsychically. I emphasize this to illustrate that we are dealing with a relationship in action and reaction. This is far more difficult to understand than the mother-child dyad, for example, although frequently containing major remnants from early childhood.

Dr. Kaufman starts with the reassuring information that some researchers have documented the possibility that some married couples find their relationships satisfactory in later life. With the enormous divorce rate, and the tremendous number of patients coming for consultation about marital difficulties, this is indeed a reassuring note for all professionals as well as married couples. Certainly those of us who treat couples can easily feel that many marriages these days are in serious difficulty. Perhaps this is due partially to the fact that more and more people are seeking professional help, and that less stigma is attached to treatment. This, however, does not explain the increasing divorce rate in all socioeconomic groups and strata.

Dr. Kaufman, too, has read an article that troubled me when I saw it in the *Boston Globe*. I found it to be unfortunately superficial. I felt that the emphasis on education and the breezy style hardly did justice to the complexities of the subject and smacked of "pop culture" with easy answers that really say very little. In fact, the article contains a number of distortions including the notion that "the feeling that it's all over really bothers a great many men." I think that the author of the article believed that men in middle age were sexually finished. This is an example of a misconception Dr. Berezin and others have written about, yet it continues as a myth about the aged as well as the middle-aged. What also interests me is how blithely Professor Hallberg skips over the issue of the last child going off to college when he describes the sudden change in the middle-aged father. He ascribes the reaction of the man to sexual changes and to the realization that advancement at work is no longer possible. Dr. Hallberg seems to mix middle and old age into quite a stew, as he brings in the issue of retirement, which seems to be hardly a central topic for a 40-year-old man.

I would prefer to consider the narcissistic and object problems that Dr. Kaufman has referred to in his paper. If I saw the man Hallberg was describing in the newspaper article, I would certainly have had more than a passing interest in the fact that the father was now chasing 18-year-old girls and sounded quite depressed. It would not have taken me very long to speculate that rather than copying the life style of a changing generation, this man was, perhaps, suffering from the loss of his last daughter who had just gone off to college. Furthermore, as a form of restitution, he was directly seeking a substitute for the missing object as well as identifying with her. I certainly would have been tempted to consider the possibility of a grief reaction that was being handled by substitutive gratification while this father was acting like a suitable object for a young girl to be intersted in. I am afraid that my point of view would not meld well with advocating that we all go through predictable crises and should expect to continue to grapple for further education. If Hallberg believes that one must learn from life as well as from one's own reactions and patterns, and that it is never too late for this kind of emotional education, then I would agree with his ideas, but not the way he states them.

I have some questions regarding the survey of Stinnett, Carter, and Montgomery (1972). It is not clear to me whether these are all long-married, never-divorced people, or whether some of them have been divorced and have remarried. I shall make some comments about the sample since they are all attending a senior citizen center. The fact that the couples are attending together indicates a commonality of interests and a degree of social relatedness and interaction as a marital pair that perhaps explains why so many of them regard themselves as happily married and more satisfied at this period of their lives than ever before. A sample selected in this fashion is more likely to have this attitude than a random sample of couples with diverse interests and a different pattern of social interaction.

Notably, in this sample there was a continuing need and desire to be in love. I am not so surprised at the continuing need or the desire, but I wonder, perhaps skeptically, about the 48 percent who reported that they were in love. Not only Freud had difficulty defining the term; I think most people have trouble with it, and I have often seen people who were in love but hated to use the words and felt uncomfortable with them. I am curious as to what the respondents meant when they said they were in love, and also whether the couples felt they had to give certain socially approved answers to the examiners. I do not know whether the types of questions or the attitudes of the examiners may have produced this very positive response about marriage. From my own clinical experience, I know that the degree of involvement, consideration, respect, and love felt by individuals and couples can vary tremendously over a period of time and is much influenced by both intrapsychic shifts and external pressures. I think most of us would not believe that love is a static state, but rather that there are changes and fluctuations which most people would honestly acknowledge.

From the standpoint of working with patients, it is not uncommon to find people more uncomfortable about expressing genuine tender feelings and love with appropriate affect, than about aggressive and hostile impulses. I do not believe that only men have difficulty in expressing tender and positive feelings, but I would agree that they are more likely to be inhibited and that there is a prevailing feeling that it is unmasculine to display and acknowledge positive feelings. All of which makes it even more startling to read that 48 percent of the elderly couples report they are in love. Even considering that by this age the most dissatisfied and unhappy marital partners have long ago divorced or separated, and that we are left with a group of the most positive people, I still cannot account for these results.

It is equally startling that sexual satisfaction, although ranked fourth in importance, is only mentioned by a minimal number of the couples as an ingredient of a successful marriage. Again we may have a situation where people feel uncomfortable with questions like this, and do not acknowledge the importance of sexual gratification in their lives.

I can honestly say I have never seen an elderly couple in consultation where this was not a major and significant issue. If they were not currently sexually active, they usually spoke longingly of past activity and gratification. As a rule those who were not currently active sexually generally were unhappy about it, unless this had been a lifelong style in the marriage.

Having concluded that some marriages work, Dr. Kaufman has turned to some of the recent pressures on marriage as an institution that tax the adaptive capacity. He raises the issue of changing life styles, the new role of women, and changing attitudes about sexuality, communal living, and divorce.

Perhaps we might consider for a moment some of the social changes that have been occurring and that have influenced various institutions in our time. These changes have had enormous impact on ego functioning and represent challenges and stresses that were not present to the same degree in a bygone age. In our lifetime, for example, we have seen for the first time in the Western world mass provision for retirement. Prior to this time people worked until old age and beyond if they were lucky enough to survive disease. The disabled were cared for by their families or in institutions, and there was no concept of enjoying unstructured leisure time. Now we are seeing the effects of enforced retirement and the emotional impact of the loss of highly valued roles in a society that still has to rethink the wisdom of imposing a certain way of life on people regardless of their needs or capabilities.

Within our lifetime we have seen widespread employment of married women, a phenomenon that emerged during World War II and now is thoroughly accepted. Before, only professionals and unmarried women worked; this is no longer the situation.

We have also seen enormous increases in population with greater mobility and access to large numbers of objects and gratifications previously not possible.

Modern methods of contraception with the resulting freedom from pregnancy have made a major impact on sexual mores and conduct. All of these changes, and I have only mentioned a bare minimum, have presented new challenges to adaptation. There are increasing possibilities for greater expression and gratification as well as increasing challenges, conflicts, and anxieties. For example, instead of concerns about sexuality these days, one more frequently encounters young couples with concerns about closeness, meaningfulness, and communication of feelings. Sexual gratification is taken for granted.

Whom shall we hold responsible for the changes that I have mentioned? It is fashionable to talk about the young people when we describe the large social changes that have occurred within our lifetime. This is a delusion shared by many members of our culture. We have been witnessing a gradual evolution of social change over a considerable period of time without having been aware of it. The major social changes were not produced solely by young people, but could only have occurred through the cooperation and assistance of all generations. The time was apparently ripe for many social changes and for rethinking the meaning of institutions that had been accepted without question. The Church, the Army, Marriage, and many other sacred and important institutions have been under close scrutiny for some time.

I do not believe that great social changes have ever come about entirely at the instigation of the young. They certainly have participated and provided the energy and assistance, but many of the changes that we have seen are the result of collaboration between the generations occurring at a time when society was prepared to go off in new directions in the search for a different way of dealing with old problems. Whether all of these changes will ultimately prove to be adaptive is, of course, a moot point. As we know from adolescent development, progress is rarely straightforward and frequently consists of both progression and regression. Social change is often similar.

Some years ago, in discussing the dissent and upheaval taking place on some of the local college campuses, I talked with a wise senior colleague. My colleague was in her sixties and was known to be liberal about sexual matters and the rights of women. She asked me what I thought of the current upheaval, and I said that if it would produce some serious examination of our institutions and their functions, it was well worth the trouble. I told her I felt that many institutions were too much taken for granted, and that people had the right to rethink their meaning. I did not advocate tearing things down while the thinking was going on, nor did I advocate the unreserved worship of institutions. I was somewhat surprised that my colleague shook her head and did not agree with me. I recently realized that colleges were sacred institutions for her.

In the last part of his paper, Dr. Kaufman turns to clinical material which is personally more familiar and from which it is easier to launch a discussion. Much of it is material with which I would agree. Dr. Kaufman emphasizes the need for meshing of the patterns of the marital partners, and that marriage is a dynamic process and not a static one. The problems and the intrapsychic situations of the two partners may be shifting, and

[209]

the balance between them, which is always delicate, needs tuning and adjusting. Dr. Kaufman describes a family where the wife was the giving and protecting figure and the husband and children were more dependent and passive. The wife clearly had her own need to be in this position and the husband and children had theirs. Losing a child to college precipitated marital disequilibrium. The nurturing mother became depressed and felt unneeded, and the dependent husband struck out on his own and became independent, capable, and successful in his business. He was involved with other women and resented his depressed wife.

In contrast with the *Boston Globe* article on metamenopause, we see a very rich and complicated relationship described. Dr. Kaufman deals with it primarily in terms of narcissistic and object supplies and the balance of the needs of the two partners. I, myself, am tempted to move in a different direction. I advance the possibility that we are dealing here with the reaction of both parents to the loss of the child who went to college. In my experiences with families and couples, the central problem is often the same for both partners. Let us consider the possibility that the mother is depressed at losing her daughter and that the father is handling his feelings by greater activity, mobility, and increasing social contact with other people. They are both responding to "a family problem." It might be worthwhile under these circumstances to point out that both parents are coping with the emotional meaning of this child's going off to college, using whatever defenses and mechanisms of adaptation they have available. This suggests, further, that we try to understand what this particular child means to each parent. As we know clinically, there can be a very intense relationship with a child when one or both parents have found a deficiency in the marriage and have attempted to obtain missing gratification from this child. If one parent is thus bound up with the child, this may lead to trouble when the other resents their close relationship, and further escalation of the difficulties between the parents ensues. In addition, the husband, in this particular case, felt unconsciously that he had given up a great deal of adult gratification in order to be fed and nurtured by his wife. Perhaps it would have been worthwhile to have pointed out that it really required two people to make that kind of bargain and to extract that kind of "trade-off."

I would like to give a clinical example to illustrate how chronic marital difficulties might be relieved, using another approach. About five years ago I was asked to see a man in his early sixties who came feeling guilty and embarrassed because he had caused tremendous upset and grief to his daughter. His daughter, a woman in her late twenties and unmarried, had discovered that he was having an affair. She suddenly developed physical difficulties which were diagnosed as conversion symptoms by a neurologist. The daughter then told her physician that she was extremely upset by her father's behavior, and she was urged to talk to him directly. As a result of her confronting her father, he decided to seek psychiatric consultation both to unburden himself and to be of assistance to his daughter. The father was a successful salesman, married for over 35 years, and had two daughters. Approximately two years before the consultation he had been involved in a serious automobile accident and was lucky to escape with his life. As a result of this accident he met an attractive divorcee some 15 years younger than himself. Within a few months he found himself increasingly involved with this woman and began an affair. His wife suspected that something was going on because of his late hours and neglect of her. She finally received a telephone call telling her of the affair, and she communicated this information first to her daughter and then to her husband.

In talking with this man it became obvious that his close brush with death was significant emotionally. He felt vulnerable, insecure, and perhaps was looking for a protective maternal figure. His narcissism had been assaulted and his body integrity threatened. I continued to interview this man for about three sessions and wondered why it was that his daughter had reacted so vigorously to hearing about her parent's difficulty. I asked to see the wife and interviewed the couple together. The wife was a righteous and indignant woman who clearly felt that her husband was completely in the wrong and that she was there to receive his apology and to be treated as the victim. She was shocked when I asked why she had talked to her daughter and why her daughter had gotten so upset. This question revealed the central issue in the marital relationship. It appeared that the daughter had had an extremely close relationship with her mother and had been unable to leave home even though she was earning a good living and was in her late twenties. Only recently had she been able to find her own apartment and make the move. The other daughter in this family, who was in her thirties, was married but continued to call her mother frequently from a distant Eastern state for reassurance and direction. The daughter with conversion symptoms called two or three times a day after moving to communicate with her mother, and they were "as close as sisters."

As soon as I had obtained this information concerning the mother-daughter relationship, the husband began to speak about his dissatisfaction with his wife's closeness with this child. He pointed out that they had never had any time together unless the children were present, and that his wife had consistently refused to go on vacations with him and leave the children. For the past few years he had had thoughts of retiring, but she was adamant that she would not leave this part of the country because her unmarried child still needed her. As a matter of fact, his girlfriend had been more than willing to move with him to a comfortable retirement community. His wife, on the other hand, was not interested in making the move with him. In a few sessions, jointly, it became clear that the wife had become involved with the children during the early years of the marriage because she felt neglected by her husband, who was attempting to establish a lucrative business. She expressed her resentment that he was never available, and made it clear that she had increasingly turned to the children as a substitute for the gratification she had missed in her marriage. The husband, on the other hand, excused himself by saying he had to build up his business. He maintained that he continued to be interested in his wife and still found her sexually desirable. His main complaint was that she would not share her life with him. He pointed out that he had admired her stability and economical manner and that he had even turned over all of his money to her for the management of their finances. Their bank account was in her name, even though he had considered breaking up the marriage he had not made a move to obtain this money.

By the third joint interview the couple had decided that they wanted to remain together, and the wife indicated she was willing to consider moving to a retirement community. They made a trip, explored the situation, and wrote me they had decided to begin a new life in that area of the country.

The therapy was brief. I saw the husband three times individually, and the couple jointly three times. The pathology was obvious, and it was clear that one of the unconscious reasons the husband had been attracted to his girlfriend was that she had a son and that he only had daughters. She was also young, vigorous, very interested in sex, and showed a decided positive interest in him. His wife, on the other hand, felt that he didn't love her. She needed reassurance that he continued to care for her, and clarification that it was his disappointment because she was not emotionally available to him that made him seek other sources of gratification.

In the final part of the paper, Dr. Kaufman, too, talks about retirement and some of the problems that can arise. He describes how a man who appeared to be looking forward to retirement suddenly found himself depressed and irritated with his wife. Planning for retirement and thinking about it in advance might have made some difference to this man. Individual differences should be considered, and some people ought not to retire. Others may require structured leisure time which is very similar to a job and has fixed hours and goals.

One final point of minor difference is that Dr. Kaufman has a tendency to think of men as more concerned with narcissistic supplies and women with object relations. I do not think that this distinction is so clear-cut. For many women what appears to be the need for supplies from an object is really also narcissistic. Although this is a relatively minor point, I believe that it is often very difficult to separate the two and, of course, in a good marriage they are wedded.

PART THREE

Review of the Literature

Sex and Old Age:
A Review of the Literature

MARTIN A. BEREZIN, M.D.

MANY OF THE ARTICLES dealing with sex, especially sex in old age, are introduced by defensive and apologetic statements. The cultural attitude toward sex life among aged people is such that, to repeat a phrase used by Heiman (1967), the word "sex" in this context becomes a four-letter word.

Rubin (1965) says, "The fullest expression of the sexual needs and interests of men and women over sixty cannot take place in a society which denies or ignores the reality of these needs and interests, or in an atmosphere which prevents full and open inquiry into them. Nor can it take place in a soil which nourishes every kind of myth and misconception about these later years. . . . Sexuality after sixty is not an invention of those who are studying it and discovering its extent and its variety of manifestations."

Further evidence of the biased cultural attitude is evident in the statement that what is virility at 25 becomes lechery at 65. Jackson (1966) quotes a London biologist who remarked on the book *Human Sexual Response* by Masters and Johnson (1966): "If we are inclined to regard sexual union as something so sacrosanct that it should not be open to investigation, we

[217]

should remember that a similar view was taken regarding the stars in Galileo's day."

The widespread notion persists that old age is a sexless era, or if it is not, it should be. One of the origins for this image is the timelessness of oedipal reactions. The oedipal child fiercely clings to his conviction that his parents do not indulge in sexual activity, that they are and must be sexless. Claman (1966) tells the story of Sam Levenson, the schoolteacher and homespun philosopher of television fame, who once said, "'When I first found out how babies were born, I couldn't believe it! To think that my mother and father would do such a thing!' Then after reflection, he added, 'My father—maybe, but my mother—*never!*'" Such an attitude not only influences the cultural value system, but is also the basis for much countertransference resistance on the part of researchers and therapists.

Feigenbaum, Lowenthal, and Trier (1967) note that there is a paucity of factual data on the sex attitudes and habits of older people and attribute this to a "feeling among physicians, psychiatrists, and research workers that it is indelicate, indeed almost 'indecent,' to probe into the sexual proclivities of persons old enough to be their parents." They add that elderly people "are vitally interested, terribly confused, and hunger eagerly for information about the norms of sexuality in the geriatric age population."

A further consequence of this attitude is that older people themselves adopt a negative view of their own sexual desires, fantasies, and feelings. In other words, the myth of sexless older years held by young people becomes a self-fulfilling prophecy when they themselves reach old age. Many elderly people who find they have strong sex desires are overwhelmed with guilt and shame and feel that they are oversexed. This observation is noted by a number of authors (Bowman, 1963; English and Pearson, 1955; Kleegman, 1959; Rubin, 1965; Wolff, 1957).

The stereotype of sexless older years is in fact a myth, as those who work with older people know and as this survey of the literature demonstrates; and this myth is deleterious, for it interferes with the health and welfare of millions of old people. As Goldfarb (1965) states the case:

> . . . conflicts over sex or sexuality, however broadly defined, are not the sole basis of maladaptation at any age, and people who firmly believe their problem to be "sexual" are often chagrined by the discovery that this is not the case. Nonetheless, the widespread ignorance about sex and the high frequency, in our society, or excessive inhibition with respect to behavior that can lead to gratifying heterosexual relationships and the relief of sexual tensions make sexual problems one of the most common causes of helpless feelings among the aging. Misguided search for relief of tension and for ways to decrease feelings of helplessness generally lead to unsatisfactory relationships which are costly of time and energy and burdensome to others.

Many observers also point out that those elderly people who have always been vigorous and who have a high capacity for interest and pleasure are not influenced by the calendar and do not retreat from sexual activity. In my own writings (1963) I have stated this point by referring to the timelessness of drives and wishes.

The available data and the methodology of data collection raise certain issues. For example, to assume that sexual intercourse is the only fact of a sex life is to oversimplify the problem and to do an injustice to an overview of the situation.

Claman (1966) states, "The medical literature provides very little information concerning sexual activity in older people." As an example, he points out that although the two Kinsey reports (1948, 1953) are prodigious, out of 1,700 pages only three are devoted to the old-age group, and the sampling is small so that only impressions are permissible. However, I be-

[219]

lieve that the impressions gained from the Kinsey reports and other reports add up significantly and permit reasonable inferences to be drawn.

Sexual activities studied in the various reports include intercourse and masturbation as two significant variables of sex behavior. In addition, the reports include studies on the existence of and the degree of erotic feelings, desires, fantasies, and dreams and an evaluation of the degree of sexual satisfaction. Some of the reports are divided into different studies of aging men and aging women. Moreover, such factors as aging changes, organic conditions, and availability of sexual partners are significant. Some of the articles are oriented to sociological, statistical surveys; some relate to organic conditions; and others include psychological and psychiatric considerations. The various studies emphasize that the sex urge and sex behavior of persons of advanced years correlate strongly with their individual comparative sex life when younger (Busse et al., 1954). Thus old age as a variable and as a determinant with respect to change in sex life does not play as significant a role as is commonly assumed.

The statistical reports in the various studies are essentially sociological. They do not include the psychological and psychiatric diagnostic categories, nor do they deal with the psychodynamics in individual cases. There is, therefore, a significant omission involved in these statistics. It is already well known that age offers many elderly men and women who had sexual conflicts in their youth an acceptable alibi to release themselves from the burdens of anxiety connected with sexual behavior. Such men and women accept with relative ease the cessation of their sex lives. Nevertheless, the statistical reports in our current phase of studies are significant and offer a springboard for further refined studies in the future.

Many of the articles appearing in books and journals dealing with sex and old age make reference to the pioneering research of Kinsey and his colleagues (1948, 1953). Due credit should also be given to an early study by Pearl (1925). This study was based on a questionnaire sent to 257 men who had undergone prostatectomies. The findings were quite limited and are rarely quoted. Pearl was influenced by a mid-Victorian attitude, and references are made to coitus and sexual behavior with a conspicuous lack of detail as to what these terms connote. Pearl's book contains many pejorative statements about sex.

In his study, Pearl gives the mean age at prostatectomy as 64.53 and the mean age at marriage as 28.33. He found that with "unrestricted legitimate opportunity the peak of sex activity is prior to age 20" (p. 191).

His statistics indicate a curve of decline in frequency of intercourse with each advancing decade. He collected some data of the sex activities of 67 men married in the age period of 20-24 years. He reported a decline from the peak frequency of intercourse of 14.7 times per month at ages 20-29, to 6.3 times per month at ages 50-59, 3.1 at ages 60-69, and 1.2 at ages 70-79. Pearl states that the declining frequency "is an expression almost solely of the physiological changes of senescence" (p. 189), although he contradicts himself by referring to the role of psychological factors when he states, "Complex psychological factors are the determiners of sex activity" (p. 195).

Later he goes on to say that his statistics show that in a study of occupational groups, with "farmers, where the economic status was lowest, the intellectual content of life the least varied and interesting, and the outlets for nervous and emotional tension most restricted, the average frequency was highest at all periods of life. In the professional group, where the economic status was high, the intellectual content of life most varied and interesting, and the pleasant and satisfactory outlets for nervous energy most manifold, the average frequency of sexual activity was lowest. The merchant and banker group was intermediate to the other two groups in all these respects save economic status, where the level was about the same as in the professional group" (p. 202).

In another early reference to sex life in the aged, Hamilton

(1939) refers to the regression in psychosexual life and to the frustrated aging person who repeats early life behavior—oral, anal and urethral pleasures. He tends to believe that the decline in sexual potency in both men and women is related to glandular changes. Hamilton did a clinical study on 200 people, from which he arrived at certain impressions about their psychosexual behavior. He, too, is wary of generalizations, but he feels "reasonably certain" that masturbation occurs in both married and unmarried elderly people, and adds that "women, even more than men, show a definite tendency to increase their masturbation during the seventh decade" (p. 476). He refers to several clinical and psychotherapeutic experiences in which elderly men and women previously impotent and frigid were able to resume sexual experiences to orgasm and mentions, among others, one woman in her eighties who, after 22 years of complete frigidity, had a reawakening of sexual desire and capacity for orgasm. Barker (1939) points out that clinicians are aware that masturbation frequently occurs among sexagenarians, but he adds that in his experience it is much more common in late life among men than among women (p. 727). This last observation is not confirmed by later authors.

The Kinsey reports are valuable, but their sampling is small and incomplete. Claman (1966) states that the reports of Kinsey and others have shown that "sexual interest, capacity, and response is at its height by the age of 19 in the male (and slightly later in the female) and from then on there is a gradual lessening of these functions with age." Hirt (1966) adds:

> Although socially and psychologically incomplete, Kinsey's work was valuable in two ways. It opened the door to a kind of minute statistical examination of one aspect of human activity, and provided important raw data in the field of sexual research. . . . However, the glaring omission in the studies of Kinsey and his colleagues was the denial of, and a

lack of exploration into, the emotional aspects of the sexual relationship. In addition, it is interesting to note that in the book on the male only two pages are devoted to sex in the aged and one-half page is given to the same subject in the study of women.

The omission of a history of sexual relations in aged patients is further noted in my experiences with psychiatric residents. In the usual nongeriatric case history workup conferences, the psychiatrist includes routinely the psychosexual history in addition to all the other necessary data. However, it was noted in the case of geriatric patients that this part of the history was missing. When attention was called to the omission, the residents subsequently obtained and presented the psychosexual history—but only for male patients. The necessity of obtaining a psychosexual history of the female patient was pointed out, and it was only then that a psychosexual history in the case of male and female patients became standard routine procedure.

Christenson and Gagnon (1965) feel that Kinsey dealt with the subject in only a minor way. Le Witter and Abarbanel (1961) quote Kinsey et al. (1953): "Even in the most advanced ages there is no sudden elimination of any large group of individuals from the sexually active. This is astounding for it is quite to the contrary to the general conception of the aging process of sex." Kinsey is quoted further as saying that he found that women retain their sex potential longer than men.

Botwinick (1959) treats the Kinsey reports at much greater length. He refers to Kinsey's classification of six variables in the study of sex behavior in men: (1) ability to reach repeated climax, (2) frequency of morning erections, (3) duration of erection, (4) angle of erection, (5) speed of reaching full erection, and (6) amount of precoital mucous secretion.

Using these measurements Kinsey reported that with advanced age there was increased impotence and decreased

[223]

erotic responsiveness. He reported further that while the sex drive in the human male decreases with age, the origin of the decrease is not well established. Kinsey et al. (1948) felt that the primary factor is an altered physiological capacity, but added that it is "affected also by psychologic fatigue, a loss of interest in repetition of the same sort of experience, an exhaustion of the possibilities for exploring new techniques, new types of contacts, new situations" (p. 227).

Kinsey is quoted further: "In numerous cases change of sex partners and sexual techniques increased frequencies in older males, although in a relatively short time previous rates were re-established." This last point is mentioned here as especially significant when applied to the study of the effects of various drugs, aphrodisiacs, special health foods, etc., an issue treated in great detail by Rubin (1965). The effect of social and biological factors in the sex drive of the human male remains unclear.

As Freeman (1961) states: "Marriage was the dominant feature in the sexual picture; habit, convenience, and the combined experiences of both partners determined the nature of the older age sex pattern. In all instances, single individuals did not have nearly as satisfactory a sex life, particularly in older age. Nothing in a study of sexual behavior in the aging suggests any deviation from personal capacities and the normal physiologic trends of the senescent state."

In the human female, the problem of determining the effects of age on the sex drive is more complex. There are greater cultural restrictions on female sexuality. In addition, observations on female sexuality are not as conclusive for "a considerable portion of the female's sexual activity does not result in orgasm" (Kinsey et al., 1953, p. 45). Kinsey et al. concluded that "there is little evidence of any aging in the sexual capacities of the female until late in her life," (p. 353) and that "the human female ages slowly and to a relatively small extent" (p. 716).

Newman and Nichols (1960) present some data collected from 250 volunteer geriatric subjects whose ages ranged from 60 to 93. Some of their findings confirm and some conflict with what has been reported above. One hundred and one of their subjects were either single, divorced, or widowed. In this group only seven percent were sexually active. By contrast, in the still-married group 54 percent indicated they were sexually active. The frequency of sexual relations in this group varied from once every other month to three times weekly. Men were found to be more active than women. Black subjects were more active than Caucasians, and persons of low socioeconomic status were more active than those of high socioeconomic status—although the authors caution on too much generalization from such observations. Evidently the authors were puzzled as to why women reported less sexual activity than the men and suggested the possibility that "the women were somewhat more reluctant to give factual data about their sexual activity." Another possibility to explain this finding is that husbands on the average were four years older than their wives and therefore less active—for example, a 70-year-old man would have a 66-year-old wife, but a 70-year-old woman would have a 74-year-old husband. The availability of a socially sanctioned or legally approved sexual partner is a significant influence with respect to maintaining sexual activity, as is borne out by the marked difference between the divorced-widowed-single group and the still-married group. *The decreased sexual activity in the former is not, therefore, a function of age.*

Chronic illness in the group over age 75 places limitations on all activities including sex, and in their study the authors found that many in this group had sexual feelings in the absence of sexual activity, which had stopped because of poor health, either in themselves or in their spouses. In their conclusions, Newman and Nichols feel that their ratings show "a remarkable constancy of the experiencing of the sexual drive within individual persons throughout life," and that "given the

[225]

conditions of reasonably good health and partners who are also physically healthy, elderly persons continue to be sexually active into their seventh, eighth, and ninth decades."

In a brief paper Amulree (1954) reports the same impression. He refers to Pearl's (1925) statistics and questions the term "normal sex life," as to "whatever that may mean."

Amulree's reference to the male climacteric introduces here an issue which is discussed in many papers with various frames of reference: endocrinology, psychology, biology, physiology, etc. A few writers hold the opinion that there is such an entity in the human male, but the majority do not. This issue is not strictly within the scope of this review so that the various arguments and reference works will be omitted. Amulree, however, does refer to the phenomenon of regression, without labeling it as such, when he says that sexual powers do wane at the end of life and that "young men boast of their satisfying sexual experiences whilst old men boast of the regularity and copiousness of their bowel movements."

Bowman (1954) quotes Kinsey, Stokes, and others and arrives at some generalizations and assumptions which do not appear warranted. For example, he refers to the possibility that sexual deprivations in old age may affect longevity — a correlation not borne out by others, not by any currently known facts. He also puts the cart before the horse in his assumption that married men are healthier than single or widowed men by reason of being married. On the other hand, Bowman warns of the dangers of preoccupation with sex by elderly men and women, and is concerned that a lack of satisfactory sexual relationships during adulthood may account in part for the high number of sex offenders among old men. Along with Amulree and others, he pleads for understanding and for better management by physicians of sex life among aged people.

Interestingly enough, more papers deal with the sex life of aging males than with that of aging women. (See Ellis and

Grayhack, 1963; Finkle et al., 1959; Finkle and Moyers, 1960; Finkle and Prian, 1966; Hsu and Chen, 1965; Masters and Johnson, 1966; Stokes, 1951; and Wilson, 1956.)

Stokes's paper was written in 1951, but historically it is considered an "early" paper. Stokes is critical of the Kinsey findings; he questions the effect of endocrines on sex activities and asks for clearer definitions of sexual potency. In addition, he correctly views the sex behavior of the aging male on a longitudinal life history basis, suggesting a lifelong pattern of psychodynamics. He reminds his readers that male fertility may be carried to a very advanced age. In his summary Stokes mentions that "sex potency is held to be an aspect of total personality functioning"—a simple statement, but one which requires constant repetition.

Finkle et al. (1959) present three statistical tables noting occupational status, the frequency of intercourse per year, and marital status for (1) "sexually potent men," (2) "sexually inactive men," and (3) "sexual activity related to advancing age." Their findings for the 55 through 80 plus age group averages are summarized below.

Age Group	Percent Sexually Active	Annual Frequency of Intercourse
55-89	69	29
60-64	63	28
65-69	63	12
70-74	39	25
75-79	24	11
80 +	40	10

Although the sample is small, the findings are generally consistent with those of other studies. The authors comment:

Age is an indisputable factor relating to decline in the frequency of sexual intercourse. It is not an invariable agent, however, as emphasized by Stokes (1951), since some elderly men averred remarkable sexual aggressiveness.

. . . It is often presumed that men engaged in "physical" occupations indulge in sexual activity more frequently than those in "sedentary" or "clerical" occupations. Our data do not support this presumption; individual variations are so great as to preclude generalizations. . . . Within our definition of sexual potency about twice as many men up to 70 years of age were sexually active as those over that age. Among sexually potent men marital status was more influential than occupation or age in encouraging continued sexual activity.

In the Finkle and Prian (1966) paper on the effects of prostatectomy, the statistics are of considerable interest because of the often expressed conviction that prostatectomy causes impotence. In their study they found that of 68 potent men "subjected to prostatectomy, 84 percent retained potency postoperatively." In addition, two men who had been impotent before operation became potent postoperatively. Of those who did become impotent postoperatively, the authors feel such impotence could not be attributed to a single cause. In some it was psychological, while in others it was organic; but in most cases it was a combination of the two factors.

A significant corollary to these findings is found in a paper by Bowers, Cross, and Lloyd (1963).

Among 157 males aged 60 through 74 years, the incidence of impotence was found to rise progressively from 30 per cent to 60 per cent. However, the potent males at these ages continued to experience coitus approximately twenty times per year. The incidence of urologic symptoms or disease, past or present, in these elderly men, was the same for the impotent as for the potent. Likewise, the incidence of non-urologic disease was similar for both groups. *Impo-*

tence in the elderly male is usually independent of physical condition. [Italics added.]

It was not my intention to cover the foreign literature, but the paper by Hsu and Chen (1965), which appeared in an English translation, presents interesting cross-cultural comparisons. Suffice it to say that the observations in this paper are remarkably consistent with the observations and findings of Western cultures.

The sensational work of Masters and Johnson (1966) is of considerable value for this survey. It helps to update our knowledge and thinking with respect to sex and old age. It has the futher significance of presenting facts that go beyond interviewers and the verbal statements of subjects, statements which are often held suspect, for the facts presented by Masters and Johnson derive from direct and minute observations. While the clinical facts are beyond dispute, there are, however, questions about their explanations.

In the chapter entitled "The Aging Male," the authors state:

As the male ages, the major differences in sexual response relate to the duration of each of the phases of the sexual cycle. As opposed to the younger man's well-established reaction pattern of immediate erection, early mounting, and rapid ejaculation, the older man (particularly over 60 years old) is slower to erect, to mount, and to ejaculate. The resolution-phase refractory period also lengthens for the male past the age of 50 years [p. 248].

In short, clinical material gathered to evaluate sexuality of males in the geriatric population has been totally inadequate. This statement should not be construed as reflecting adversely upon prior investigations, but rather should serve to emphasize the difficulties inherent in any attempt to

[229]

evaluate the aging male's sexuality. In order to understand the rigid social resistance expressed toward any investigation of the aging male's sexuality, it may be helpful to recall that Victorian influence upon our society has decreed for years that the aging male possesses little or no socially acceptable sexuality [p. 260].

Briefly, if elevated levels of sexual activity are maintained from earlier years and neither acute nor chronic physical incapacity intervenes, aging males usually are able to continue some form of active sexual expression into the 70- and even 80-year age groups. Even if coital activity has been avoided for long periods of time, men in these age groups can be returned to effective sexual function if adequate stimulation is instituted and interested partners are available [p. 263].

It is clear that these statements are in general concurrence with the observations of other investigators.

Masters and Johnson also advanced six categories to explain their understanding of waning sex in the male.

Under detailed probing the individual basis for alteration in male responsive ability usually falls within one or more of six general categories: (1) monotony of a repetitious sexual relationship (usually translated into boredom with the partner); (2) preoccupation with career or economic pursuits; (3) mental or physical fatigue; (4) overindulgence in food or drink; (5) physical and mental infirmities of either individual or his spouse; and (6) fear of performance associated with or resulting from any of the former categories [p. 264].

This listing would require detailed discussion, because from a psychodynamic point of view their listing is more symptomatic and descriptive than etiological.

Another area of direct observation of sexual behavior in old men comes from the studies of Fisher (1966; Fisher, Gross, and Zuch, 1965), and other sleep-dream researchers. Fisher's papers provide an excellent bibliography for those interested in pursuing this subject further. The erection cycle in a group of relatively healthy men over age 70 was observed by Fisher and his co-workers. In their sleep and dream studies they have noted the occurrence of regular penile erections in sleep. As a result of this observation, ingenious methods to measure the frequency and magnitude of the erection have been devised. From their studies there is no doubt of the elderly male's capacity for erection and sexual arousal. Fisher (1966) cautions that "there was no particular relationship between extent of nocturnal erection and the degree of activity in their sexual lives" (p. 577). So far as I am aware, no comparable observation of measuring device is available for the study of female sex arousal during sleep and dreaming.

The number of papers dealing with sex and aging females is much smaller than those dealing with the aging male. In one such paper, Christenson and Gagnon (1965) present data gathered from 241 white females aged 50 to 90, covering six areas of sexual behavior — coitus, petting, masturbation, nocturnal sex dreams, homosexual contacts, and contacts with animals. (They do not report on the last two items.) The sampling was also broken down by age groups, religious differences, and marital status.

At age 50 marital coitus was the major sexual activity in seven-eighths (87.5 percent) of the married women, occurring on an average of once a week. At age 55 the frequency had decreased slightly, but the percentage still participating had not changed. By the age of 60, however, participation in marital coitus had dropped to 70 percent, and at age 65 it was 50 percent. The incidence of self-masturbation among these same married women remained fairly constant: 30 percent reported masturbation at age 50, and 25 percent masturbated at age 65. Nocturnal sex dreams to orgasm occurred at a similar rate

[231]

to that of masturbation: 27 percent at age 50 and 19 percent at age 65.

For women no longer married the statistics are different, for obvious reasons. At age 50, however, 37 percent were having postmarital coitus, but this percentage dropped sharply in the next decade. The compensatory activity for these women was masturbation, the incidence of which doubles that for women who were still married. Dreams to orgasm, on the other hand, were very similar in frequency in both married and unmarried women.

Christenson and Gagnon pointed out that there is a consistency of life style in women, as in men, that those who were strongly motivated to sexual experience when younger continued to be so in old age. "The capacity to have orgasm seems to be a strong factor in the desire of the female to continue coitus after marriage ends." They also suggest that since sexual behavior does continue in late life, it should be examined as part of the general adjustment of the older female.

Masters and Johnson include a chapter on "The Aging Female." They feel "it will require at least another decade to obtain the cooperation of aging women in numbers sufficient to provide biologic data of statistical significance" (p. 223), and that we are currently dealing only with clinical impressions.

Their observations on aging females include the same factors observed in young women, the physical details of which are left to the reader to examine—such factors as the flush, reaction of nipples and clitoris, the external labia, etc. However, "Regardless of involutional changes in the reproductive organs, the aging human female is fully capable of sexual performance at orgasmic response levels, particularly if she is exposed to regularity of effective sexual stimulation" (p. 238). (In this connection Kinsey et al. report the case of a woman of 90 who responded regularly to masturbation.) Also: "It has become increasingly evident that the psyche plays a part at least equal to, if not greater than, that of an unbalanced endocrine system in determining the sex drive of women during the post-menopausal period of their lives," and that "elevation of sexual responsiveness rarely results directly from the administration of estrogen or estrogen-like products" (p. 242).

I refer here to the effects of the menopause, for there are many myths and conflicts as to its effects on the sex life of women. Scattered throughout the literature are reports indicating that some women believe that the sex response is finished at the time of the menopause. On the other hand, there are more women, freed from the fear of pregnancy, who intensify their sex activity and experience a second honeymoon in their fifties.

Masters and Johnson confirm again what has been reported by many others, that a woman who has had a happy marriage and enjoyed sex relations in her early years will continue in the same way in her postmenopausal years. The converse is also true. Reference is made to the trend in our population toward an aging society of women without men. In regard to such women, Masters and Johnson reaffirm what others have said: "Deprived of normal sexual outlets, they exhaust themselves physically in conscious or unconscious effort to dissipate their accumulated and frequently unrecognized sexual tensions. . . . In short, there is no time limit drawn by the advancing years to female sexuality" (pp. 246-247).

There are a number of miscellaneous articles in the literature which deal with topics related to sex and the elderly. One of the persistent ongoing lines of research deals with studies of endocrine effect in menopausal and postmenopausal years. As mentioned earlier, the effect of endocrine replacement therapy is a debatable issue — whether it affects libido, cosmetic appearance, or the general state of well-being has not been definitively established. Masters and Ballew (1955) make reference to the third sex, a neuter sex among the aged, which they feel is helped by endocrine therapy. A peripheral problem

[233]

is the search, more by elderly men than women, for drugs and special foods designed to increase potency. Such people are easv prey for quacks and gimmick advertising. Rubin (1965) deals adequately with this topic.

An article by Natter (1964) deserves passing comment. He states that while there have been reports of women giving birth at 60, 62, and 83 years of age, such reports have not been verified. The author himself reports delivery of viable children from two women at ages 50 and 52.

Greenblatt and Scarpa-Smith (1959) report on two women, ages 51 and 65, with strong sexual urges. The authors use the term "nymphomaniacal compulsion" more as a pejorative than as an accurate description, and nowhere do they adequately define the term. The authors' attitude is revealed when they report that by endocrine therapy the sex drive was held in "complete abeyance," which is termed a "beneficial" result. I find this a debatable conclusion.

A sociological problem linked to the issues discussed in this survey is one highlighted by Dean (1966). He refers to the finding, which had been reported in newspapers throughout the country, that many aged men and women were living together without benefit of marriage because legal marriage might deprive them of pensions or Social Security benefits. This situation arose out of an inequity in the Social Security Act, which states that a widow will receive 82.5 percent of her deceased husband's benefits only if she does not remarry. In some cases remarriage would mean that the combined dole would be smaller than her original one. In 1964 statistics showed that more than two million widows and widowers over 62 were drawing Social Security, yet only 6,000 or 0.3 percent remarried! It follows, says the author, that because of this restrictive clause old people are "forced to live alone in loneliness or together in sin." A bright note about this problem is that legislation is being passed to correct the legal inequity.

Kassell (1966) presents a fascinating suggestion for the solution of many of the problems of the aged. Because of the greater ratio of older women to older men, he feels that there is a need for polygyny. If a man could marry two, three, four, or five women over age 60, such marriages would be beneficial in the following ways: (1) They would create the opportunity to re-establish a meaningful family group. (2) Diets would improve. Married couples subsist on a more adequate diet than do widows and widowers. (3) The polygymous marriage offers the opportunity to pool funds so that there is enough money for all. (4) In matters of illness many aged persons would not need nursing home care if responsible people at home were available to nurse the infirm person. (5) Two or more women working together would lighten the burdens of housework. (6) And finally, with respect to sex, polygymous marriage offers a solution to a number of sexual problems, especially the legal availability of partners. In any event, the author advances his suggestion seriously with full recognition of all the social and psychological obstacles to its fulfillment.

A survey such as this would not be complete without reference to one more condition of sexuality in the aged. Several authors (Levin, 1965; Stokes, 1951; Wilson, 1956) comment on the issue of the sexual interest of older men in young female children — an interest or behavior often viewed, unfortunately, as taboo or criminal.

In this connection, Levin makes an astute observation: "It is worth noting that the elderly female is usually given greater permission to obtain direct satisfaction of libido by means of bodily contact with children, either through sleeping arrangements or otherwise, whereas elderly males are apt to be considered perverted in either a heterosexual or homosexual direction if they seek such contacts."

Wilson expresses a similar view: "Innocent fondling and petting of children by old men is often misinterpreted as an attempt to seduce them. Old men can love children with no aberrant sexual thoughts." Wilson also feels that the incidence

[235]

and intent of such "crimes" is exaggerated, although the fact is that sex crimes do indeed occur.

In summary, the results of studies in the literature demonstrate that there are many invalid conclusions, myths, and misconceptions about sexuality in old age. Reports and surveys of sex and old age are still accompanied by some defensiveness, and these reports are essentially sociological and statistical. The studies conducted so far should be regarded as a basis for further refined studies, particularly of individual experiences. There is a need for greater sophistication in theorizing with respect to the psychology and emotional aspects of sex and old age. A greater understanding of the significance of the psychosexual life in old age will undoubtedly enable those who are in a position to help old people to evaluate and assess more accurately the total personality organization of the elderly person. Studies on sex in old age singularly have not referred to love, affection, tenderness, and object relationships as part of the total psychosexual picture. Sexual intercourse by itself cannot tell the whole story of a human condition. It is to be hoped that future studies will consider the total person, of whom the sex life is but a part, an instrument serving to express the success or failure of the total human relationship.

A revealing and still relevant comment on old age was made by Plato 2,000 years ago in his dialogue between Sophocles and the aged Cephalus. Sophocles is asked: "How does love suit with age . . . are you still the man you were?" He replies that he is glad to have escaped the "mad and furious master" of the passions and that he has developed a clear sense of calm and freedom. Cephalus affirms what modern writers have said about the genetic and psychodynamic view of the longitudinal continuation of earlier interests and the capacity for enjoyment in old age when he adds, ". . . for he who is of a calm and happy nature will hardly feel the pressure of age, but to him who is of an opposite disposition youth and age are equally a burden."

[236]

Sex and Old Age: A Further Review of the Literature

MARTIN A. BEREZIN, M.D.

MY FIRST SURVEY on "Sex and Old Age: A Review of the Literature" (1969) covered the literature through 1967. One might reasonably suspect that during the last nine years a great deal more on the subject would have appeared, especially in view of the liberalized attitude toward sex on the part of the general populace and the more open and explicit depiction of sex in the theatre, movies, and other forms of popular culture.

But in reviewing the scientific literature since 1967, we note that publications on the topic of sex and old age continue to show very little variation in content from my first survey. The earlier studies repeatedly indicated that the most consistent factor in the consideration of sex and old age was the individual's comparative level of sexual activity. Those who are sexually active when young are sexually active when old; those who are not sexually active when young are not sexually active when old. Subsequent studies have confirmed this point repeatedly.

Another finding revealed the defensiveness among those who were studying this subject. For instance, it was considered to be "indecent" for a young person to study the sex life of an aged person, that is, a person old enough to be his parent. This was especially true in discussing or investigating the sex life of elderly women. The carry-over of taboo from the nineteenth century with respect to female sexuality has persisted for many decades. And while it is true that there is more openness with regard to sex in general, this taboo still persists in a variety of ways despite sex education and explicit portrayals of and references to sexuality in the media.

One significant change is that articles on sex and old age are appearing more frequently in the popular literature, such as newspapers and magazines. They usually take on a tone of exhortation, demanding that elderly people should have the right to have a sex life without being stigmatized by society. Obviously, the scientific literature has made the general public more aware of the social taboos and prejudices which have for so long troubled many people about sex in old age. But the defensive tone of these articles demonstrates that the prejudice they are decrying still exists.

One example of this is seen in another medium, the movies. In the motion picture *Harry and Tonto*, a particular scene was apparently shocking to many viewers. An elderly man who has been hitchhiking is picked up by an attractive young woman in a convertible car. He is grateful to her for the ride. Within minutes she informs him that she is a "hooker" and that she wants to have intercourse with him because, as she says, she feels "horny." Whereupon he says to her, in effect, "But I'm too old for you," and she blithely replies, "Oh, I've had them older than you; don't worry." In the next scene the convertible is closed, and the implication is clear that sexual intercourse takes place. The audible gasps from the audience that this scene elicited shows that for many sex in old age is still a shocking revelation.

During a television program depicting the life of the elderly, one woman in her late seventies, a widow twice over, remarked she had a lover who was 79 years old, and that they frequently engaged in sexual intercourse. She made the statement that if she did not have sex she would rather be dead for, she said, life was not worth living without sex.

[238]

As an indication of the changing mores among elderly people regarding their sex life, I am reminded of a bumper sticker which read: "I am not a dirty old man. I am a sexy senior citizen."

In the book, *Masturbation: From Infancy to Senescence* (1975), I wrote the chapter on "Masturbation and Old Age." It is unique that a whole chapter on this topic could have been written, indicating the growing interest in the sex life of the elderly.

In spite of the residue of defensiveness, the general public is becoming more aware of some of the conditions, statistics, factors, myths, misconceptions, and prejudices about sex in general, and specifically about sex in old age.

One condition I referred to in my first review of the literature on sex and old age still persists. Studies on sex in old age are concerned with the physical aspects of sex, such as the fact that elderly people can continue to have sex, that elderly people enjoy sex, that elderly people masturbate. The earlier articles were generally statistical and physical observations. What was missing was any sense that an aged person's sexual relations are in the service of a love relationship, an object tie in which tenderness and affection are significant. The articles published since my original review of the literature exhibit the same one-sidedness. They refer to frequency, the physical aspects, statistics, and so forth.

One particular paper is disappointing in that it promises something more in its title — "Factors Influencing Sexual Behavior" (Greenblatt and Leng, 1972). However, instead of referring to the possibility of love as a factor in sexual behavior, the paper has an endocrine-organic approach. The authors list some factors which affect the intensity and direction of human sexuality, such as "gonadal integrity, chromosomal determinants, external genital adequacy, socioeconomic influences, endogenous and exogenous hormonal dependency, and possibly hypothalamic sensitization during fetal life"

[239]

(p. 49). Even though the authors refer to the "psyche," their comments in this direction are scanty and superficial. Libido, they say, "is a chemical test-tube equation," but is not further defined. They report on several cases in which endocrine therapy played a significant role, but each of the cases is a pathological condition to begin with, such as "male pseudohermaphroditism" treated by surgery and endocrines. In a situation where a frigid woman was treated with endocrines, the authors state that the substance was no better than a placebo and that "of all the hormonal preparations, androgens alone consistently intensified her desire for sexual relations; the direction was always heterosexual, and gratifications could be equated with dosage" (p. 53). This finding is not consistent with the results reported by other researchers, especially those of Masters and Johnson (1966). In addition, Greenblatt and Leng reveal a pejorative value system in their use of the terms "nymphomania" and "satyriasis."

Comfort (1974) takes the exhortative approach in his paper "Sexuality in Old Age." This short paper offers no new information about sex and old age. Comfort states repeatedly that sex in old age is acceptable and even desirable. He indulges in a number of caveats against those who fail to realize that sex for old people is a natural phenomenon. He gives no bibliography, although he quotes and refers to Simone de Beauvoir, Tom Lehrer, and Richard Burton, the Victorian anthropologist. For the most part Comfort states the obvious. For example: "The elderly have been in a sense hocussed out of continuing sexual activity by a society which disallows it for the old . . ." (p. 440). His popular approach may be seen in his final statements: "It is rather nice, too, that a lot of older people have been resexualized — or even fully sexualized for the first time — by turned-on sons and daughters. That is a service we can do for the elderly in the recreational and relational use of sex which compensates in part for the service which they did us in its reproductive use" (p. 442). This article adds nothing new

[240]

or useful to the literature on sex in the old, and the title promises more than it delivers.

One foreign contribution is a paper entitled "Sex in the Aged" (de Nicola and Peruzza, 1974), a study which comes out of Pavia and Venice, Italy. References are made to already-known conditions and factors about sex in the aged, and the authors add some specific cultural determinants. Early in the paper they comment that unfortunately sex is "still considered a duty and not a free exhibition of the personality. . . ."

I suspect that a loose correlation with respect to a determining influence is made in another way when they refer to the following: "A negative influence is often exerted on young persons by pornography with obscenities but not true eroticism. This sets a wrong pattern for ideal sexuality and leads to secondary impotence, especially in those who have 'ejaculatio praecox' or have bad experiences during their first sexual intercourses. A physiologic balance during youth may therefore influence the patterns of aging" (p. 380, italics added).

They go on to state that as the man ages his erection may be less strong and the ejaculant less abundant, but there is no loss of interest and satisfactory effect. In women, however, they add — and this sounds like an old Victorian approach — there is "always the possibility that, during adulthood, sexual intercourse has been a passive, painful or even disgusting duty and experience. Thus they are induced to forget about sex as soon as their age permits" (p. 380). We shall see later that this comment is in contradiction to another finding in this same paper.

The authors make an important point — again one that is well known — that sexual impairment does not occur because of advancing age but because of certain inhibiting factors. In one survey the authors studied 53 men and 32 women between the ages of 62 and 81. They were not affected by disease. With regard to sexual activity, 45 men and 17 women were still active "with a maximum of five intercourses weekly and a minimum of one intercourse monthly." In the 62-71 age group

[241]

the mean frequency was twice a week, and for ages 72-81 it was three times a month. The contradiction about female sexuality is contained in their observation that the women "masturbated more often than did the men and with more satisfaction in some cases."

One encouraging note in this paper is the statement made at the end, referring to the fact that social prophylaxis of many conditions, such as promoting home care of aged persons, helping them financially, and adding comfort without exerting authority in nursing homes and hospitals, can be very helpful. Under these conditions "any inhibition of loving and sexual activities is harmful, and it is appropriate to promote the formation of new couples and their living together" (p. 382). What is encouraging here is the reference to loving and to couples living together.

In a paper called "Crime and Delinquency Among the Aged in Israel" (Bergman and Amir, 1973), I found some comments about sex and old age that may be of peripheral interest. First they state: "The available criminal statistics permit only a general orientation in regard to 'aged criminality,' a category consisting of offenses committed by persons 60 years of age and older . . ." (p. 149). Listed among the various offenses are "sexual offenses." This category includes both first offenders and recidivists "who from relatively early age were sexually maladjusted." In other words, it is consistent, as we have noted before, that what happens in old age is part of a continuum in the lifelong process. Among the sexually maladjusted are homosexuals, compulsive exhibitionists, and pedophiliacs. The explanation offered for first offenders is the deterioration of inhibitions consistent with the aging process. Under the category "offenses by women" is the following succinct comment: "Some of the women in the 'criminal population' are petty thieves. Some are compulsive offenders. Some are old courtesans turned 'madam'" (p. 152). This last statement leaves room for philosophical reflection and definition of what are sex offenses and criminals. With respect to crime among the aged, Weiss (1973) indicates what happens to the aging psychopath as he mellows: his criminal tendencies diminish with time.

S. Kent's (1975) paper, "Being Aware of a Patient's Sexual Problems Should Be the Concern of Every Physician," considers "Sex After 45." It is not as superficial and naïve as the title may lead one to suspect. The author makes some important points. Aside from reporting much of what is already known, such as the fact that most sexual disorders are primarily psychogenic in origin, even in elderly patients, or that older people are not expected to have sexual needs or desires, he makes reference to the ' "dirty old man' [who] has long been considered curious and depraved; [and] now with women's liberation, the 'dirty old woman' has emerged" (p. 140).

Kent refers to a survey by Burnap and Golden (1967), from which the information emerges that "the most common problems reported were lack of orgasm, frigidity, concern over frequency of intercourse, lack of general sex information, impotence, dyspareunia, and *lack of affection during intercourse*" (p. 142, italics added). A significant finding is the reported attitude of the physician during the interview. The 29 physicians who routinely asked about sexual problems while taking a history encountered almost twice as many as the 31 who asked about such problems *only* when indicated. The 18 physicians who showed obvious signs of discomfort such as blushing, fidgeting, and looking away frequently during the survey interview reported only one-fifth the number of patients with sexual problems that the other 42 physicians did. Furthermore, the authors report that when the physicians were asked how they treated such problems, 22 said they just "talked" with the patient; 18 gave reassurance or allayed misconceptions, or both; two gave placebos, that is, hormone injections; 13 offered no therapy; and five used specific measures. When asked about their training in managing sexual

[243]

problems, seven percent replied they had some training in medical school; 10 percent had some at the postgraduate level; and 83 percent had none. Ninety percent felt more training was needed.

Kent goes on to add that among the situations in which the physician may seek information about a patient's sex life are:

1. When he is performing a general medical workup on a new patient with no specific complaint.

2. When a patient comes to him with a specific sexual problem.

3. When a patient's disease or physical condition affects sexual behavior.

4. When he suspects that a patient is using a complaint to mask a sexual problem [p. 142].

The author then elaborates on the conditions that are inherent and intrinsic to each of these four situations. Finally, he states: "In all the described situations, regardless of whether the physician chooses to treat the problems, he should consider detecting them a matter of responsibility" (p. 142). It is indeed unfortunate that such a caveat should be necessary, but it is encouraging that it is being made.

Some of the more intensively pursued research studies on the sex life of the elderly have been carried out by the Duke University Center for the Study of Aging and Human Development. The studies are reported in several papers. Two of these (Verwoerdt, Pfeiffer, and Wang, 1969a, 1969b) are longitudinal studies going back to 1954. The data the authors report are part of a larger, interdisciplinary study of physiological, psychological, and social changes occurring in old age. Their subjects were 260 community volunteers, aged 60 or more at the beginning of the project. The data were taken at three different times, separated by an interval of three to four years. The initial studies were done between 1955 and 1957 (study I); they were repeated between 1959 and 1961 (study II); and

[244]

again in 1964 (study III). It is noted that 67 percent of the sub-jects were white and 33 percent black. Further, no subjects who were hospitalized, bedridden, or otherwise immobilized were included in the study, and the ages of the subjects at the time of the first study ranged from 60 to 94. There was a naturally expected attrition in the number of subjects over the years. The focus was on sexual *activity* and sexual *interest*. The findings were broken down into categories of degree of sexual activity, incidence of sexual activity, and patterns of sexual activity; and degree of sexual interest, incidence of sexual interest, and patterns of sexual interest. There was a

> tendency toward a gradual decline of sexual activity with advancing age. . . . The decline of activity in the group was such that by the late 80's the frequency of intercourse ap-proached zero. Nevertheless, individual exceptions oc-curred. Among male subjects surviving into the 80s and 90s continued sexual activity was no great rarity; about one-fifth of these men reported having sexual intercourse once a month or less [Verwoerdt, Pfeiffer, and Wang, 1969b, p. 140].

The subjects were grouped into two categories depending on whether they had no sex activity or some sex activity "re-gardless of the degree." According to the statistics in the various studies the "incidence of sexual activity approached zero by the late 80s." With advancing age, "there was a grad-ual decline in the proportion of sexually active subjects. For all age groups, the incidence of sexual activity was higher in men than women" (pp. 141-142). The authors also include the effect of marital status on the incidence of sexual activity. The female groups showed the most obvious differences. Sexual activity among unmarried women was almost negligible.

In contrast to this, the unmarried men reported a signifi-cant amount of sexual activity (35, 80, and 55%, respec-

[245]

tively, in the three studies). In fact, in studies II and III, the unmarried men had higher proportions than married men. Of course, the number of unmarried male subjects was too small for definite conclusions. The incidence of activity among married men, for the three studies, was 57, 53, and 36% respectively; for the married women these figures were 43, 41, and 42%. Thus, in the course of the three studies, male subjects showed greater change in the incidence of activity than did the women. Married men were more active than married women in studies I and II, but, by the time of study III, the activity of married women was slightly greater [pp. 142-143].

We learn that the degree of sexual interest was restricted to interest in sexual intercourse, and this was rated on a four-point scale: 0, no interest; 1, weak; 2, moderate; 3, strong. The degree of sexual interest "declined with age in such a manner that a strong degree of sexual interest became exceptional after the age of 70 and was practically nonexistent after 75" (p. 145). However, exceptions were noted. One finding was that in the older age group there was more interest than in other groups, but the average degree of sexual interest in this group of subjects was weak in all three studies. "The higher mean score for study III reflected the preservation of mild to moderate degrees of sexual interest among subjects surviving to the time of study III" (p. 145).

The incidence of interest declined in women more than in men with advancing age. "For all age groups, women had a lower incidence than men" (p. 146). The authors do not overlook a significant variable in referring to an increased rate of interest in subjects in study II, and attribute this to the fact that these subjects were biologically advantaged in the sense of their greater longevity. Reference is made to unmarried women: "The increasing incidence of sexual interest among unmarried women . . . was probably related to the increasing proportions of recently widowed women" (p. 147).

[246]

Some special features of sexual behavior in the aging are summarized:

1. Men were generally more sexually active than women, but in the married group, the differences became smaller in the course of the three studies and by the time of study III, married women had higher incidence of sexual activity.

2. Among men surviving into the 80s, and 90s, continued sexual activity was no great rarity; about one-fifth of these men reported they were still sexually active.

3. Although the degree of sexual interest declined with age, about one-half of the subjects surviving into the 80s and 90s reported sexual interest of mild or moderate degree.

4. In women, sexual interest tended to be at a relatively low ebb during the late 60s and early 70s.

5. In both men and women, the incidence of interest usually exceeded that of activity. This interest-activity discrepancy was greater for men than for women. In men, the discrepancy tended to become greater with age, but in women, it remained approximately the same.

6. Unmarried men had approximately the same level of activity and interest as married men. What is especially interesting is the finding that unmarried men more often reported a pattern of increasing activity and interest.

7. In women, the incidence of continuously absent activity patterns steadily increased with age, in contrast to the pattern of continuously absent interest. In men, on the other hand, the pattern of continuously absent interest became more frequent with age.

8. The difference between men and women with regard to sustained interest became less with increasing age to the point where, after the age of 78, women had a higher incidence of this pattern.

9. The configuration of decreasing activity and inter-

[247]

est patterns occurred, in women, most frequently during the 60 to 65 age range, as compared to the 72-77 age range for men.

10. In men, the incidence of increasing activity or interest patterns changed relatively little with age. In other words, even though the overall picture in the subjects was one of decline, in roughly one-fourth of the male subjects an increase in the degree of activity or interest or both was observed, regardless of age [pp. 151-152].

In a paper entitled "Sexuality in the Aging Individual," Pfeiffer (1974) reconfirms the various findings about sex in the elderly as reported in the literature, both his own and cohort writings as well as those of others. He makes reference to the existing sense of taboo in society toward sex life in the aged. He refers to the fact that there is no biological limitation to sexual capacity and that persons who have been active in their younger years tend to be active in their later years as well. Pfeiffer urges clinicians to understand the needs of the elderly and to respect the continuation of the aged person's life style, including his or her sex life. He points out that certain conditions such as depression or myocardial infarction may interrupt sexual capacity, but need not cause permanent cessation. Finally, he makes a special plea for privacy for the elderly, so as to assure the opportunity for sexual expression. There also should be greater acceptance of the solitary sex life of the nonpartnered elderly. Pfeiffer's paper does not in essence say anything new, but his plea for the nonpartnered elderly is consistent with the times and mores with respect to sexuality today.

Another paper, entitled "Determinants of Sexual Behavior in Middle and Old Age" (Pfeiffer and Davis, 1972), reconfirms that early sex life activity is a determinant for sexual behavior in the elderly. Pfeiffer and Davis used a different methodological approach in that stepwise multiple regression analyses were made permitting the emergence of a number of variables which might otherwise be missed.

The authors add another variable in what is considered to be a determinant — not only early sexual activity, but also the factor of enjoyment with respect to sexual relations in the younger years. They state: ". . . for women, the enjoyment of sexual relations in younger years, rather than frequency or level of sexual interest in younger years, seems to be of particular importance in determining the extent of present sexual interest and frequency of intercourse" (p. 156). This comment comes closer to the thesis I have tried to suggest in terms of determinants of sexual behavior, namely, object relations. We hope yet to see a study on sex life in the elderly that can work postdictively back to the issue of object relations and the significance of frequency, interest, and enjoyment of intercourse as an indicator of a love relationship.

The authors point out a significant statistical observation, one that is known but not sufficiently emphasized in other papers: The average life expectancy of women exceeds that of men by seven years (Metropolitan Life Insurance Company Statistical Bulletin, August, 1967). In addition, women marry men who are on the average some four years older. Therefore, women can expect to experience an average of 11 years of widowhood, and only a very small proportion of widowed women remarry. A much larger percentage of widowed men remarry. With each passing year women in our society become increasingly supernumerary.

Thus, according to the 1970 census figures, at age 65 there are 138.5 women for every 100 men in the United States, and at age 75 this ratio has risen to 156.2 women for every 100 men. It is the authors' interpretation that much of the decline in sexual interest among aging women is not physiologic but is defensive, that is, protective. It may well be adaptive to inhibit sexual strivings when little opportunity for sexual fulfillment exists. With advancing age, fewer and fewer women have a sexual partner available. The remedy would seem to lie in efforts directed at prolonging vigor and extending the life span of men [pp. 157-158].

In a paper entitled "Emotional Quality and Physical Quantity of Sexual Activity in Aging Males," Finkle (1973) points out that the male is generally the lifelong aggressor in sexual relations, but "the wife usually regulates the frequency of intercourse by granting and denying coitus." Finkle reaffirms some previous writings (Finkle and Moyers, 1960; Finkle, Moyers, Tobenkin, and Karg, 1959; Finkle and Prian, 1966) that impotence in elderly men is usually independent of physical condition. He adds that some men feel that it is necessary to continue to behave in a sexual way reminiscent of earlier years. In other words, some men have a "self-deprecating appraisal of 'what should be right.'"

Finkle includes two case reports in his paper. He disclaims any special psychiatric training, but he has an objective approach. The first patient was a college graduate, healthy, active, who had a reasonably good relationship with his wife except for sexual relations. The only thing that was discovered on physical examination was a mild congestive prostatitis. The physician explained to the patient that this was not the cause of his impotence, and had a long discussion with him about prostatitis in general. When the prostatic inflamation improved and the patient was reassured, a new problem was encountered: the patient's wife remained reluctant to attempt intercourse because, she claimed, he was unable to succeed. Moreover, she refused to come in for further interviews on her own, and she preferred to "utilize sexual inactivity as a tool by which she [could] control or irritate her husband. . . . His straitlaced background and his marriage [led] him to fear the personal and social stigmata of seeking an extramarital sexual outlet. Thus, he will, unfortunately, continue to suffer sexual denial at home" (p. 76).

[250]

The second case was a 51-year-old, black bus driver who complained of dysuria following extramarital sexual contacts. It turned out that during the 15 years of his first and only marriage, intercourse had occurred about twice a week, but "because his wife was a very religious woman" she was sexually unenthusiastic and grudging about sexual relations. So he had separated from his wife and for 18 months had lived with one paramour. His dysuria had occurred during these 18 months. Finkle put the patient on a health regime which he responded to satisfactorily. Following this, the patient returned to his wife. For two months his wife refused sexual intercourse because she was fearful of infection, and so he masturbated once a week as his only sexual outlet. Sometime later the patient was seen again, and a carcinoma of the prostate was revealed. A radical perineal prostatectomy was done and recovery was uneventful. At six weeks postoperatively the patient was informed he could resume sexual activity. Four months later he found another girlfriend and successfully engaged in intercourse twice in the next month. "The sensation of pleasure with ejaculation was identical to his preoperative status, but there was, of course, no fluid ejaculate at the time of climax owing to the usual retrograde ejaculation secondary to the prostatectomy" (p. 77).

One important point among others that Finkle makes here is that it is erroneous to believe that impotence invariably follows radical perineal prostatectomy. The cooperation of a willing partner accomplished reinstatement of this man's sexual competence with a minimum of psychological support. Finkle points out that there may at times be an iatrogenic impact on sexual potency:

It is probable that those urologic surgeons who believe that impotency is an unavoidable sequel to radical prostatectomy transmit their pessimism either directly or by implication to their patients. Thus, the physician's attitude serves to suppress, inadvertently or otherwise, any prospect for

[251]

postoperative resumption of coitus that the patient may have anticipated [p. 77].

The information about radical perineal prostatectomy as opposed to simple prostatectomy is a new addition to the literature. In summary, Finkle recommends supportive measures and encouragement for people who have problems of impotence.

Christenson and Johnson (1973) present data that is reasonably new in their paper on "Sexual Patterns in a Group of Older Never-Married Women." The authors report that never-married women at older ages are relatively uncommon in the general population, and they make up less than nine percent of the total population of white women of that age group. The interviews done in this group were very sensitive and very difficult, and had to be done with great professional skill. This is especially true because the generation presented in this paper were people who were born largely before the turn of the century. The authors express the hope that in future years such data gathering will become much easier both for the interviewer and the subject.

Christenson and Johnson refer to a serious methodological problem that has been referred to in other papers with respect to the study of female sexuality: if coitus alone is to be representative of the state of affairs, then there is a serious problem. A bias is evident in the infrequent attention given to the less obvious female outlets such as masturbation, dreams to orgasm, and homosexual activities. The authors give a description of the sample of their never-married women.

Another variable measured is "attitudes toward marriage." Of the entire sample of 71 women studied, only 10 stated they had never wanted to marry. Twenty others expressed some desire to be married. The remainder reported they had very much wanted to be married, usually when they were younger. This is striking in comparison to the statistics in a college

[252]

sample, in which 90 percent of over 4,000 women indicated a strong desire to marry. It appears, therefore, that the lack of a wish to be married is an important determinant in remaining single.

The interviewees expressed a number of reasons for their failure to marry. Some of the reasons referred to inhibitions, while others appeared to be rationalizations. Explanations included:

"My mother always possessed me and prevented me from marrying. . . ." "My mother made me fear and dread marriage because of its frequent pregnancies. . . ." "I was just too busy in my work to have any boy friends." "I did not want to lose my identity in marriage." "There is no hunger in me for it unless it is an intellectual union with a man" [p. 85].

A low self-image was a variable that accounted for a negative effect on social and sexual expectations. Some of the women were markedly overweight, some were exceptionally tall, two were very thin, one had gray hair since she was 15. What stands out is that 30 percent had actually at some time or another considered themselves engaged, usually during their twenties. They reported that the engagements ranged from a period of several months to 17 years.

Another variable involved was that strong homosexual interests on the part of several of the subjects may have played a role in sidetracking them from marriage.

The authors refer to the work of Pfeiffer, Verwoerdt, and Davis (1972) and the latter's report of the lack of data on sexual behavior among older never-married women. There is a methodological problem, and Christenson and Johnson state:

From the viewpoint of a male investigator, it is perhaps difficult to envisage a life span of 50 to 60 years virtually devoid of either heterosexual or homosexual responses and

[253]

also of solitary sexual behavior. Certainly the majority of older single women in the present sample do not report such a low profile. But, of our 71 subjects, almost a third (23 cases) revealed that they had never experienced any overt sexual activity beyond simple petting [p. 85].

In fact, five of these people had never even experienced petting, and 11 had not gone beyond kissing. Erotic arousal had been minimal. All of the 23 women mentioned above were, of course, virgins. "Moreover, none of them had ever experienced an orgasm from any source—masturbation, sex dreams, petting, or homosexual experiences" (p. 85).

It is striking also to hear the descriptions from these women about their lack of sexual experience.

> "I have not missed sex ever."
> "I worked hard and didn't need sex."
> "I was trained against sex as a young girl. I think I'm rather cold perhaps...."
> "I have never been loved by anyone."
> "My father was wonderful. He taught me about all the things to avoid. . . ."
> "Mother told me to avoid all sex, never even talk about it . . ." [pp. 85-86].

It is perhaps not surprising to learn that these same virginal women reported a much higher degree of religious devoutness than the remainder of the sample.

The authors make a statement, which may be prophetic and certainly deserves to be passed on, namely, these "histories were collected more than two decades ago, and it is just possible that they will prove to be the last of their kind—true museum pieces—for today we are surely in the midst of a change toward freer life styles for single women" (p. 86).

Of the rest of the sample, over three-fourths of the subjects had at some time masturbated to orgasm, almost two-thirds had experienced intercourse, and more than half had reported having orgasmic sex dreams. In addition, eight subjects described fairly extensive homosexual contacts.

The authors point out that there is a diminishing sexual activity with aging. One significant statistic here is that at age 50 the incidence of masturbation had decreased by only five percent. By age 60, however, among the remaining single women, some of them still masturbated, and one engaged in coitus twice a year. The authors state cogently: "Since masturbation activity was used as one measure, obviously one cannot attribute the lessening of this particular sexual outlet with the passing of years to the unavailability of a coital partner" (p. 88)

In a comparison with previously married women, it was discovered that after the termination of their marriages formerly married women might retain more contact with eligible male partners and could also use a higher degree of social skill in developing these contacts, possibly with the aim of remarriage; this is in contradistinction to the never-married women.

The authors record the differences in early sexual levels and compare these with late sexual behavior. As noted in other situations for sex in old age, comparative activity persists, so that in this group of women the early "highs" (sexually active) showed over 80 percent masturbating at age 45 and 70 percent at age 50 and 55. In contrast, 21, 18, and 12 percent, respectively, were reported by the "lows" (less sexually active).

Studies on the aging homosexual are extremely rare.[1] The authors report eight cases with extensive homosexual histories, and yet none of them was exclusively homosexual, for all reported heterosexual experience in coitus as well. Strikingly, in the case of two women, homosexual relations did provide the first social-sexual outlet, taking place more than 50 times in

---

[1] We hope that with the openness of the Gay Liberation Movement we shall be able, in the near future, to make further studies of homosexuality and aging.

one case and several hundred in the other, all before age 30. In neither case did it recur after that age. One of these subjects reported coitus first at age 41, following a 10-year interval of occasional heterosexual petting to climax. The other woman told of a four-year break between the change from homosexual to heterosexual behavior.

With regard to their findings on menopause, Christenson and Johnson report the usual variations. One fourth of the women experienced an increase, another fourth reported a decrease, and the remainder, 50 percent, felt no change in erotic levels at the termination of menopause. Pfeiffer, Verwoerdt, and Davis (1972) report that in 41 women, aged 51-55, 22 percent felt no decline in sexual interest or activity.

In summary, it appears that recent studies of sex and old age essentially confirm the findings reported in earlier studies. There has, however, been a shift in the public awareness of sex and old age. Consistent with the current attitudes and mores about sex as portrayed and depicted explicitly in the various media, the public has become more aware and knowledgeable about the real facts concerning sex and old age.

Discussion

ADRIAN VERWOERDT, M.D.

RESEARCH ON SEX IN OLD AGE is relatively recent. Publications on adult sexuality began to appear in the late nineteenth century, on adolescent and child sexuality 20 to 30 years later (1920s), and on sex in senescence again some 20 to 30 years later (1950s). This development is related to several factors. As Dr. Berezin has elaborated, the social attitudes toward the sexual activity of older people have been marked by taboos, prejudices, and denial. Despite this, the increasing numbers of older people and the emergence of gerontology and geriatrics have focused attention on the problems of living in old age, including those of sex. Finally, attention has been focused on old age as a phase with its own opportunities for leisure and recreation. As time goes on, more healthy people who are vigorous, look forward to leisure, and enjoy sex, will reach old age. In my discussion of Dr. Berezin's review of studies in this important area, I would like to single out the following for further elaboration: (a) the effects of aging on sex, (b) the quality of sexual experience in later life, and (c) the sexual problems of old age.

THE EFFECTS OF AGING ON SEX

The final common path of human sexual behavior is under the influence of many factors, including biological endowment, developmental and age-related changes, psychodynamic forces, interpersonal relations, and sociocultural factors. It is no surprise, therefore, to find a great deal of *variability* among the aging with regard to their sexual behavior. Several types of individual variations are pointed up by some of the Duke research data, and have been reviewed by Dr. Berezin. For example, elderly men are sexually more active than women, but in the course of time the differences become smaller; although sexual interest declines with age, about one-half of the subjects surviving into their eighties and nineties report that they still have sexual interest of mild to moderate degree; unmarried men have about the same level of sexual activity and interest as married men; and, about one-fourth of the men, regardless of age, report an increase in the degree of activity or interest, over a period of several years.

Since sexual potency declines consistently beginning in the early adult years until well into old age, it follows that increased sexual activity in aging men is likely to be due to psychological or social factors (an exception, of course, would be increased sexual activity due to improved physical health). Among such we may see the following:

1. Personality growth and emotional maturation, on the basis of general life experiences or due to psychotherapy, may result in a *lessening of earlier sexual inhibitions.*

2. Attempts to *compensate* for, or deny, the age-related decrease in potency (overcompensation, counterphobic behavior, denial) tend to increase sexual activity or cause compulsive hypersexuality.

3. Certain emotional crises (depression, boredom, and monotony, a sense of existential meaninglessness, work pressures, etc.) may prompt a *quest for oblivion* by way of losing oneself in exciting experiences, including sex.

4. *Success in one's life work* may bring about a sense of "having arrived." The reality of actually "having it made," combined with the increased self-esteem, makes it possible for

one to take more time out for all sorts of enjoyable activities, including sex.

5. *Economic success* may enable one to create those settings conducive to increased sex, e.g., vacation trips with spouse or an extramarital relationship.

6. Changes in the family, e.g., when children begin to leave the home, may leave the middle-aged couple with more time and fewer responsibilities.

7. Many important factors pertain to the marital relationship. The *wife's menopause* may have a favorable effect when there no longer need to be concerns about the risk of unwanted pregnancies. But loss of the spouse's childbearing capacity may be felt as a loss by the man himself, in which case the wish to deny his own aging and to feel young again may lead to pseudo hypersexuality or extramarital sex with younger partners.

Among men surviving into the eighties and nineties, continued sexual activity is no great rarity; about one-fifth of these men are still sexually active. The Duke research data suggest that continued sexual activity is characteristic of vigorous people who may represent a biological elite. These aged people tend to be still married, retain physical and psychological health, and remain socially, as well as sexually active. Thus, continued sexual activity is a correlate of continued vigor.

The Quality of Sexual Experience in Later Life

It is important to keep in mind that the Duke project, from which the above data were obtained, studied groups of subjects at different points in time. Thus, data reflect the "average profile" of specific groups rather than longitudinal changes in the sexual behavior of particular individuals. In addition, as Dr. Berezin has pointed out, the nature of the research data is quantitative rather than qualitative. Research involving quantifiable variables is "objective," in that it permits statistical validation and replication by other investigators. However, if sex in the postmature years (following middle age and covering as much as one-third of the life span) is to continue playing an important role, then its quality is a pertinent issue. The subjective quality of sexual experience is more relevant than the quantity. Our attempt to understand some of the qualitative aspects is facilitated by keeping in mind certain considerations.

1. When sex is no longer procreative, there may be more emphasis on its recreational aspects. In spite of the anatomic and functional decline of the genital apparatus, interest in sexual activity tends to persist.

2. Because of involution of the genital organs, there may be a shift of interest away from traditional sex (sexual intercourse with orgasm), in the direction of other types of sexual activity, i.e., sexual drives and behavior not primarily aimed at discharging genital excitation through orgasm. These pregenital needs and activities include sexual excitations from many parts of the body (e.g., oral, touch, and temperature stimulation).

3. Such a relative predominance of pregenital drives in an older person cannot be simply compared with the sexual immaturity of children or adolescents. Old age is not a second childhood. A lifetime of experience makes the difference.

4. The aim of sexual activity may not be primarily orgastic release of sexual tension, but rather the developing or maintaining of excitation. In this context, sexual activity may also serve more general aims, for example, the need for intimacy and warmth, or a sense of being alive.

5. Many patients suffering from a variety of chronic physical disabilities continue to have sexual interest, and maintain sexual activity. Chronic illnesses such as heart disease, stroke, neurological and urogenital diseases, interfere to some extent with sexual interest and activity. But this interference is not necessarily a total one. Most men, for example, who have had

a coronary attack or a prostatectomy are able to continue sexual activity. Certain problems, however, may arise in these situations. Physical disability may interfere with the capacity to take sexual initiative and to perform sustained activity. An example of what might be a difficult readjustment is the change from an active mode to a less active or passive mode in the case of highly aggressive, independent or self-assertive men. Such situations require, in both partners, open-mindedness and cooperation that permit experimentation with new sexual "techniques" to discover new ways of intimacy.

SEXUAL PROBLEMS IN OLD AGE

Lifelong sexual problems may be carried over into later years or may recede in old age. On the other hand, sexual problems may begin with the aging process. People with a background of good lifelong sexual adjustment and maturity of personality tend to have few, if any, sexual problems in old age. In keeping with our general topic of the "Normal Psychology of the Aging Process," I will discuss briefly some psychological problems that may arise in response to expectable sexual involution, and the occurrence in later years of sexual symptoms that serve to express nonsexual psychopathology.

Pathological Responses to Involution

In these cases, sexual involution acts as a pathogenetic factor. Loss of any capacity, including sexual functions, gives rise to a grief reaction, to anxious concerns about disruptions in intimate relationships, and can be perceived as a narcissistic injury resulting in lowered self-esteem. A variety of coping behavior and defense mechanisms can be used for the purpose of adapting to the loss (e.g., substitution, denial, projection, regression, withdrawal). Whether these coping techniques are adaptive or maladaptive depends not only on the type of mechanism selected (i.e., its appropriateness), but also on the

[261]

intensity with which it is employed. Associated with maladaptive responses are specific emotional-behavioral patterns, such as "hypersexuality," jealousy, embarrassment, identity crisis of late life, and so forth.

Personal identity is closely related to one's self-concept as a man or woman. Therefore, decline or loss of sexual functions may pose a threat to an individual's sense of identity. The resulting identity crisis of late life may be quite disruptive. Frequently, we find that earlier psychological problems (dating back to adolescence and childhood) are reactivated.

The person who tries to deny his sexual decline may appear to be hypersexual. This facade of overcompensating should not be confused with true hypersexuality, which is very rare.

Decline of sexual function may lead to fears concerning loss of love. Some persons are bothered by a nagging fear that they will lose their hold on the spouse. Possessiveness, the attempt to have a permanent hold on the other person, is based on pathological apprehension about the possibility of alienation of affection. Excessive projection frequently plays a role in the psychodynamics of involutional depressions.

A protective retreat as a response to feeling of sexual inadequacy can manifest itself as a regression into self-absorption and hypochondriasis. The physical symptoms provide an alibi for the alleged inadequacy.

Avoidance of sexual opportunities may lead to another risk—withdrawal from the other person. After some time, a new relationship becomes solidified, with the two partners now being further apart.

The fear of failure associated with feelings of sexual inadequacy is often the result of an all-or-none view: if sex is viewed as an all-or-none business, without a place for intermediate sexual activities (sex short of orgasm through intercourse), then the options are limited.

Embarrassment and shame can originate in several ways. Most people feel that the aged body is less beautiful than the young body. Whereas in earlier years looking at the partner's body was a source of sexual stimulation, this is no longer so; by the same token, being looked at by one's partner may evoke feelings of embarrassment. No longer is the emphasis on showing and showing off, but more on the need to cover and have privacy, from one's own eyes and those of one's partner. The ideal of dignity has as its counterpart the risk of shame. Loss of face may be the result of acting inappropriately, that is, not acting one's age. Another source of shame or guilt is related to the relative predominance of pregenital strivings.

It is interesting that nowadays older persons are often advised to relax their inhibitions and not worry about guilt regarding sex. One gets the impression that older persons are being encouraged to enjoy the kind of sex that younger people have, as if age made no difference at all. Thus, a new stereotype may develop, replacing the previous one of the sexlessness of old age. This new stereotype might be more damaging than the old one, because it tends to set a standard of behavior beyond the reach of the majority of old people.

Sexual Symptoms as an Expression of Nonsexual Pathology

Sexual disturbances (sexual deviations, sexual acting out, etc.) may be due to nonsexual age-related changes. The latter include, for example, changes in the ego and superego, changes in object relations, physical illness or iatrogenic factors. Decreased impulse control may result from age-related changes in the ego and superego. The importance of possible iatrogenic factors is illustrated by the case of a 60-year-old man, concerned about impotence, and being treated for depression. He reported that any time he would take imipramine he had a "nearly uncontrollable urge to phone the little girls in the neighborhood and make sexual propositions to them."

Geriatric patients in institutions may present problems of sexual acting out. What is acted out through sexual behavior can be a variety of impulses or psychological conflicts. For example, a patient may express hostile, defiant, or rebellious tendencies through provocative sexual acts. Another patient discovers that exhibitionism is a guaranteed attention-getting device. Again, another type of patient learns that the only certain opportunity to be touched by human hands is the forceful restraint that follows his attack on somebody else, or being cleaned up after soiling himself.

Patients with organic brain damage often present sexual problems. Because of the brain damage, there may be psychological impairments such as poor judgment and poor impulse control. Such elderly patients may show sexual behavior that is inappropriate with regard to time and place, and social context. Examples of such behavioral disturbances are exhibitionism, masturbation in public, and pedophilia.

Sexual preoccupations may cover up death anxiety. Thus, for example, delusions pertaining to sex, and life or death are not uncommon in aged patients close to death.

An 82-year-old schizophrenic woman had been preoccupied for years with sex and pregnancy. She had the delusion of being two and one half months pregnant. She also complained, "When I put my hand on the red knob of the railing, my thumb becomes swollen." Her underlying wish is probably to be pregnant which, in turn, represents a denial of death's approach. The pregnancy is to come about through contact with the phallic object; the hard railing with the red knob (glans). Touching the phallic symbol causes part of her body to swell. The swelling represents pregnancy, but it is displaced to her thumb, another phallic symbol. Thus, through symbolic representation and displacement, an underlying fantasy is highly distorted and condensed into a brief somatic delusion.

Some aged women complain of feeling "sex-starved." This may represent an instance of hypersexuality, where the emphasis on Eros is defensively used to cover up the approach of Thanatos. A corollary of this phenomenon is found in the phrase "learning the facts of life." The facts of "life" are usually learned in preadolescence; what is overlooked, however, is that it is around this same time that the facts of death are fully discovered. Thus, the phrase "facts of life" is a euphemism, involving a certain element of denial of death.

References

Ahrens, R. J. (1972), The White House Conference: An assessment. *Perspect. Aging*, 1:11-13.

Alvarez, W. C. (1969), The problems faced by geriatricians. *Geriat.*, 24:45-46.

Amulree, L. (1954), Sex and the Elderly. *Practitioner*, 172:431-435.

Anastasi, A. (1974), Individual differences in aging. In: *Aging: Its Challenge to the Individual and Society*, ed. W. C. Bier. New York: Fordham University Press, pp. 84-95.

Atkin, S. (1940), Discussion of M. R. Kaufman, "Old Age and Aging: The Psychoanalytic Point of View." *Amer. J. Orthopsychiat.*, 10:79-84.

Barker, L. F. (1939), Aging from the point of view of the clinician. In: *Problems of Ageing*, ed. E. V. Cowdry. Baltimore: Williams & Wilkins, pp. 717-742.

Barron, M. (1961), *The Aging American*. New York: Crowell.

Bender, M. B., Green, M. A., & Fink, M. (1954), Patterns of perceptual organization with simultaneous stimuli. *Arch. Neurol. Psychiat.*, 72:233-255.

Beres, D. (1971), Ego autonomy and ego pathology. *The Psychoanalytic Study of the Child*, 26:3-24. New York: Quadrangle.

Berezin, M. A. (1963), Some intrapsychic aspects of aging. *This Volume*, pp. 75-97.

――――― (1969), Sex and old age: A review of the literature. *This Volume*, pp. 217-236.

――――― (1972), Psychodynamic considerations of aging and the aged: An overview. *Amer. J. Psychiat.*, 128:33-41.

――――― (1975), Masturbation and old age. In: *Masturbation: From Infancy to Senescence*, ed. I. M. Marcus & J. J. Francis. New York: International Universities Press, pp. 329-347.

――――― & Cath, S. H., eds. (1965), *Geriatric Psychiatry: Grief, Loss, and Emotional Disorders in the Aging Process*. New York: International Universities Press.

[267]

_____ & Stotsky, B. A. (1970), The geriatric patient. In: *The Practice of Community Mental Health*, ed. H. E. Grunebaum. Boston: Little, Brown.

Bergman, S. & Amir, M. (1973), Crime and delinquency among the aged in Israel. *Geriat.*, 28:149-157.

Bexton, W. H., Heron, W., & Scott, T. H. (1954), Effects of decreased variation in the sensory environment. *Canad. J. Psychol.*, 8:70-76.

Bibring, E. (1941), Theory of instincts. *Internat. J. Psycho-Anal.*, 22:102-131.

_____ (1953), The mechanism of depression. In: *Affective Disorders*, ed. P. Greenacre. New York: International Universities Press, pp. 13-48.

_____ (1954), Psychoanalysis and the dynamic psychotherapies. *J. Amer. Psychoanal. Assn.*, 2:745-770.

Bibring, G. (1956), Psychiatry and medical practice in a general hospital. *New Eng. J. Med.*, 254:366-372.

Bier, W. C., ed. (1974), *Aging: Its Challenge to the Individual and to Society*. New York: Fordham University Press.

Blood, R. O. & Wolfe, D. M. (1960), Resources and family task performance. In: *Sociology of the Family*, ed. M. Anderson. Baltimore: Penguin Books, pp. 259-271.

Bossard, J. & Boll, E. (1955), Marital unhappiness in the life cycle. *Marr. Family Living*, 17:10-14.

Bott, E. (1955), Urban families: Conjugal roles and social networks. In: *Sociology of the Family*, ed. M. Anderson. Baltimore: Penguin Books, pp. 217-232.

Botwinick, J. (1959), Drives, expectancies, and emotions. In: *Handbook of Aging and the Individual*, ed. J. E. Birren. Chicago: University of Chicago Press, pp. 739-768.

Bowers, L. M., Cross, R. R., Jr., & Lloyd, F. A. (1963), Sexual function and urologic disease in the elderly male. *J. Amer. Geriat. Soc.*, 11:647-652.

Bowman, K. M. (1954), The sex life of the aging individual (Editorial). *Geriat.*, 9:83-84.

_____ (1963), The sex life of the aging individual. In: *Sexual Behavior and Personality Characteristics*, ed. M. F. DeMartino. New York: Citadel Press, pp. 372-375.

Brenner, C. (1955), *An Elementary Textbook of Psychoanalysis*. New York: International Universities Press.

Burnap, D. W. & Goldin, J. S. (1967), Sexual problems in medical practice. *J. Med. Educ.*, 42:673-680.

[268]

Busse, E. W., Barnes, R. H., Silverman, A. J., Shy, G. M., Thaler, M., & Frost, L. L. (1954), Studies of the process of aging: Factors that influence the psyche of elderly persons. *Amer. J. Psychiat.*, 110:897-903.

Cameron, N. (1945), Neuroses of later maturity. In: *Mental Disorders in Later Life*, 2nd edition, ed. Oscar J. Kaplan. Stanford, Cal.: Stanford University Press, 1956, pp. 201-243.

Cameron, P. & Biber, H. (1973), Sexual thought throughout the life span. *Gerontologist*, 13:144-147.

Caplan, G. (1961), *An Approach to Community Mental Health*. New York: Grune & Stratton.

Christenson, C. V. & Gagnon, J. H. (1965), Sexual behavior in a group of older women. *J. Gerontol.*, 20:351-356.

_____ & Johnson, A. B. (1973), Sexual patterns in a group of older never-married women. *J. Geriat. Psychiat.*, 6:80-98.

Claman, A. D. (1966), Introduction to panel discussion: Sexual difficulties after 50. *Canad. Med. Assn.*, 94:207.

Clow, H. E. & Allen, E. B. (1951), Manifestation of the psychoneurosis occurring in later life. *Geriat.*, 6:31-39.

Cohen, E. S. (1960), Cultural attitudes toward aging and their implications for public planning. *J. Amer. Geriat. Soc.*, 8:337-344.

Comfort, A. (1974), Sexuality in old age. *J. Amer. Geriat. Soc.*, 22:440-442.

Connelly, M. (1929), *The Green Pastures*. New York: Farrar & Rinehart.

Cumming, E. & Henry, W. E. (1961), *Growing Old*. New York: Basic Books.

Cutner, M. (1950), Analysis in later life. *Brit. J. Med. Psychol.*, 23:75-86.

Davies, A. D. M. (1972), The effects of age, sex and occupation on selected variables: Some preliminary results of a longitudinal study. In:*Aging of the Central Nervous System: Biological and Psychological Aspects*, ed. H. van Praag & A. F. Kalverboer. Haarlem: de Erven F. Bohn N. V., pp. 101-122.

Davis, R. H. (1975), Television and the image of aging. *Television Quart.*, 12:21-24.

Dean, S. R. (1966), Sin and senior citizens. *J. Amer. Geriat. Soc.*, 14:935-938.

de Nicola, P. & Peruzza, M. (1974), Sex in the aged. *J. Amer. Geriat. Soc.*, 22:380-382.

Dunbar, F. (1957), Immunity to the afflictions of old age. *J. Amer. Geriat. Soc.*, 5:982-996.

[269]

Eissler, K. R. (1955), *The Psychiatrist and the Dying Patient*. New York: International Universities Press.

Ellis, W. J. & Grayhack, J. T. (1963), Sexual function in aging males after orchiectomy and estrogen therapy. *J. Urol.*, 89:895-899.

English, O. S. & Pearson, G. H. J. (1955), *Emotional Problems of Living*. New York: Norton.

Epstein, G. & Bronzaft, A. (1972), Female freshmen view their roles as women. *J. Marr. Family*, 34:671-672.

Erikson, E. H. (1950), *Childhood and Society*. New York: Norton.

———— (1959), *Identity and the Life Cycle* [*Psychological Issues*, Monogr. 1]. New York: International Universities Press.

Feigenbaum, E. M., Lowenthal, M. F., & Trier, M. L. (1967), Aged are confused and hungry for sex information: A report of a study. *Geriat. Focus*, 5 (20):2.

Feldman, H. (1964), Development of the husband-wife relationship. Preliminary report. Cornell Studies of Marital Development: Study in the transition to parenthood. Ithaca, N.Y.: Cornell University, Dept. of Child Development and Family Relationships, New York State College of Home Economics.

Finkle, A. L. (1973), Emotional quality and physical quantity of sexual activity in aging males. *J. Geriat. Psychiat.*, 6:70-79.

———— & Moyers, T. G. (1960), Sexual potency in aging males. IV. Status of private patients before and after prostatectomy. *J. Urol.*, 84:152-157.

———— ———— Tobenkin, M. I., & Karg, S. J. (1959), Sexual potency in aging males. I. Frequency of coitus among clinic patients. *JAMA*, 170 (12):113-115.

———— & Prian, D. V. (1966), Sexual potency in elderly men before and after prostatectomy. *JAMA*, 196:139-143.

Fisher, C. (1966), Dreaming and sexuality. In: *Psychoanalysis— A General Psychology*, ed. R. M. Loewenstein, L. M. Newman, M. Schur, & A. J. Solnit. New York: International Universities Press, pp. 537-569.

————, Gross, J., & Zuch, J. (1965), Cycle of penile erection synchronous with dreaming (REM) sleep. *Arch. Gen. Psychiat.*, 12:29-45.

Freeman, J. T. (1961), Sexual capacities in the aging male. *Geriat.*, 16:37-43.

———— (1963), Sexual aspects. In: *The Care of the Geriatric Patient*, ed. E. V. Cowdry. St. Louis: Mosby, pp. 156-179.

Freud, A. (1936), *The Ego and the Mechanisms of Defense.* New York: International Universities Press, 1946.

Freud, S. (1913), The disposition to obsessional neurosis. *Standard Edition*, 12:311-326. London: Hogarth Press, 1958.

―――― (1914), On narcissism: An introduction. *Standard Edition*, 14:73-81. London: Hogarth Press, 1957.

―――― (1918), From the history of an infantile neurosis. *Standard Edition*, 17:3-122. London: Hogarth Press, 1955.

Fried, E. & Stern, K. (1948), The situation of the ages within the family. *Amer. J. Orthopsychiat.*, 18:31-54.

Gill, M. M. & Brenman, M. (1959), *Hypnosis and Related States: Psychoanalytic Studies in Regression.* New York: International Universities Press.

Gitelson, M. (1948), The emotional problems of elderly people. *Geriat.*, 3:135-150.

Goldfarb, A. I. (1955), Psychotherapy of older persons. *Psychoanal. Rev.*, 42:180-187.

―――― (1965), Foreword. In: *Sexual Life after Sixty*, ed. I. Rubin. New York: Basic Books, pp. v-ix.

――――, Kahn, R. L., Pollack, M., & Gerber, I. E. (1960), The relationship of mental and physical status in institutionalized aged persons. *Amer. J. Psychiat.*, 117:120-124.

―――― & Turner, H. (1953), Psychotherapy of aged persons. *Amer. J. Psychiat.*, 109:916-921.

Gordon, M. (1960), Changing patterns of retirement. *J. Gerontol.*, 15:300-304.

Gorman, W. & Vetter, J. (1961), Psychiatric medical management. *J. Amer. Geriat. Soc.*, 9:288-293.

Greenblatt, R. B. & Leng, J. J. (1972), Factors influencing sexual behavior. *J. Amer. Geriat. Soc.*, 20:49-54.

―――― & Scarpa-Smith, C. J. (1959), Nymphomania in postmenopausal women. *J. Amer. Geriat. Soc.*, 7:399-342.

Grotjahn, M. (1951), Some analytic observations about the process of growing old. In: *Psychoanalysis and the Social Sciences,* 3:301-312, ed. G. Róheim. New York: International Universities Press.

―――― (1955), Analytic psychotherapy with the elderly. *Psychoanal. Rev.*, 42:419-427.

Hamilton, G. V. (1939), Changes in personality and psychosexual phenomena with age. In: *Problems of Ageing*, ed. E. V. Cowdry. Baltimore: Williams & Wilkins, pp. 459-482.

[271]

Hartmann, H. (1939), *Ego Psychology and the Problem of Adaptation*. New York: International Universities Press, 1958.

———— (1951), Technical implications of ego psychology. *Psychoanal. Quart.*, 20:31-43.

———— (1964), *Essays on Ego Psychology*. New York: International Universities Press.

Heiman, M. (1967), Introductory remarks. Panel on female sexuality. Annual Meeting of the American Psychoanalytic Association, Detroit, Mich., May 6.

Heron, W., Bexton, W. H., & Hebb, D. O. (1953), Cognitive effects of a decreased variation in the sensory environment. *Amer. Psychol.*, 8:366-372.

———— Doone, B. K., & Scott, T. H. (1956), Visual disturbances after prolonged perceptual isolation. *Canad. J. Psychol.*, 10:13-18.

Hirt, N. B. (1966), The psychiatrist's view. Panel discussion. Sexual difficulties after 50. *Canad. Med. Assn. J.*, 94:213-214.

Hoch, P. & Houston, R. E. (1958), *Report on Psychiatric Services for the Aged—Comments by Commissioners of Mental Hygiene and Social Welfare*. New York State (mimeo).

Hollander, M. H. (1951), Role of the psychiatrist in homes for the aged. *Geriat.*, 6:243.

———— (1952), Individualizing the aged. *Soc. Casework*, 33:337.

Howell, T. H. (1973), Geriatrics one hundred years ago. *Med. Hist.*, 17:432-445.

Hsu, C. J. & Chen, P. H. (1965), Sexual activities in older male. *J. Formosa Med. Assn.*, 64:129.

Jackson, D. D. (1966), Forbidden ground. Book review of *Human Sexual Response*. *Med. Opinion Rev.*, 2:32-33.

Jones, H. B. (1959), The relation of human health to age, place, and time. In: *Handbook of Aging and the Individual*, ed. J. E. Birren, Chicago: University of Chicago Press, pp. 336-363.

Kahn, R. L., Goldfarb, A. I., Pollack, M., & Peck, A. (1960), Brief objective measures for the determination of mental status in the aged. *Amer. J. Psychiat.*, 117:326-328.

———— ———— ———— ———— (1961), Factors in selection of psychiatric treatment for institutionalized aged persons. *Amer. J. Psychiat.*, 118:241-244.

————, Zeman, F. D., & Goldfarb, A. I. (1958), Attitudes toward illness in the aged. *Geriat.*, 13:246-250.

Kassell, V. (1966), Polygyny after 60. *Geriat.*, 21:214-218.

Kaufman, I. (1976), Marital adaptation in the aging. *This Volume*, pp. 187-201.

Kaufman, M. R. (1940), Old age and aging: The psychoanalytic point of view. *Amer. J. Orthopsychiat.*, 10:73-79.

Kent, D. P. (1968), Aging within the American social structure. *J. Geriat. Psychiat.*, 2:19-32.

Kent, S. (1975), Sex after 45. Being aware of a patient's sexual problems should be the concern of every physician. *Geriat.*, 30: 140-142.

Kinsey, A. C., Pomeroy, W. B., & Martin, C. I. (1948), *Sexual Behavior in the Human Male*. Philadelphia: Saunders.

―――― ―――― ―――― & Gebhard, P. H. (1953), *Sexual Behavior in the Human Female*. Philadelphia: Saunders.

Kleegman, S. J. (1959), Frigidity in women. *Quart. Rev. Surg. Obstet. Gynecol.*, 16:243-248.

Kohut, H. (1972), Thoughts on narcissism and narcissistic rage. *The Psychoanalytic Study of the Child*, 27:360-400. New York: Quadrangle.

Kris, E. (1952), *Psychoanalytic Explorations in Art*. New York: International Universities Press.

Lawton, G. (1940), Old age and aging: The present status of scientific knowledge. *Amer. J. Orthopsychiat.*, 10:85-87.

Leeds, M. (1960), Senile recession: A clinical entity? *J. Amer. Geriat. Soc.*, 8:122-131.

Levin, S. (1965), Some comments on the distribution of narcissistic and object libido in the aged. *Internat. J. Psycho-Anal.*, 46: 200-208.

―――― & Kahana, R. J., eds. (1967), *Psychodynamic Studies on Aging: Creativity, Reminiscing, and Dying*. New York: International Universities Press.

Levinger, G. (1968), Task and social behavior in marriage. In: *A Modern Introduction to the Family*, ed. N. W. Bell & E. F. Vogel. Toronto: Free Press, pp. 355-367.

Le Witter, M. & Abarbanel, A. (1961), Aging and sex. In: *The Encyclopedia of Sexual Behavior*, 2:75-81, ed. A. Ellis & A. Abarbanel. New York: Hawthorn Books.

Lilly, J. C. (1956), Mental effects of reduction of ordinary levels of visual stimuli on intact healthy persons. *Psychiat. Res. Rep.*, 5:1-9.

Linden, M. E. (1953), Group psychotherapy with institutionalized senile women: Study in gerontologic human relations. *Internat. J. Group Psychother.*, 3:150-170.

―――― (1957), Effects of social attitudes on the mental health of aging. *Geriat.*, 12:109-114.

_____ & Courtney, D. (1953), The human life cycle and its interruptions: A psychologic hypothesis. Studies in gerontologic human relations. I. *Amer. J. Psychiat.*, 109:906-915.

Lipman, A. (1961), Role conceptions and morale of couples in retirement. *J. Gerontol.*, 16:267-271.

Lowy, L. (1974), The White House Conference on Aging; two years later. *Internat. J. Aging Hum. Devel.*, 5:205-211.

Masters, W. H. & Ballew, J. W. (1955), The third sex. *Geriat.*, 10: 1-4.

_____ & Johnson, V. E. (1966), *Human Sexual Response.* Boston: Little, Brown.

Meerloo, J. A. M. (1955), Psychotherapy with elderly people. *Geriat.*, 10:583-587.

_____ (1961), Modes of psychotherapy in the aged. *J. Amer. Geriat. Soc.*, 9:225-234.

Meissner, W. W. (1977), *The Paranoid Process.* New York: Jason Aronson.

Meyer, A. (1890-1945), *The Collected Papers of Adolf Meyer*, ed. E. Winters. Baltimore: Johns Hopkins University Press, 1950-1952.

Nadelson, T. (1969), A survey of the literature on the adjustment of the aged to retirement. *J. Geriat. Psychiat.*, 2:3-20.

Natter, C. E. (1964), Pregnancy after fifty. *Obstet. Gynecol.*, 24: 641-643.

Newman, G. & Nichols, C. R. (1960), Sexual activities and attitudes in older persons. *JAMA*, 173:33-37.

Oberleder, M. (1957), Attitudes related to adjustment in a home for the aged. Unpublished doctoral dissertation. Columbia University.

Orwell, G. (1949), *1984.* New York: Harcourt Brace.

Pearl, R. (1925), *The Biology of Population Growth.* New York: Knopf.

Pfeiffer, E. (1974), Sexuality in the aging individual. *J. Amer. Geriat. Soc.*, 22:481-484.

_____ (1975), Sexual behavior. In: *Modern Perspectives in the Psychiatry of Old Age,* ed. J. Howells. New York: Brunner/Mazel.

_____ & Davis, G. C. (1972), Determinants of sexual behavior in middle and old age. *J. Amer. Geriat. Soc.*, 20:151-158.

_____, Verwoerdt, A. & Davis, G. C. (1972), Sexual behavior in middle life. *Amer. J. Psychiat.*, 128:1262-1267.

Plato (n.d.), *The Republic,* Book I (Jowett translation). New York: Modern Library, 1948.

Pollack, M, Kahn, R. L., & Goldfarb, A. I. (1958), Factors related to individual differences in perception in institutionalized aged subjects. *J. Gerontol.*, 13:192-197.

Rapaport, D., ed. (1951), *Organization and Pathology of Thought.* New York: Columbia University Press.

—— (1958), The theory of ego autonomy. In: *The Collected Papers of David Rapaport*, ed. M. M. Gill. New York: Basic Books, 1967, pp. 722-744.

Riese, W. (1971), Changing criteria of old age. *Bull. N.Y. Acad. Med.*, 47:1398-1400.

Rochlin, G. (1965), *Griefs and Discontents: The Forces of Change.* Boston: Little, Brown.

Rockwell, F. V. (1946), Psychotherapy of the older individual. In: *Mental Disorders in Later Life*, 2nd edition, ed. O. J. Kaplan. Stanford, Cal.: Stanford University Press, 1956, pp. 423-445.

Rollins, B. & Cannon, K. (1974), Marital satisfaction over the family life cycle: A reevaluation. *J. Marr. Family*, 36:271-283.

—— & Feldman, H. (1970), Marital satisfaction over the family life cycle. *J. Marr. Family*, 32:20-28.

Rosen, J. & Neugarten, B. (1960), Ego functions in middle and later years: A thematic apperception study of normal adults. *J. Gerontol.*, 15:62-67.

Rosenbaum, G. S. (1959), Living arrangements and mental disorders among the aged. *Amer. J. Orthopsychiat.*, 29:699-707.

Rubin, I. (1965), *Sexual Life after Sixty.* New York: Basic Books.

Sanders, H. J. (1972), Human aging: The enigma persists. *Chem. Engin. News*, 50:13-16.

Saphilios-Rothschild, C. (1967), A comparison of power structure and marital satisfaction in urban Greek and French families. *J. Marr. Family*, 29:345-352.

Schaie, K. W. (1973), Methodological problems in descriptive developmental research on adulthood and aging. In: *Life-Span Developmental Psychology: Methodological Issues*, ed. J. R. Nesselroade & H. W. Reese. New York: Academic Press, pp. 253-280.

Schuster, D. B. (1952), A psychological study of a 106-year-old man. *Amer. J. Psychiat.*, 109:112-119.

Sextus, C. (1893), *Hypnotism, Its Facts, Theories and Related Phenomena, with Explanatory Anecdotes, Descriptions and Reminiscences.* Hollywood: Wilshire, 1957.

Sheps, J. (1959), New developments in family diagnosis in emotional disorders of old age. *Geriat.*, 14:443-449.

Shock, N. (1960), Concepts of the medical profession in relation to aging. *J. Amer. Geriat. Soc.*, 8:206-215.

Shrut, S. D. (1958a), Evaluation of two aged populations living under two modes of institutional residence within the same institution. *J. Amer. Geriat. Soc.*, 6:44-59.

―――― (1958b), Attitudes toward old age and death. *Ment. Hyg.*, 42:259-266.

Somerville, R. (1971), Family life and sex education in the turbulent sixties. *J. Marr. Family*, 33:11-35.

Spitz, R. A. (1946), Anaclitic depression. *The Psychoanalytic Study of the Child*, 2:313-342. New York: International Universities Press.

Steinbeck, J. (1939), *The Grapes of Wrath*. New York: Viking.

Stinnett, N., Carter, L., & Montgomery, J. (1972), Older persons' perceptions of their marriages. *J. Marr. Family*, 34:665-670.

――――, Collins, J., & Montgomery, J. (1970), Marital need satisfaction of older husbands and wives. *J. Marr. Family*, 32:428-434.

Stokes, W. R. (1951), Sexual function in the aging male. *Geriat.*, 6:304-308.

Swartz, F. C. (1960), What is aging? *J. Amer. Geriat. Soc.*, 8:194.

Szasz, T. (1952), On the psychoanalytic theory of instincts. *Psychoanal. Quart.*, 21:25-48.

Townsend, P. (1957), *The Family Life of Old People*. London: Routledge & Kegan Paul.

Tuckman, J., Lorge, I., Steinhardt, R. W., & Zeman, F. D. (1953), Somatic and psychological complaints of older people in institutions and at home. *Geriat.*, 8:274-279.

―――― ―――― & Zeman, G. (1961), The self-image in aging. *J. Genet. Psychol.*, 99:317-321.

Verwoerdt, A., Pfeiffer, E., & Wang, H. S. (1969a), Sexual behavior in senescence: Changes in sexual activity and interest of aging men and women. *J. Geriat. Psychiat.*, 2:163-180.

―――― ―――― ―――― (1969b), Sexual behavior in senescence. II. Patterns of sexual activity and interest. *Geriat.*, 24:137-154.

Waelder, R. (1936), The principle of multiple function: Observations on overdetermination. *Psychoanal. Quart.*, 5:45-62.

Weinberg, J. (1959), *Personal and Social Adjustment to Psychological Aspects of Aging*. Washington, D.C.: American Psychological Association.

Weiss, J. M. A. (1973), The natural history of antisocial attitudes: What happens to psychopaths? *J. Geriat. Psychiat.*, 6:236-242.

Wilson, J. G. (1956), Signs of sexual aberration in old men. *J. Amer. Geriat. Soc.*, 4:1105-1107.

Winnicott, D. W. (1960), Ego distortion in terms of true and false self. In: *The Maturational Processes and the Facilitating Environment.* New York: International Universities Press, 1965, pp. 140-152.

Wolff, K. (1957), Definition of the geriatric patient. *Geriat.*, 12: 102-106.

Zinberg, N. E. (1964), Geriatric psychiatry: Need and problems. *Gerontologist*, 4:130-135.

_____ (1970), The mirage of mental health. *Brit. J. Sociol.*, 21: 262-272.

_____ (1975), Addiction and ego function. *The Psychoanalytic Study of the Child*, 30:567-588. New Haven: Yale University Press.

_____, Boris, H. N. & Boris, M. (1976), *Teaching Social Change: A Group Approach.* Baltimore: Johns Hopkins University Press.

_____ & Kaufman, I. (1963), Cultural and personality factors associated with aging: An introduction. *This Volume*, pp. 7-55.

Index

Abarbanel, A., 223
Adaptation and adjustment
  concept of, 109-113, 126
  marital, 187-201
  psychopathology and, 108-109
  regression as, 15-17, 52-53, 83, 149, 173
  social interaction and, 113-115, 174-176
  threats to, 113-115
  see also Ego; Libido, equilibrium of
Adolescence
  creativity and, 102-103
  drives during, 91-92
Aged
  attitudes of younger people toward, 70-74, 148
  consultative position of, 93-97
  need for psychiatric care of, 3-5, 8, 11, 44-47, 54-55, 65-69, 74, 105, 176
  see also Aging; Treatment
Aggressive drive, 21, 26-27, 152-153
  narcissism and, 183
Aging
  definition of, 58-59, 75, 94-95, 187
  emotional conflict in, 10-11, 47, 116-121
  intrapsychic aspects of, xv-xvii, 11-21, 76-97
  normal, 52, 76-77, 99-105, 148-149, 155

personality factors in, 7-30
physical deterioration in, 9-11, 24-27, 29-30, 36-38, 47-48, 50-52, 57-60, 63, 65-66, 76, 101, 117, 142
psychobiologic aspects of, 151-154
psychodynamics of, xvii, 21-30, 64, 76-77, 99-105
  see also Aged; Gerontologic psychiatry; Psychopathology; Society and culture
Ahrens, R. J., 160
Allen, E. B., 22
Alvarez, W. C., 159
Amir, M., 242
Amulree, L., 226
Anastasi, A., 160
Atkin, S., 142
Autonomy, 169-171, 173-174, 178-182; *see also* Ego; Independence

Ballew, J. W., 233
Barker, L. F., 222
Barron, M., 191
Baruch, B., 96
Bender, L. F., 61
Beres, D., 180
Berezin, M. A., xiii, xiv, xvi-xvii, xix, xxi-xxii, 3-5, 75-97, 135, 147, 149, 151-154, 157-161, 204, 217-257, 259
Bergman, S. 242

[279]

Berkeley, B., 169
Bexton, W. H., 171
Biber, H., 160
Bibring, E., 97, 127, 135, 153-154
Bibring, G., 77, 135
Bier, W. C., 160
Blau, D., xix, xxi, 203-214
Blood, R. O., 187
Boll, E., 188
Boris, H. N., 175
Boris, M., 175
Bossard, J., 188
Bott, E., 198, 199
Botwinick, J., 223
Bowers, L. M., 228-229
Bowman, K. M., 159, 218, 226
Brenman, M., 15, 126
Brenner, C., 92
Bronzaft, A., 195
Browning, R., 154
Burnap, D. W., 243-244
Burton, R., 240
Busse, E. W., 220

Cameron, N., 21, 47
Cameron, P., 160
Cannon, K., 188
Caplan, G., 62
Carter, L., 188, 191-192, 205
Cath, S. H., xiv, 161
Chen, P. H., 229
Christenson, C. V., 223, 231, 232, 252-256
Chronic brain syndrome, 63-67
Cicero, 57, 97
Claman, A. D., 218-220, 222
Clow, H. E., 22
Cohen, E. S., 31, 45
Collins, J., 193
Comfort, A., 240
Compartmentalization, 18, 30, 65, 101; see also Defense(s)
Connelly, M., 21
Consultative position, 93-97
Cozzens, J. G., 131

Creativity, 102-103, 105
Cross, R. R., Jr., 228-229
Cultural attitudes; see Society and culture
Cumming, E., 160
Cutner, M., 39

David, 70
Davies, A. D. M., 160
Davis, G. C., 248-250, 253, 256
Davis, R. H., 160
Dean, S. R., 234
Death and dying
  fear of, 60
  preparing for, 9, 14, 53-54, 154, 183-184
  psychoanalytic view of, 152-153
  society's attitude toward, 73-74
de Beauvoir, S., 240
Defense(s)
  psychological levels of, 112
  psychosis and, 116-117, 119
  role in social interaction, 30, 172
  sexual drive and, 22-24, 93
  see also specific defenses
Denial, 18-19
de Nicola, P., 241
Depression, 37, 47, 50-51, 81
Descartes, R., 169-170
Drive(s), 11-13, 86
  concept of, 91-93
  see also Aggressive drive; Instinct; Libido; Sex
Doone, B. K., 171
Dunbar, F., 10

Ego
  aging and, 13-20, 77
  autonomy of, xix-xx, 169-171, 173-174, 178-180
  creativity and, 102-105
  drive and, 91, 99-101, 142
  levels of, 110-111
  psychosis and, 116-117
  regression and, 125-127, 136, 173